1. a

Students' Book

the Intermediate CHOICE

nd Richard Acklam

Longman

Unit Colour Key:
- Focus on Present
- Focus on Past
- Focus on Future
- Focus on Modals
- Consolidation
- Zero unit or 'surprise'

An extended map of the contents of *The Intermediate Choice* can be found at the front of the Teacher's Book, featuring:
- the pronunciation syllabus
- the skills work, unit by unit
- the detailed contents of each Consolidation Unit

The Teacher's Book also includes Check What You Know tests 1–4.

0 *What do you know?*

DO THESE EXERCISES TO SEE HOW WELL YOU ALREADY SPEAK ABOUT THE PAST, THE PRESENT AND THE FUTURE IN ENGLISH.

Focus on the past

1 Look at the photographs of family life in the 1940s. What was each member of the family doing when the photographs were taken?

2 Tell your partner about life in the past for someone in your family.

1 What is the relationship of this person to you?
2 What time in the past are you talking about?
3 What was her/his life like then? How is life different for your family now?

Example: When my grandmother was a young girl, she . . .

3 Ask questions about your partner's more recent past. Find out what she/he did yesterday/last weekend.

Focus on the present

1 Look at the photographs of a modern family. What are the different members of this family doing?

2 Answer these questions together. Say how you think life has changed between the time of the first and the second group of photographs.

1 What technological changes have there been?
2 What important historical events have taken place?
3 In what ways is life now probably better/worse than before?

3 Tell another student about important changes in your life in the last five years. How is your daily routine different now?

Focus on modals

1 **Work in groups. Imagine the names, ages, occupations and relationships of the people in the modern photographs.**

2 **On your own, imagine more about *one* of the people in the photographs. Make notes about:**

a) her/his main interests and talents.
b) what she/he does on a typical day/at the weekend.
c) what she/he has to do at home. Are there any things she/he mustn't do?
d) what she/he enjoys most/least about family life.

3 **Tell other students in the group about your person. Together, form a picture of this family and describe it to the class.**

Focus on the future

1 **Tell other students about your family and some of their plans for the future.**

2 **Discuss the headlines above. What do you think?**

1 Which ones are possible in the near future?
2 What major changes will there be in your lifetime?
3 In what ways will life be better/worse?

3 **Write a letter to your teacher. Tell her/him a little about your:**

a) past, e.g. education/jobs.
b) present, e.g. family and/or work responsibilities.
c) future, e.g. hopes and plans for the next five years.

1 *What an experience!*

WHEN WAS THE LAST TIME YOU DID IT?

WHATEVER YOU LIKE DOING ON A SHORT BREAK, YOU'LL FIND MORE OF IT IN BRIGHTON.
PHONE FREE ON 01800 512711 OR FILL IN THE COUPON FOR OUR SHORT BREAKS BROCHURE.

NAME ______________________
ADDRESS ____________________
____
POST CODE __________________
SEND TO: Arts & Leisure Services
Room 84, Marlborough House, 54 Old Steine,
Brighton, East Sussex BN1 1EQ

DO IT BRIGHTON STYLE

1 Diagnosis: Past Simple vs Present Perfect

1 Look at the advertisement and answer these questions.

1 What place is it advertising? Is it by the sea or in the mountains?
2 What different things can you do there?

2 Ask and answer these questions with another student.

1 Which seaside, lake or mountain resorts have you been to?
2 Which of the activities in the photos have you ever/never done?

3 Find out when your partner last did some of the activities above. Ask the question at the top of the advertisement, changing the verb as necessary.

Example: When was the last time you ate out?

4 Ask questions and complete the form in the advertisement for your partner. Make sure your spelling is correct.

5 Introduce your partner to the class and say one or two things you have found out about her/him.

There is a Revision exercise for Past Simple vs Present Perfect on page 127.

NB Irregular verbs

Present	*Past Simple*	*Past participle*
go	went	been/gone
buy	. . .	. . .
eat	. . .	. . .
meet	. . .	. . .
have	. . .	. . .
drink	. . .	. . .
see	. . .	. . .
make	. . .	. . .
do	. . .	. . .
take	. . .	. . .
put	. . .	. . .

Complete the chart.

How do you form a) the past participle of regular verbs and b) the Present Perfect?

Present Perfect (experience) vs Past Simple; *ago*; *already/yet*; *at*; *before*; *ever/never*; *in/on*; countries; hobbies

2 Grammar: past + time expressions

1 the wine. **But that was a year ago, two years ago.** A
2 [A] **Brush your teeth.** [B] **I've already done that.** I'
3 ... erm ... **She was with him at the weekend** ... ar
4 nd ... **I think I've seen them before.** They have bee
5 ... light on. **Well, have you ever seen that?** ... I
6 ... then. **Also we got married in May** and they say m
7 d blouse they've got ... **I've never seen it.** Each b
8 r seen it. **He showed it to me on Tuesday.** We erm ar
9 . **I mean, we haven't drunk it yet** ... we'll leave t

From the *British National Corpus* (Spoken)

1 Look at the sentences above with another student. Find examples of a) the Present Perfect, and b) the Past Simple.

2 Answer these questions about the highlighted time expressions.

1 Which ones are used with a) the Present Perfect, b) the Past Simple?
2 Which ones go a) before, b) after the main verb?
3 Which one is used before a) months/years, and b) days/dates?

3 Find and correct six mistakes in the conversation below. They are all mistakes to do with the language above.

A: Where have you gone at the weekend?
B: To Hungary, on business. I've flown there on Saturday.
A: Lucky you! I never went there. What's it like?
B: Great! But I went there before. I went to Hungary and Poland on June. Have you ever been to Poland?
A: No, not yet, but I went to the Czech Republic.

4 Find out about your partner's travel experiences.

1 Which towns/countries has she/he been to?
2 When did she/he go there?
3 What did she/he enjoy most about each place?

3 Vocabulary: hobbies

1 Name hobbies by matching a word in column A to a word in column B. Use each word once only.

A	B
horse	collecting
sun	jumping
bird	shopping
bungee	skiing
water	surfing
rock	racing
wind	climbing
stamp	bathing
window	seeing
sight	watching

2 Listen, check your answers and repeat. Where is the stress on these compound words?

Listening

1 Listen to two people talking about an exciting experience. Answer these questions for each person.

1 Which hobby in the photographs below does she talk about?
2 When and where did the experience take place?
3 What made it so exciting?

2 Talk to other students about their hobbies. Who has the most similar hobbies to you?

4 Key word: *get*

1 Normally I **get** home by four o'clock.
2 s? You can **get** them in other shops a
3 at! Go and **get** your coat then. Okay,
4 girl. She **gets** up off the ground ..
5 My tea is **getting** cold. What's it y
6 . Have you **got** any money on you? Not
7 Anyway, I **got** this lovely letter ba
8 well. He's **got** three children too ..

From the *British National Corpus* (Spoken)

1 Look at the forms of *get* above with another student. Find one example where:

a) *get* means
- to buy
- to arrive
- to receive
- to collect/fetch
- to become

b) *get* + *preposition* shows movement.

c) *have* + *got* is used to talk about
- possessions
- family relations

d) *got* is the Past Simple form of *get*.

2 Now make questions to ask your partner from these prompts. Note her/his answers.

1 What/get last time/go shopping?
2 How many children (brothers and sisters)/got?
3 What time/usually get up in the morning?
4 How often/get letters from friends (family)?
5 What/get/last birthday?
6 How/usually get to and from/English class?
7 What/think is a good age to get married?

3 Tell other students something interesting you found out about your partner.

5 Reading

1 Before you read, what do you think?

1 In what order do most people do these things?
get pregnant get to know someone
get married get engaged
get divorced

2 Who are the people in the photographs? What is the special occasion?

2 Work in two groups. Each group, read one article below and decide if these statements are true (T), false (F), or you don't know (DK).

1 The Japanese people knew all about this romance.
2 Many people attended the official wedding ceremony.
3 Masako's Japanese wedding dress was unusually light.
4 She has studied in Britain and the USA.
5 There was wide TV coverage of the event.
6 Masako has worked for the Japanese government.
7 She has learned at least three foreign languages.
8 She is the first 'non-royal' to marry a Japanese prince.
9 She didn't hesitate at the chance of marrying him.

3 Ask a student who read the other article about anything you didn't know.

4 Look at the pictures opposite of the secret ceremony. What happened to:

a) Masako? b) Naruhito? c) both of them?

5 Tell other students what happens at a traditional wedding in your country.

Royal romance

JAPAN has been stunned by a royal romance kept secret from its people: Crown Prince Naruhito is to marry a commoner, and first news came from a newspaper report abroad.

For almost a year, the Japanese media had kept silent on all stories about 32 year-old Naruhito and his 29 year-old Oxford educated bride-to-be, Masako Owada.

Masako, whose father is a former diplomat, has spent 14 years living in Europe and the United States.

She went to school in Boston, and to Harvard and Tokyo University, as well as attending Balliol College, Oxford for two years from 1988. She is fluent in English, German and French.

The wedding will be the biggest event since the 1959 wedding of Naruhito's parents, Emperor Akihito and his bride, Michiko, the first commoner to marry into the Japanese royal family.

Crown Prince Naruhito, dazzlingly rich, is probably the Eastern World's most eligible bachelor. He is amiable, open-minded and well-educated.

6 Pronunciation: numbers

1 Find these numbers in the articles and say them. What does each number refer to?

32 29 14 1959 1,500 8th 30 200,000

2 Put these words in the correct order to make one large number. Where do you put *and*?

two hundred/seventy-four thousand/two/ one million/twenty/and

3 Listen, check and write the number in figures. Where do you put the commas?

4 Now say the numbers below. Which is a telephone number, a time, a price, a decimal, a percentage and a fraction?

3.4 £3.60 1/4 0130 584 9726 7.45 pm 5%

5 Ask questions to find out:

a) your partner's telephone number.
b) her/his birthday.
c) how much she/he spends on clothes a month.
d) what percentage of her/his friends speak English.
e) what time she/he normally goes to bed.

7 Grammar: prepositions in questions

a) In which year did she get married?
b) Which year did she get married in?

1 What do you think?

1 Which question above is the most formal and not often used in spoken English, a) or b)?
2 Where does the preposition often go in spoken questions?
3 Is the preposition stressed or unstressed?

2 Listen and repeat the spoken question.

3 Complete the questions below with one of these prepositions. Use each preposition once only.

with for from to in

1 Where in your country do you come . . . ?
2 Who in your family do you live . . . ?
3 Which clothes are you most comfortable . . . ?
4 What are you learning English . . . ?
5 Which English-speaking countries have you been . . . ?

4 Ask another student the questions.

THE SECRET CEREMONY

1. The bride has her body purified with holy water.
2. Her hair is set in traditional style.
3. The bridegroom bows four times to sacred mirror.
4. The couple takes turns to sip sacred sake.
5. Each eats one rice cake to ensure a son.

Bride ancient and modern

JAPAN has gained a new Crown Princess. Crown Prince Naruhito's marriage to Masako Owada took place in secret, with all the formality and ritual of his 1,500 year-old dynasty. Not even the Emperor or Empress of Japan were present.

Bride and groom wore flowing robes styled from the eighth century. Masako's green and gold outfit weighed 30lb and she needed two ladies-in-waiting to help her move. Naruhito wore the scarlet of the land of the rising sun.

But as the newlyweds, in formal Western dress, left for their honeymoon in an open-top Rolls Royce, they looked a thoroughly modern couple.

Almost 200,000 well-wishers lined the streets to see the newlyweds emerge and millions more watched on television as Japan's six channels devoted most of the day to the event.

Masako, a 29 year-old Western-educated Foreign Ministry official, agreed to marry Naruhito after initially refusing him. But yesterday, her father said her decision was prompted by love not duty. 'Our daughter looked forward to her marriage with great happiness,' he added.

From *The Daily Mail*

english in action

YOU ARE GOING TO EXPLORE DIFFERENT LANGUAGE LEARNING EXPERIENCES.

1

First find out how other students learned languages.

1 How many languages can each of you speak? How well can you speak them?

2 Which of the ways illustrated on this page have *you* used to learn English? Which other ways have you tried?

3 Which did/didn't you enjoy?

4 What do you think? What helped you learn best?

2

Before you hear about a 'language corpus', what do you think? Is the answer to each question below a), b) or c)?

1 Is a language corpus real language kept a) in a book b) in a language laboratory c) on computer?

2 Is the language for a spoken corpus recorded by a) actors and radio personalities b) people in the street c) all kinds of people?

3 How many words do they think there are in spoken English? a) about 55, 000 b) about 500,000 c) about 5,000,000

4 Do the ten most frequent words make up a) about 25% b) about 50% or c) about 75% of everyday spoken English?

3

Now listen to a language researcher talking about the British National Corpus. Were you correct?

4

Listen again and answer these questions.

1 How big is this spoken corpus?

2 How has the data been collected?

3 What are the ten most common spoken words in English?

4 Which of these areas of language learning can the spoken corpus help us with?
- pronunciation
- reading
- grammar
- vocabulary
- functional language

5

Look at pages 7 and 8 and find examples from the spoken corpus. Which areas of language learning was it used for in this unit?

Language review 1

1 Verbs: Past Simple vs Present Perfect + time expressions

Use Present Perfect to talk about general experience.
Use Past Simple to talk about specific time/detail.

Present Perfect is often used with expressions of indefinite time.
e.g. ever/never   yet/already   before

I've	*already*	been to America.
	never	

Have you	*ever* been there(?)
I haven't	

Have you been there	*yet*?
	before?

I haven't been there	*yet*.
	before.

Past Simple is often used with expressions of definite time.
e.g. *yesterday*   an hour *ago*   *in* 1993
at the weekend   *on* Friday   *last* week

He went there	*yesterday/last* Monday. two weeks *ago*.
He didn't go there	*at* Christmas. *in* the summer.
Did he go there	*on* 8th May?

a Choose the correct alternative in these sentences.

1 Jo had a party in/on June 20th.
2 I haven't read that book yet/already.
3 No more coffee, thanks. I've before/already had two cups this morning.
4 I last saw him two weeks before/ago.
5 I haven't ever/never been to Chile.
6 I haven't seen a watch like that before/yet. It looks great!

b Make the sentences in this letter grammatically complete and correct.

Dear Wendy,
I/get/Athens/July 1st. Deborah/arrive/plane/two days later and/meet her/airport.
We/spend/about/week/the/capital/see/famous sights/then/take/boat/the islands.
In the end/we/stay/on/island/call/Naxos. I/never/see/such/beautiful place!
We/leave/Naxos/three days/get/another boat/Turkey.
We/already/visit/Ephesus and/few other interesting places/but/get/Istanbul/yet.
We/hear/so many stories/Istanbul/I can't wait/see it! We/go/Izmir/last weekend/and/visit/zoo/there/Saturday. We/enjoy/very much.
We/probably/be back/end/next week. So, until then,
Lots of love, Steve

2 Prepositions in questions

Prepositions are often put at the end of questions in English, especially in spoken language.

What can I write this letter *with*?
Where do you come *from*?
What is it used *for*?

c Complete these short conversations with an appropriate question word and preposition in each case.

1 . . . did she go . . . ?	The bank.
. . . did she go. . . ?	Her friend, Mary.
. . . did she go . . . ?	To get some travellers' cheques.
2 . . . is he talking . . . ?	Politics, as usual.
. . . is he talking . . . ?	That couple who moved in next door.
3 . . . did you buy it . . . ?	A man at work who wanted to sell it.
. . . did you buy it . . .?	The money my father gave me at Christmas.
. . . did you buy it . . .?	Us, of course!
4 . . . was it written . . . ?	Orwell, a famous English writer.
. . . year was it written . . . ?	1936.

2 Memorable words

Name:	CARY GRANT
Occupation:	actor
Age:	in his late fifties
Health:	fine
Appearance:	attractive hair: brown (dark) eyes: blue
Character:	friendly; good sense of humour
Hobbies:	golf; old movies

Famous lasting words ...

A magazine preparing an article on screen-star Cary Grant wired his agent urgently requesting information ...

HOW OLD
CARY GRANT?

Grant himself opened the telegram and promptly replied ...

OLD CARY
GRANT OKAY,
HOW YOU?

Of course, nowadays International Telegrams are even transmitted via satellite. But they're still the most memorable way to get your message across. And so simple to send, just pick up the 'phone and dial 190. So if you have friends or family overseas, remember that receiving an International Telegram from you will leave a lasting impression.

DIAL 190 *international* TELEGRAMS

Don't you know someone who deserves one?

1 Diagnosis: describing people

1 Read the first part of the advertisement for international telegrams and answer these questions.

1 Who is the man in the photograph?
2 Why is the second telegram funny?

a) What question did the magazine writer ask?
b) What question did the actor answer?

2 Answer these questions about Cary Grant in the advertisement, using the notes above it.

1 How is he?
2 How old is he?
3 What is he like?
4 What does he look like?
5 What does he like doing?

3 Ask another student the questions above about her/his best friend or someone in her/his family. Tell the class what you found out.

There is a Revision exercise for 'asking for descriptions' on page 127.

2 Pronunciation: sentence stress

1 Listen to someone sending an international telegram and complete the form below.

INTERNATIONAL TELEGRAM FORM

FROM:	TO:
ADDRESS:	ADDRESS:
POSTCODE:	
TEL NO:	POSTCODE:

PLEASE PRINT YOUR MESSAGE IN BLOCK CAPITALS BELOW

2 Read the telegram and answer these questions.

1 Which words below are often unnecessary in a telegram message?
2 Which are often stressed in a sentence?

nouns	adjectives/adverbs	*I/me/my*
be/can/have	main verbs	prepositions
a/the	negatives	

3 Write a telegram to someone in the class.

4 Read the telegram you receive. Tell another student the message, like this:

Cary Grant says he's okay.

5 Guess the words on your partner's telegram.

3 Key word: *be*

1 Look at the advertisement again. Put the correct form of the missing verb *be* in the correct places in the telegrams.

**2 Find ten examples of the verb *be* in the sentences below. In each example, in your language, do you use:
a) the verb *be*, b) another verb, or c) no verb?**

Example: In my language, we say *I have hot*, not *I am hot*.

1 **[A] Aren't you too hot? [B] Yes, I am.** Switch ...
2 **It's made of glass and metal.** It's not made of plas
3 **[A] I was wrong. [B] I was right** ... at co ... the
4 **They were burgled four times.** Well and that they ge
5 **Don't be so noisy. They will be frightened then.** ..
6 **He's being really nice to me at the moment.** He's re
7 **Oh, I haven't been in there for years,** not C and A

From the *British National Corpus* (Spoken)

3 Make personal questions with the verb *be* to ask another student. What was the most interesting thing you found out?

Grammar: Present and Past Simple passives

1 Look again at the verbs in sentences 2 and 4 above.

1 What do they have in common? How are they formed?
2 Why is this form used?

2 Talk about the things below with another student.

1 What are they usually made of?
2 If you have one, what is it made of and where was it made?

a watch   a chair   a wallet   shoes   a sweater   a shirt   a bag

4 Vocabulary: materials

1 Work together. Which is the odd word out in each group below?

cotton/silk/nylon   wood/gold/silver   plastic/wool/leather
glass/pottery/china   fire/water/grass

2 Read the poem and put one word above in each of the first four gaps.

3 Now put one of these words in each gap at the end of the poem.

earth   toenails   hair   linen   skin

4 Listen to the poem and check your answers. Which words are stressed?

5 Read the poem to another student.

5 Writing

1 Now write some more verses for the first part of the poem. Write about *wood*, *silk* or some other material.

2 Read your verses to the class. Pause before you name the material. Can they guess what 'stuff' you are talking about?

I like that stuff

Lovers lie round in it
Broken glass is found in it
...
I like that stuff

Tuna fish get wrapped in it
Legs come wrapped in it
...
I like that stuff

Elephants get sprayed with it
Scotch is made with it
...
I like that stuff

Cigarettes are lit by it
Pensioners get happy when
they sit by it
...
I like that stuff

... on my hands
... on my head
... on my feet
And ... on my bed

Well I like that stuff
Yes I like that stuff
The earth
Is made of ...
And I like that stuff

Adrian Mitchell

Dance music; adjectives; adverbs of manner and degree

6 Listening

1 Before you listen to a song, talk to other students. What country do you associate with these types of dance music?

- the tango
- rock 'n' roll
- reggae
- the flamenco
- the waltz
- the bossa nova
- the polka

2 Close your book and listen to the song. What do you think?

1 Which of the music above is it an example of?
2 Is it about a person, a place or a thing?

3 Listen again. One word in each line below is different in the song. What is it?

4 Listen again. Sing or follow the corrected words of the song.

Tall and tan[1] and fun and lovely
The girl from Ipanema goes working
And when she passes, each one she glances goes aah!

When she talks she's like a Samba
That sings so cool and sways so gently
That when she dances, each one she passes goes aah!

Oh but he washes so sadly
How can he tell her he loathes her?
Yes, he would give his hat gladly
But each way when she walks to the sea
She looks right ahead not at he[2]

Small and tan and young and lovely
The girl from Ipanema is walking
And when she passes he sighs
But she mustn't see

Poetic licence

1 *tan* should be *tanned*
2 *he* should be *him*

7 Grammar: adjectives and adverbs

1 Put these words from the song in the correct column below. Which word can go in both columns?

tall sadly lovely young gladly straight tanned gently

adjective	adverb

2 With another student, decide if these statements are correct.

a) Adverbs are often formed by adding *-ly* to an adjective.
b) Adjectives never end in *-ly*.
c) Some adverbs have the same form as the adjective.

3 Make these adjectives into adverbs and add them to your columns. What happens to adjectives that end in *-y*?

slow/fast angry/happy
nervous/confident quiet/loud

4 Play this game in two teams. Take it in turns to:

1 Choose one of the actions below, or another action, and mime it in the manner of one of the words above.

sing a song
make a cup of tea
turn on the radio
play the piano
put on a tie
eat spaghetti
climb a ladder

2 Guess the action and the adverb of students in your team.

Example: You are making a cup of tea quietly.

5 Look at these words. Which ones generally make the adjectives and adverbs after them a) stronger, b) less strong?

really very a bit extremely quite

6 Now complete these sentences with personal information.

1 I speak very fast when . . .
2 I'm a bit nervous about . . .
3 I'm quite good at . . .
4 I feel extremely happy when . . .
5 I react really angrily when . . .

Tom Jobim with Helo (left) and her daughter

Now a pop classic, *The girl from Ipanema* was the first big hit to come from the *bossa nova* movement of Brazilian singers and composers. In the mid-1960s, the voice of Brazilian singer Astrud Gilberto put Brazilian popular music on the map and brought instant fame to composer Tom Jobim and lyricist/poet Vincius de Moraes.

But what about the girl, or was there ever a 'girl from Ipanema'? There was indeed and, in fact, there still is. The song and lyrics were inspired in 1962 by the beauty of the 14 year-old Heloisa Pinheiro. She regularly walked past the Veloso Bar sidewalk cafe on Montenegro Street in Ipanema on her way home from school. After several weeks following Helo's daily passage, Jobim and Moraes felt sufficiently inspired to write the song that made them famous. Today, the street has been renamed after the poet Moraes, and the bar is appropriately called *A garota de Ipanema* (The girl from Ipanema).

Looking back with a smile, Helo today, still strikingly beautiful, attributes her immortalisation to 'being in the right place at the right time'. Other observers, however, most notably Jobim himself, insist that Helo represented the image of stunning Rio beauty. Says Jobim, 'She had long golden hair, beautiful bright green eyes and a fantastic figure...'

From *Insight City Guides: Rio*

8 Reading

1 Read about *The girl from Ipanema* in the extract from a travel guide and answer these questions.

1 Why is this song important?
2 Did 'the girl' really exist?
3 What did *The girl from Ipanema* represent to the composer?

2 Now complete this catalogue entry for the song with names from the text.

	sung by	music composed by	lyrics written by	inspired by
The girl from Ipanema (1962)				

Grammar: adjective order

1 Look at the description of Helo at the end of the text. Number the information below in the order it generally goes before the noun.

colour size/age/shape opinion

2 Write a description of someone in the class. Use *she* or *he* instead of the name, and some of the words below.

light/fair/dark
curly/wavy/straight
smart/casual
easy-going/amusing/serious
in her early/mid/late 20s, etc.

3 Listen to other students' descriptions. Guess who they are describing.

4 In Rio, you can buy *multi-coloured cotton* swimwear and *Brazilian leather* shoes.

Which order is correct, a) or b)?
a) colour, material, nationality + noun
b) colour, nationality, material + noun

5 Put these words in order.

1 an doctor moustache elderly a black He French with was
2 silk bought dress expensive She red an
3 boots wore leather They Spanish
4 in a fantastic stayed farmhouse old We Portuguese
5 woman bright met with eyes middle-aged I Greek blue a

NB Describing people

He's an attractive young man with short blond hair.

Only two or three adjectives usually go before a noun. Which word can introduce extra information?

english in action

YOU ARE GOING TO HAVE A 'BRING AND BUY SALE'.

1
First, listen to people phoning to find out about some of the items advertised on this page. Match each conversation to its advertisement.

2
Now write a short advertisement for something you would like to sell. What parts of speech will you need/not need to include?

DISPLAY YOUR ADVERTISEMENTS.

3
Look at other students' advertisements. Find things you are interested in buying and note:

- the owner
- the price
- other information you need

HAVE A 'BRING AND BUY SALE'.

4
Work in two groups. Take it in turns to be buyers and sellers.

BUYERS: How much are you prepared to spend on each item/in total? Go to the sellers of things you are interested in and ask your questions. Write down what you would like to buy.
SELLERS: Give extra information and try to persuade the buyers to buy what you have for sale.

5
Tell the class what you sold and what you agreed to buy.

Language review 2

1 Verbs: Present and Past Simple passives

Active verb forms stress the subject of a sentence. Passive verb forms stress the object. (The subject is often unknown or unimportant to the speaker.)

Seiko watches are made in Japan. (passive)
The Japanese make Seiko watches. (active)

	Be		Past participle		(Preposition)
Present	am/is/are	+	opened made done	+	*by* + subject *of* + material *in* + country/ time
Past	was/were				

a Make the following sentences grammatically correct and complete.

1 This chair/make/Germany/15th century.
2 This kind/cotton/grow/Egypt/then/export.
3 The parts/this car/manufacture/Japan/then/ assemble/Britain.
4 1500 new houses/build/the south-east/England/ last year.
5 The rubbish/collect/6.30/Thursday/every week.
6 These toys/made/wood/local children.
7 The room/clean/yesterday.
8 When/telephone/invent?
9 My bag/steal/last week.
10 She/born/Africa.

2 Adjectives and adverbs

• **adverbs of manner**

Adverbs of manner describe verbs.

He walked *slowly*.

• **Regular**

Adjective	**Adverb**
bad	badly
easy	easily

• **Irregular**

Adjective	**Adverb**
good	well
fast	fast

Some adjectives end in *-ly*, e.g. *friendly*.
Some adverbs have the same form as adjectives, e.g. *hard, fast, straight, early, late*.

• **adverbs of degree**

Adverbs of degree can describe adjectives or other adverbs.

She's *really* intelligent. She works *very* hard.

+	++	+++	++++	+++++	++++++
a bit shy(ly)	quite shy(ly)	shy(ly)	very shy(ly)	really shy(ly)	extremely shy(ly)

• **adjective word order**

When adjectives come before a noun, they usually have to go in a particular order, like this:

opinion	size/age/ shape	colour	nationality	material	noun
(a) nice			Egyptian	cotton	scarf
(an) ugly	old				man
lovely	straight	black			hair

If there are more than two or three adjectives, then we often use *with* to add extra information.

It's a large brown dog with beautiful, floppy ears.

b Decide if the underlined word in each sentence is correct. If it isn't, correct it.

1 My parents are happy married.
2 She speaks very well English.
3 My father speaks German fluent.
4 Are you always unfriendly when you meet new people?
5 He was a bit shy and talked quite nervous.

c Complete each sentence below with ideas of your own.

1 I am extremely sorry to hear . . .
2 It was quite hot because . . .
3 She came home very late because . . .
4 They spoke really loudly because . . .
5 She was a bit surprised when . . .

d Describe the person and the various objects in the picture in as much detail as possible.

Example: On the left there is a black, leather handbag with gold straps.

Bossa Nova

LEARN TO DANCE THE BOSSA NOVA.

1 Look at the feet in the pictures for the man's part. Put these instructions in order.

a) Put your left foot forward.
b) Put your left foot back.
c) Keep your left foot where it is and move your weight onto it.
d) Put your right foot forward.
e) Put your right foot back.
f) Keep your right foot where it is and move your weight onto it.

2 Practise the man's part to a *Slow Quick Quick* rhythm.

3 Look at the pictures of the woman's feet. Change the instructions above to match her part.

Example: 1 Put your left foot back.

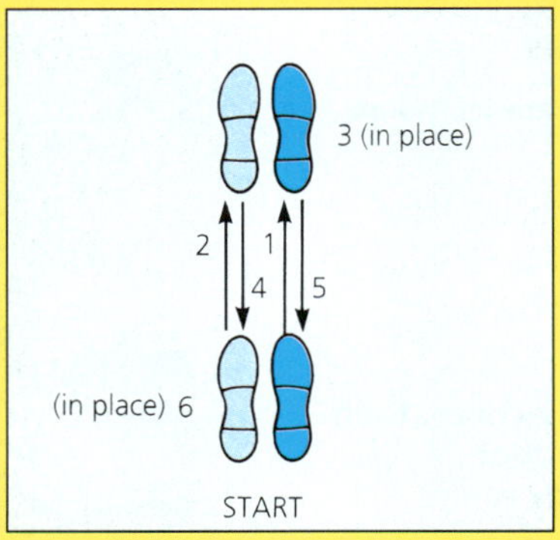

Man's part

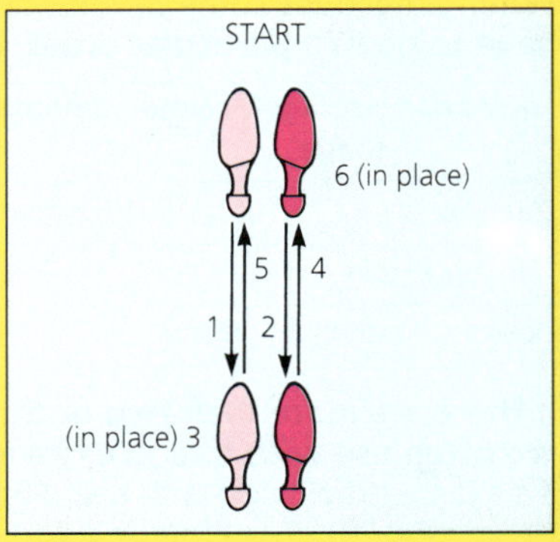

Woman's part

4 Work in groups of three. Take it in turns to look at the book and teach the other two students how to:

a) stand and hold each other.
b) move from the hips.
c) move their feet.

5 Find a partner and practise the Bossa Nova.

PLAY 'THE GIRL FROM IPANEMA' AND ENJOY THE DANCE!

3 Difficult decisions

American Airlines

1 Diagnosis: *will* vs *going to* (decisions)

1 Make quick decisions. You have $150 to spend. Tell another student what duty-free goods you will buy some of these people.

your partner/best friend your son/daughter yourself
your mother/father your brother/sister

2 Ask your partner why she/he decided to buy each thing. Tell the class one or two of her/his reasons.

Example: Marc is going to get his mother a scarf because she loves new clothes.

3 Complete this conversation with *am/are/is going to* or *will*. Use contracted forms if possible.

A: What . . . (you) get Carmela for her birthday?
B: A box of chocolates.
A: That's a good idea. I . . . get her some flowers then.

4 Have similar conversations about people in your class.

- Divide a list of students between you and your partner.
- Write an idea for a birthday present for each person.
- Take it in turns to ask about people on your partner's list. Decide what you'll get them when you hear your partner's idea.

There is a Revision exercise for *will* vs *going to* (decisions) on page 127.

2 Vocabulary: describing clothes

1 Use each word below once only to complete these word pairs.

shoes and . . .	a t-shirt and . . .	a coat and . . .
a shirt/jacket and . . .	a bra/vest and . . .	a scarf and . . .
a skirt and . . .	a sweater and . . .	a dressing-gown and . . .

slippers socks pants tie hat blouse gloves shorts jeans

2 Listen and check your answers. Which word is stressed in the pair? How do you pronounce *and*?

3 Work with another student. Look at these words for describing clothes. Which of the clothes above can each one go with?

Example: You can say tight-fitting shoes, but you don't usually say baggy shoes.

baggy/tight-fitting long-sleeved/short-sleeved
checked/striped/plain round-necked/v-necked

4 Take it in turns to describe someone in the class by the clothes they are wearing. How soon can other students guess who you are describing?

Presents; *will* and *going to* (predictions); *I think/definitely/probably* (word order)

3 Reading

1 Read the magazine article below quickly. What occasion and whose present are *all* the people talking about?

2 Read the article again and complete this chart.

Name	Present last year	Present this year	Romantic/practical?
Terry Reid		?	
Sophie O'Neill			
Sam Rahman	*jewellery*		
Isabel Martin			*romantic*

3 What do you think?

1 What will you give your best friend next birthday?
2 What will she/he give you for *your* birthday?

4 Grammar: *will/going to* (predictions 1)

a) It will *probably* be something practical.
b) I *think* she'll get me something for the house.
c) He's *definitely* going to buy me something expensive.

Look at the position of *probably*, *think* and *definitely* in the predictions above. Rewrite:

a) the *will* sentences using *going to*.
b) the *going to* sentences using *will*.
c) each sentence in its negative form.

Pronunciation

1 What do you think? Are *probably*, *think* and *definitely* stressed or unstressed in sentences a), b) and c) in the last exercise?

2 Listen and check the answer.

1 Which two words have main stress in each sentence?
2 How is unstressed *will* pronounced?

3 Predict some of these things with another student. Make a note of your answers.

- the weather tomorrow
- the next report of something in today's news
- the next episode of your favourite TV serial
- the result of a sporting event next weekend
- the film at your nearest cinema next week
- your teacher's clothes next lesson

4 Next week, tell the class how many of your predictions came true.

One from the heart

It's that time of year again when you are wondering what on earth to buy your loved one. Chat's Fiona Thompson finds out what people plan to give their partners for Christmas.

TERRY REID, surveyor
'I haven't a clue what I'll buy her this year. She'll drop some heavy hints, but I'll get her something practical. Romance went out of the window years ago! Last year I bought her a dishwasher.'

SOPHIE O'NEILL, lawyer
'I'm going to buy him a woolly jumper because he likes woolly things. I'll choose it, though. Last year I bought him some boxer shorts and lots of little things – a mixture of practical and romantic items. It's got to be something quite special, hasn't it?'

SAM RAHMAN, student
'I'll buy her gold or some clothes. It will be something she'll be able to keep for sentimental value. Last year I brought her some gold jewellery back from Cairo. She's probably the hardest person to buy for because you want to get her something really special.'

ISABEL MARTIN, unemployed
'It will probably be a bracelet. I usually buy romantic things at Christmas. He's the worst person I have to buy a present for because he's so awkward. He says he's pleased with what I buy him but after a couple of months he'll bring up the fact that he didn't like it!'

From Chat

Key word: *if*; *if/when/unless/if . . . not* + future time; first conditional

5 Key word: *if*

1 Make short dialogues by matching a sentence containing *if* in column B to a sentence in column A. Use each sentence once only.

A	B
1 Shall I come round?	a) Yes, if he wants to.
2 Will you both help Basil?	b) What if she is?
3 She's sure to be angry.	c) Yes ... except if it rains.
4 Give her my love.	d) Yes, if you like.
5 Can he come with you?	e) Yes, if we can.
6 Will it be outside?	f) If only!
7 You could go on holiday.	g) Yes, if I see her.

2 Check your answers by taking it in turns to begin each dialogue with another student.

3 Work with your partner. Take one of the dialogues above and write the four or five lines of conversation that came before and the four or five lines that came after.

Example:
A: But why did you lose your job?
B: They said I was rude to my boss.
A: And were you?
B: Well, a little. But he's always so nasty to me. Anyway, I don't know what I am going to do now.
A: **You could go on holiday.**
B: **If only!**
A: What do you mean?
B: I haven't got any money.
A: Couldn't you stay with your brother in Scotland?
B: He's on holiday in America!

4 Now take a part each and act out your dialogue.

a) Read your dialogue out loud together.
b) Read it again, but look up as you say each line.
c) Have the dialogue without reading!

6 Listening

1 Listen to some people talking about difficult decisions they have to make in the near future. Complete the first part of this chart.

	The decision	To be made by	Depends on
PERSON 1			
PERSON 2			
PERSON 3			

2 Listen again and complete the rest of the chart.

Grammar: *if/when/unless*

He'll go to university
- *when* he leaves school.
- *if* he passes his exam.
- *if* he does *not* fail.
- *unless* he fails.

1 Look at these words above: *when, if, if . . . not, unless.*

1 Which two mean the same?
2 Which one introduces what:
a) will definitely happen?
b) will possibly happen?
3 Is the verb after each one in a present or future form?

2 Complete these gaps with *if* or *when*.

1 I'll wait . . . you hurry.
2 He'll phone . . . he arrives.
3 . . . the film ends, we'll leave.
4 . . . I work harder, I'll pass.
5 We'll go later . . . it's fine.

3 Keep the same meaning and rewrite the *if* sentences in the negative.

Example: I won't wait if you don't hurry.

4 Rewrite them using *unless*.

Example: I won't wait unless you hurry.

5 Talk about your future plans for work/school and home life. What do they depend on?

"This will be your room. They'll ring if they want anything ..."

7 Speaking

1 Read these instructions and then prepare a 'balloon' debate in groups.

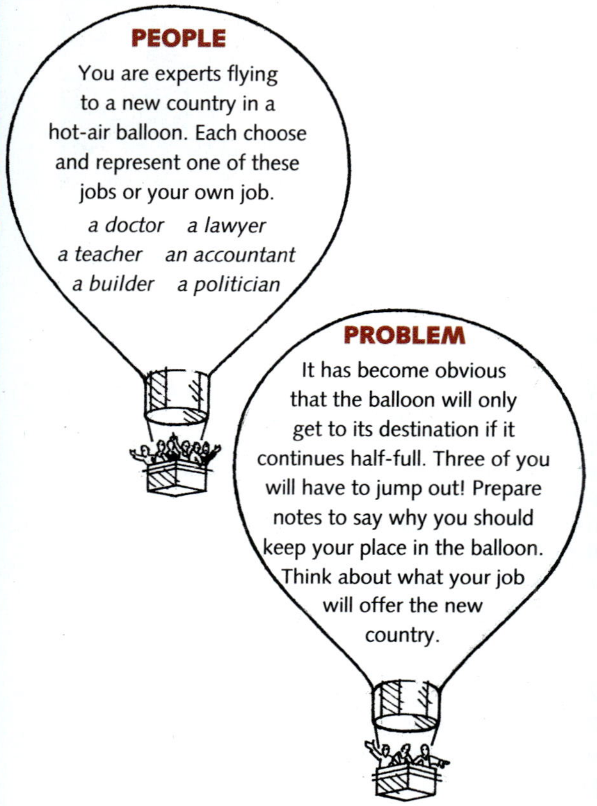

2 In turn, tell your group why you shouldn't jump.

Unless I get there, ...

When I arrive, ...

If I jump, ...

3 When you have heard everyone's case, take a vote on each job in turn.

- Each person in the group has three votes but can't vote for her/himself.
- The three people with the lowest number of votes must jump!

4 Tell the class which people your group will send to the new country and why. How far do all the groups agree?

8 Function: agreement/disagreement

1 **No, you're quite right.** Why? Because
2 **Oh rubbish!** ... It is ... No it ain'
3 **Mm mm ... that's true!** .She'd like t
4 **Yes, I think so too.** Erm, I'm not su
5 **I quite agree** ... somebody has a tak
6 **Yes I know, but** it's such a long way
7 **No, I don't agree with that.** ... No
8 **Actually, you're right,** it does ...

From the *British National Corpus* (Spoken)

1 Put the examples of agreement/disagreement above into one of these columns.

+	–
I agree (with you)	I don't agree (with you)

2 Listen and repeat each expression with feeling. Which one do you think can sound rude unless the people know each other well?

3 Discuss these predictions about the future of work within the next ten years in your country. How many of you agree with each one? What do they depend on?

1 Unemployment will definitely fall.
2 More people in companies will work from home.
3 If they want a good job people will have to speak English.
4 More young people will have to work abroad for part of their lives.
5 In many families, women will go out to work and men will look after the home.

EXCITING SUMMER JOBS IN AMERICA

If you want to spend nine weeks in the USA working in a summer 'camp' and spend additional weeks travelling (at your expense), or return home at the end of your camp stay, then we have just the programme for you. It includes:

- placement in a camp with full board and lodging
- free round trip transportation between London/Amsterdam/Frankfurt and New York
- help in securing the J-l Cultural Exchange visitor's visa
- pocket money
- independent travel time of up to 7 weeks

Camping – as American as apple pie

There are more than 12,000 summer camps in the USA which serve 7,000,000 American children aged six to sixteen. Camps are usually situated in country areas with space for swimming, sailing, water skiing and other sports and activities.

Camp counsellors

Life as a camp counsellor is not easy but is always rewarding. Some of you will be employed as specialist counsellors, others as general counsellors. A general counsellor will be responsible for overall activities and looking after a small group of children. A specialist counsellor is responsible for instructing a specific skill such as swimming, tennis or riding.

Do I qualify?

You qualify if you:

- are a bona fide student, youth worker, teacher, or someone with a specialised skill
- are calm, patient, caring and flexible
- are available for departure to the US between 1 and 30 June and available for a 9/10 week work commitment
- are at least 18 years old by June 1 of the summer for which you are applying
- are physically fit and can speak English

To apply you must:

- complete the application form in the Camp America brochure
- arrange a personal interview with an authorised interviewer

Brochures and a list of interviewers are available from Camp America, London.

YOU WANT TO APPLY FOR WORK ON A SUMMER CAMP IN THE USA.

1

Read about Camp America. Is a), b) or c) correct in each sentence below?

1 You will work mainly with:
a) children.
b) adults.
c) old people.

2 A specialist counsellor needs:
a) to have medical skills.
b) to be good at a particular activity.
c) to be a good swimmer.

3 Your stay in America will be for:
a) the month of June.
b) seven weeks.
c) a minimum of nine weeks.

4 Camp America will pay for:
a) your travel (to and from the USA).
b) your travel and something for your work.
c) your travel, work and final holiday.

5 To apply you'll need to get:
a) an application form.
b) an interview.
c) an application form and an interview.

2

Before you write for your brochure and list of interviewers, check you know how to write a formal letter in English.

- Where will you put your address?
- Where will you put the date?
- How will you begin the letter? How will you finish it?
- What opening sentences can you think of?

3

Listen and write the address of Camp America.

WRITE AND SEND YOUR LETTER!

4

While you are waiting for an answer, have a mock interview with another student. Ask and answer questions about:

- your reason/s for applying.
- the skills and expertise you can offer.
- any advantages the experience will give you.
- what you'll do when camp is over.

GOOD LUCK WITH YOUR APPLICATION!

Language review 3

1 Verbs: *will/going to*

- **Decisions**

***Going to* is often used to talk about decisions made before speaking.**

***Will* is often used for decisions made at the time of speaking.**

A: *I'm going to* get a newspaper. Do you want anything?
B: Well, I'd love an ice-cream.
A: OK. I'*ll* get you one.

- **Predictions**

Going to and *will* can both be used to make predictions.

If they win the election,	they'*ll* cut taxation.
	they'*re going to* cut taxation.

a For each sentence below decide if you can use *will*, *going to* or both.

1 I can't meet you tonight. I . . . see George.
2 What . . . (you) do if it rains?
3 That exercise isn't difficult. I . . . show you.
4 We . . . be late if you don't hurry.
5 I'm sorry I forgot to post your letter. I . . . do it now.
6 We've already started decorating. We . . . paint the kitchen yellow.

2 *Definitely/probably/I think + will/going to*

These words are often used when we predict the future.

Word order is important.

- ***I think***

+	*I think* he'll phone. *I think* he's going to phone.
–	*I don't think* he'll phone. *I don't think* he's going to phone.
?	*Do you think* he'll phone? *Do you think* he's going to phone?

- ***definitely/probably***

+	She'll *definitely/probably* phone. She's *definitely/probably* going to phone.
–	She *definitely/probably* won't phone. She's *definitely/probably* not going to phone.
?	Will she *definitely/probably* phone? Is she *definitely/probably* going to phone?

b Put the words in these predictions in order.

1 soon AIDS I find for think cure they'll a
2 will world think a don't there government I ever be
3 live old they probably 100 going people until are are to years
4 towns definitely in won't life safer get
5 people soon definitely are to on live moon going the
6 cigarettes they places ban probably won't all in public

c Use the language opposite and make three predictions for each of the things below. What will life be like in 100 years' time?

Example: I don't think anyone will wear hats.

- clothing
- education
- entertainment
- housing
- transport

3 *If/when/unless* + future time (first conditional)

***If/when/unless* + Present Simple expresses future time. *If/unless* introduces a condition.**

***If* = perhaps it will happen**

***When* = it is definitely expected to happen**

Unless* = it will happen *except if

The dog won't bite	*if*	you are gentle.
	when	it is asleep.
	unless	you frighten it. (*if* you do *not* frighten it)

d Make the following predictions grammatically complete and correct.

1 If/I/see/Tony/I/tell/him/you/home.
2 I/not/go/unless/he/ask/me/to.
3 When/meeting/finish/we/all/go out/for/drink.
4 I/be/late/for work/unless/I/take/car.
5 you phone/me/if/you/miss/9.00 train?
6 I/help/you/with/homework/when/I/get back.

4 *Power games*

Dear Miss Smith,
Could you read this letter out during assembly, it goes like this. I hate some of the fifth and sixth-year people. Boys and girls torment me about my speech and hearing. My name is Matthew Jagger and I'm in class 5S. I wear glasses and two hearing aids. I hate wearing them but I have to, to help me see and hear. But people don't seem to understand. They laugh at me and call me names which makes me very, very unhappy. I just wish it would stop and we could all be friends.
Thank you.
Matthew Jagger

From *Today*

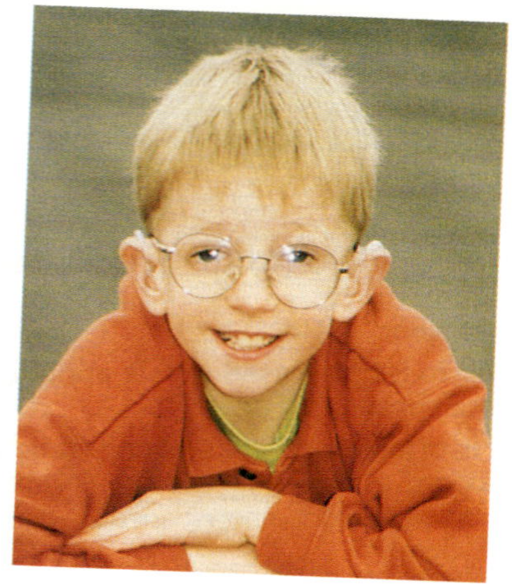

1 Diagnosis: deduction

1 Tell other students about your early schooldays and your:

favourite teacher/subject first/last day best/worst moment

2 Before you read the letter above, answer these questions.

1 What is the difference between a) a class and an assembly, b) a first-year and a sixth-year pupil?
2 What do you think? What is the possible connection between a) the letter and the photo, b) Matthew Jagger and Miss Smith?

3 Now read the letter and check the answer to the last question. What does Matthew want Miss Smith to do? Why?

4 Children who behave like the ones in the letter are called *bullies*. Work with another student and complete this definition.

A bully is someone who . . .

5 Use one word to complete each sentence about Matthew's situation.

1 The bullies . . . be bigger than Matthew because they are a lot older.
2 School . . . be much fun for Matthew because other children bully him.
3 He wears glasses so he . . . be short-sighted or he . . . be long-sighted.

There is a Revision exercise for *must/might/can't be* on page 127.

2 Grammar

Must/might/can't + verb

1 Look at the underlined words in the sentences below. Which ones say something is:

a) very improbable?
b) very probable?
c) just one possibility?

1 Matthew <u>must be</u> brave . . .
2 He <u>can't have</u> many friends . . .
3 His teachers <u>can't know</u> what's happening . . .
4 The other children <u>might feel</u> sorry for him now . . .
5 But they <u>might think</u> . . .
6 He <u>must trust</u> his teacher . . .

2 Work with another student. Complete the sentences above with logical explanations.

Example: Matthew must be brave because he isn't afraid to tell people about the bullies.

NB Logical deduction or future possibility

a) Sylvie might be at home later.
b) Sylvie might be at home. She often is at this time.

Which refers to present/future time, a) or b)?

Should/shouldn't (obligation); requests;
key word: *could; could be*

3 Speaking

1 What do you think? Which of these things might be helpful to Matthew? What should/shouldn't his teachers do?

- separate the bullies from the other children
- bully the bullies
- call the police
- provide self-defence classes for small children
- other?

2 Read what actually happened on page 124. How must Matthew and the bullies feel now?

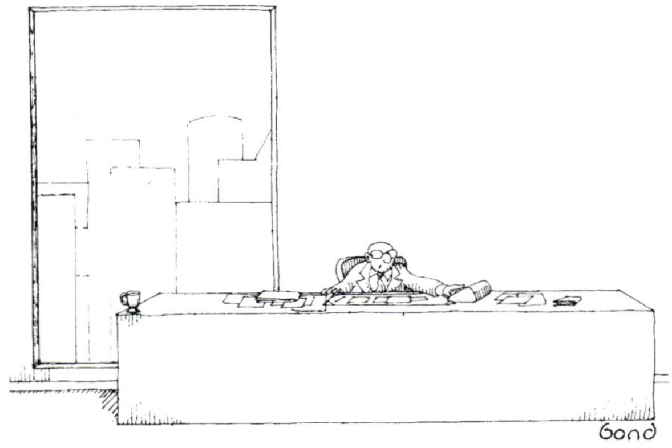

"Miss Ellis, could you come in here and pass me my coffee?"

4 Function: making requests

1 Find the request at the beginning of Matthew's letter. How many ways can you change *could you* and keep the same meaning?

2 Answer these questions about the requests below.

1 Which two look the most/the least polite?
2 Where could you put *please* in each sentence to make them all look more polite?

1 Could you go and ask her? How many b
2 Do you think you could open the door
3 Can you bring me the book? ... Post
4 Put that there, will you? ... Up her
5 Will you turn that tape recorder off
6 Would you close the kitchen doors? S
7 Would you mind doing the beans now?

From the *British National Corpus* (Spoken)

Pronunciation

1 Listen to each request above. Which two are the most polite/the least polite? Where and why were your predictions different?

2 Have short conversations for these situations.

a) A teenager asks her/his parent if she/he can borrow the new family car.
b) An employee asks her/his boss if she/he can leave work early at the end of the week.
c) A business person asks the bank manager for a big overdraft to start a new business.

5 Key word: *could*

He *could be* a bank manager but I'm not sure.

1 Look at *could be* in the sentence above, describing the man in the cartoon. Is it similar in meaning to *must be, might be* or *can't be*?

2 Look at other ways we use *could*. Match each example below to one of these groups.

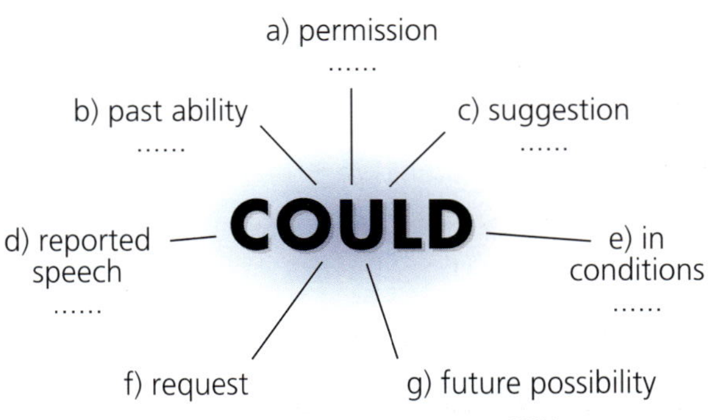

1 We could go to the cinema, what do you think?
2 Please could I go out this evening?
3 Could you open the window please?
4 You said I could.
5 Things could get worse.
6 I could read when I was three.
7 If I could afford to live here I would.

3 Make questions for your partner using *could*.

1 Ask if you can borrow something (say what).
2 Find out about her/his abilities at a particular age (say when).
3 Suggest doing something together after class.
4 Ask about her/his future job possibilities when she/he speaks fluent English.

A

B

C

6 Listening

1 Before you listen, talk to other students. Give examples of bullying behaviour by one or more of these people:

boss   policeman   parent   brother/sister   other?

2 Now listen to a woman talking about her situation.

1 Which people above were involved?
2 Was she the victim or the bully?
3 Was it physical or mental bullying?

3 Listen again and number the pictures in the order they are referred to. What is the significance of each one in the story?

Grammar: *used to*

1 Work with another student. Complete these sentences with Monica's exact words.

1 I . . . keep her (my sister) in check.
2 I . . . go upstairs and hide in the linen cupboard.
3 We . . . live near the sea.
4 I . . . make them all walk in a line.

2 Listen, check your answers and repeat. Which sound do you hear linking *used to*, /d/ or /t/?

3 Look at the completed answers with another student. Decide which of these statements are true.

We say *used to* to talk about:

a) an action which happened only once in the past.
b) past habit.
c) something which probably still happens.
d) the past only. There is no present or future form.

4 Use the correct forms of *used to* to complete each gap in these sentences about Monica's situation.

1 What . . . (Monica) do to keep her brothers and sisters in check?
2 She . . . jump out of the cupboard to frighten her sister at night.
3 She . . . hit her brothers and sisters very often.
4 Her sister . . . sleep very well because she was frightened.
5 She . . . believe there were chickens under her bed.

5 Tell other students what you remember about your own childhood or a favourite time in your past. Think about:

- the place
- the people
- activities you did regularly

NB ***used to/usually***

a) I usually go to bed at 11 o'clock.
b) I used to go to bed earlier than that.

Which sentence is about a present habit, a) or b)? Which is about a past habit?

Describing people; defining relative clauses

7 Vocabulary

Describing character

I think it was just good management.

I think I was just a good organiser.

1 Look at Monica's words above. What do you think?

1 Is it necessary to frighten people a little if you are their 'leader'?
2 What type of person should a good leader be?

2 Look at the leadership qualities opposite. Match one adjective from each pair below to its definition in the text.

adaptable/conservative
creative/practical
moody/even-tempered
optimistic/pessimistic
ambitious/unambitious
organised/disorganised
sensitive/insensitive
fair/biased
shy/self-confident
clever/stupid

3 Check your answers with another student. Where is the main stress on each adjective?

4 With your partner, write definitions for the words you didn't use, like this:

An unambitious person is someone who . . .

5 In groups, decide the qualities of a good leader.

1 Choose a type of leader to talk about, e.g. a student representative, or politician.
2 Choose seven adjectives.
3 Put the adjectives in order, beginning with the most important.

FOLLOW THE LEADER

Being a leader isn't just a matter of giving orders. Certain personal qualities are also desirable and can have a good effect on other people.

PERSONALITY TYPE	POSSIBLE BENEFITS
• *ambitious*	Someone who has a strong desire to be successful. This could encourage others to be successful too.
•	Someone who shows delicate feelings and judgement. This encourages others to say how they really feel.
•	Someone who feels hopeful about the future. This encourages general positive thinking.
•	Someone who is just and reasonable, without favourites. Everyone should feel valued and important.
•	Someone who believes in their own worth. This can act as an example to shyer, less confident people.
•	Someone who is usually in a good mood. This should encourage a happy atmosphere.
•	Someone who is intelligent and generally skilful. The benefits of these abilities can be shared by everyone.
•	Someone who can change her/his behaviour and ideas to fit new situations. This should help other people to adapt more easily.
•	Someone who keeps things in order and well arranged. This helps create an atmosphere of efficiency and calm.
•	Someone who produces new and original ideas and thoughts. This makes things more exciting and keeps motivation high.

8 Grammar: defining relative clauses

1 Listen to a poem twice with your book shut. Then write what you remember with another student.

2 Use the structure below and rewrite the poem. Which of the underlined words are used with:

a) places only b) places and things c) people?

I'd like to meet someone

<u>that</u> is . . .	<u>where</u> we'd talk about . . .
<u>whose</u> passion is . . .	<u>which</u> are made of . . .
<u>who</u> lives in . . .	<u>that</u> might . . .

3 Use this structure to write about someone you'd like to meet.

english in action

YOU ARE GOING TO TRY OUT A GROUP DISCUSSION TECHNIQUE DEVELOPED BY THE PSYCHOLOGIST EDWARD DE BONO.

1

Read the descriptions of group member 'types'. Which colour best describes you?

2

Listen to six people's comments. What colour hat do you think each person was wearing?

3

Work in groups and discuss two of the issues opposite. For each issue, each group member:

- takes a different colour.
- writes notes for ideas which suit her/his colour's character.
- joins in the discussion as that colour.

4

Choose a 'blue' group leader and one colour only for the rest of the group.

- Begin to discuss issue 3 with everyone wearing the same colour hat.
- All change colour when your leader says so and continue discussing from the new point of view.

5

What do you think? What are the advantages of groups made up of a) different types of people, and b) the same types?

'Six Thinking Hats' is a method for doing one sort of thinking at a time. Each hat has a different colour and represents a type of thinking.

WHITE – neutral viewpoint. Likes to present objective information and facts.

YELLOW – optimistic and positive viewpoint. Concentrates on why things can be done.

RED – emotional viewpoint. Reacts emotionally on instinct, and is not particularly logical.

GREEN – creative viewpoint. Has lots of new ideas but these are not always very practical.

BLACK – pessimistic and negative viewpoint. Concentrates on why something cannot be done.

BLUE – likes to be the leader and organise other group members to get the best solution to a particular task or problem.

ISSUE 1: Hiring a teacher

You interviewed a lot of people for the job of English teacher for a private language school. You offered by far the best candidate the job by phone. She has now discovered she is pregnant and needs maternity leave of at least six months in the near future. What should you do?

ISSUE 2: Smoking areas

A new leisure centre should help relieve the problems of crime and unemployment for young people in your town. The safety and health committee has decided on a no-smoking policy in the centre. Only non-smokers will get jobs. Anyone found smoking will be banned from the centre for a year. What are the views of the group?

ISSUE 3: Shoplifting

Your neighbour's only son has been caught shoplifting at the local supermarket. He is already in trouble with the police and might be taken away from his mother if a complaint is made. The manager of the supermarket says prices will continue to go up if he can't stop people shoplifting. What should he do?

Language review 4

1 *Must/might/can't* + verb (deduction)

Use *must/can't* + verb to express definite conclusions from evidence.

Use *might* + verb to express possible conclusions.

He always works overtime.	He *must feel* tired. He *might need* the money. He *can't have* a very good social life.

a Write sentences to explain each situation below. Use *must, might/could* and *can't* + suitable verbs as in the example opposite.

1 Carmela knows a lot about films.
2 Josef has got three cats, two dogs and a parrot.
3 She is always well-dressed.
4 I haven't eaten for a week.
5 Vera isn't at work today.

2 Making requests

Be less direct with people you don't know very well or if the request is strange/inconvenient.

Requests, from the most to the least direct, include:

Open *Don't open*	the door, *will you?*

Can *Could* *Will* *Would*	you open the door?

Do you think you *could*	open	the door?
Would you mind	open*ing*	

b Write an appropriate request for each of these situations.

1 Your younger brother is playing music loudly in the next room. You are trying to work.
2 You have gone to quite a formal dinner party. You don't know many of the people. You want the salt which is at the other end of the table.
3 You are in a bar and you need a light for your cigarette. Someone near you is smoking.
4 Someone is smoking in a train compartment which is marked *No Smoking*. You hate the smell of smoke.
5 Your friend is going shopping. You need some milk.
6 You need to borrow quite a lot of money from a friend. It's the third time this month!

3 *Used to*

***Used to* + verb is used to talk about finished past states and habits.**

I *used to* live there when I was a child. (state)
I *used to* smoke but I don't any more. (habit)

***Used to* always refers to the past. There is no present or future form.**

+	He	used to	smoke(?)
?	Did he	use to	
–	He didn't	use to	

c The two forms below were completed by the same person at different times. Use the information to write three positive and three negative sentences with *used to*.

A	B
Name: Sue Smith	Name: Sue Murray (née Smith)
Address: 11, Park Road	Address: 7 Bliss Close
Hobbies: stamp collecting, bird watching	Hobbies: dancing, wind surfing, bird watching

4 Defining relative clauses

These give extra information about a noun.

***Who, whose* and *that* define people:**

This is the person *who/that* wrote to me and *whose* brother lives next door.

***Which* and *that* define things and places.**

This is the house *which/that* Jack built.

***Where* means 'in which' and defines places.**

This is the town *where* I was born.

d Choose the correct alternatives in these sentences.

1 A baker is someone that/which sells bread.
2 This is the factory which/where we met.
3 She's the woman who/whose daughter phoned.
4 Is that the dog who/which bit you?
5 Lend me the pen that/who you bought yesterday.
6 I spoke to the man who/which I told you about.

5 Consolidation

C

A

B

1 Across cultures: social issues

Revises
Vocabulary: Clothes and physical appearance
Grammar: Present Perfect (indefinite time); *must/might/can't* + verb; *should/shouldn't* (obligation)

1 Look at the pictures and use your mini-dictionary on page 138 to check the meaning and pronunciation of these words.

market	(news)papers	worn-out	pride	dirt
rags	carrier bags	tea-cup	medal	
hero	lonely	loosely	ribbon	

2 Work with other students. Describe the people and their clothes in the pictures. Then use *must/might/can't* and imagine their possible:

age nationality family situation daily routine

Example: He must be about sixty. Look at his face.

3 Listen to a well-known 1970s protest song.

1 Which verse goes with which picture?
2 Which country/town are the people in?

4 Put the lines of the chorus in order.

To make you change your mind.
And say for you that the sun don't shine?
And lead you through the streets of London.
So how can you tell me you're lonely, (1)
I'll show you something
Let me take you by the hand

5 Listen to the chorus again and check your order. Does it say that you:

a) should enjoy city life?
b) shouldn't complain?
c) might become like the people in the song?

6 Sing or follow the words of the complete song on page 131.

7 Answer these questions with other students and discuss social issues in your country.

1 How serious a problem is poverty/homelessness?
2 Is a particular age-group involved?
3 Which of the following things are provided by a) the government, b) private companies? How do they compare?

- education
- health care
- housing

D

2 Thinking about learning: vocabulary

Revises
Vocabulary: Hobbies; jobs; characteristics; countries/nationalities; materials
Grammar: Passives; adjective word order

Compound words

1 Look at the words of the song on page 131 again, and find examples of compound words.

Example: newspaper (news + paper)

a) Four are spelt with a hyphen (-).
b) One is written as one word and describes a job.
c) One is written as two separate words and describes something you carry.

2 Work with another student. Match each word in column A to a word in column B to make other compound words. In which hobbies is this equipment used?

A	B
tennis	glass
face	boots
fishing	mask
surf	club
hiking	racquet
magnifying	rod
golf	board

3 Look at the compound words above with your partner.

1 What is each thing usually made of?
2 What equipment do you use to do your favourite hobby or activity? Where was it made?

Suffixes

1 Look at the endings of the words in each group below and answer these questions.

1 Which suffixes are frequently used to make:
a) adjectives b) personal nouns c) abstract nouns?
2 Where is the stress on these words?

a) active attractive expensive	b) musical political practical	c) communication imagination separation
d) teacher butcher doctor	e) photographic artistic idealistic	f) scientist biologist astrologist

2 Find the word with the incorrect suffix in the groups below and correct it. What suffixes go with which type of vocabulary?

a) banker, footballer, directer, manager
b) Japanese, Argentinese, Maltese, Lebanese
c) politician, electrician, librarian, journalian
d) socialism, democratism, communism, buddhism
e) Finland, Ireland, Tunisland, Holland

3 Play this game in groups and practise the vocabulary you know. Take it in turns to:

- Think of a famous person. Don't say who.
- Answer questions about their nationality, appearance, personality and things they are famous for. You can only answer yes or no.
- Unless the other students guess in ten questions, you win.

Prefixes

1 Work with another student. Put the opposites of the adjectives below in one of the columns. Are the words in the columns generally negative or positive in meaning?

un	dis	im	in

attractive	friendly	sensitive	loyal
experienced	caring	ambitious	adaptable
reliable	obedient	polite	tolerant
patient	selfish	decisive	faithful
romantic	lucky	fair	intelligent

2 Now choose the best adjectives to describe some of these people to your partner. Explain why you chose each word.

a) your best friend b) a member of your family
c) your boss/teacher d) a young child you know

3 Language in context: numerology

What's your

Revises
Vocabulary: Alphabet; numbers; adjectives describing people
Grammar: Adjectives/adverbs; agreement/disagreement; *will/going to*; *if/unless*

Find out how numerology can tell you about your character and future.

1 Read the information below and discover:

1 Which famous mathematician taught numerology?
2 When did he live?
3 Which numbers did he think influenced life most?
4 How can we find our personal number?

NUMEROLOGY: THE THEORY OF NUMBERS

In the sixth century BC, Pythagoras, the father of mathematics, taught 'number theory', which included geometry and numerology. He believed that everything in the universe was influenced by predictable cycles, and that the numbers one to nine were the key to these patterns. And numbers are just as significant today. As you come to understand how to work out your own and others' numbers, you will see that many of your closest friends and partners have at least one number in common with you. For example, members of the same family are often born on the same day of the month (a mother on 12th January, her daughter on 12th February).

We discover our own personal numbers by using calculations based on our names and birth date. It is these numbers which have the most influence on our numeroscope forecast.

2 Find out your partner's personal number.

1 Ask her/him what name (first and surname) she/he is usually called by.
2 Check you know how to spell these names.
3 Change every letter in the names to a number. Use the code in the conversion chart. For example, Tom Cruise becomes:
2 6 4 3 9 3 9 1 5
TOM CRUISE

1	2	3	4	5	6	7	8	9
A	B	C	D	E	F	G	H	I
J	K	L	M	N	O	P	Q	R
S	T	U	V	W	X	Y	Z	

4 Add all the numbers together. Tom's total is 42.
5 Add the numbers in the total together until you get one single number.
Tom's personal number is 6 (4 + 2 = 6).
6 Now read 'What's the score?' and see what it says about your partner's character. Which number do you think you are?

3 Tell your partner what you have found out about their character.

1 What things does she/he agree/disagree with?
2 What things is she/he most surprised to hear?
3 What new things might she/he try because of it (e.g. sport even if she/he thinks she/he is lazy)?

WHAT'S THE

ONES . . .

TWOS . . .

THREES . . .

FOURS . . .

FIVES . . .

SIXES . . .

SEVENS . . .

EIGHTS . . .

NINES . . .

number?

CORE?

are ambitious, successful and virtually unstoppable. They often put their careers before relationships and on bad days can be extremely selfish and manipulative.

are kind, artistic and hard-working. They can be dominated by their partners. Twos are a bit shy and quite possessive romantically and on bad days they can be indecisive and easily hurt.

express themselves well and amusingly and are often talented artistically. They are also good at turning difficult situations to their advantage. On bad days Threes can be a bit quick-tempered.

are practical and reliable. They are also very conservative and extremely suspicious of different ideas or lifestyles. Fours are very good with money, but not always successful. On bad days they can be moody and depressed.

are extremely affectionate and generous. They are fascinated by anything new or different. Fives are often lucky in love but on bad days can be over-confident and quite thoughtless.

are very romantic and family-oriented. They often fill their homes with beautiful things. Sixes take their time getting what they want, but are frequently successful. On bad days they can be really selfish and self-satisfied.

are a bit serious. They are thoughtful people who feel there is more to life than money. They are idealistic but don't mix with other people well. On bad days they are moody and distant.

are hard-working, emotional, clever and very adaptable. They are survivors who have often had a lot of tragedy in their lives. On bad days Eights are moody, jealous and get depressed easily.

are idealistic romantics who often act without thinking. They are attracted to big causes and enjoy helping others. On bad days they can be impatient, intolerant and accident-prone.

Now use your personal number to predict your future.

4 **Read 'Your days are numbered' below. Which dates each month match your name number and are lucky?**

YOUR DAYS ARE NUMBERED

You can even use numerology to predict your own future. You always have better luck on dates that match your name number. If you're a seven, for example, you'll do better on the 7th, 16th (1 + 6 = 7) and 25th (2 + 5 = 7) of each month.

5 **Think of an important date for you in the future. Tell your partner a) what you hope will/won't happen on that date, b) what it depends on.**

6 **Do this calculation to find out about that future date. What's your final number?**

your name number	e.g. Anna Morris		**= 5**
+ your birth date number	e.g. 15/6/75	= 1+5+6+1+9+7+5= 34 = 3+4	**= 7**
+ the date of the month	e.g. 17th (May)	= 1+7	**= 8**
Total			**= 20**
Final number		20= 2+0	**= 2**

7 **Now read 'Dates to remember'. Tell your partner what you think might happen on that day now. What can you do about it?**

DATES TO REMEMBER

ONE:	Best for action. Go for it!
TWO:	Time to organise yourself.
THREE:	For fun: parties, important meetings and social occasions.
FOUR:	Do routine things like housework.
FIVE:	Impossible to know what will happen – take a few risks!
SIX:	Good time to put an end to quarrels and misunderstandings.
SEVEN:	Good for quiet thinking and reflection.
EIGHT:	Be ambitious, especially with money and work.
NINE:	Great for everything – it's the luckiest day!

8 **Talk about your partner's future situation. What is she/he going to do?**

9 **What do you think? Discuss these questions with other people.**

1 Do you believe in numerology?
2 What about astrology? Do you read your stars in magazines?
3 What other things might influence our characters and future life?

Check What You Know!

Test what you have learned in Units 1–5 by completing Check What You Know 1. (See Teacher's Book.)

6 *Noisy neighbours*

1 Diagnosis: Past Continuous (interrupted)

1 Look at the picture of neighbours in their flats. Tell another student what each person/animal on each floor was doing at six o'clock this morning.

2 Listen and write down two noises coming from each flat. Which floor did each pair of noises come from?

3 Check your answers with your partner. Then, in one sentence, say what happened in each flat. Include both noises.

There is a Revision exercise for Past Continuous (interrupted) on page 127.

2 Vocabulary: noises

1 Match the noises on the left with the definitions on the right. Use each example once only.

You	when
1 whisper	a) you are tired
2 yawn	b) you are asleep
3 sneeze/cough	c) you've got a cold
4 cry	d) you are frightened
5 snore	e) you are unhappy
6 gasp	f) you are happy
7 groan	g) you don't want someone to hear you
8 scream	h) you are in pain
9 shout	i) you are surprised
10 laugh	j) you want to attract attention

2 Check your answers with another student.

1 What is the Past Simple form of the verbs on the left?
2 Does each one end with the sound /t/,/d/ or /ɪd/?

3 Now listen to the noises in the block of flats last night. List each noise you hear.

4 Tell your partner in one sentence what you think happened, and in which flat.

NB ***you* and *they***

You cry when you are unhappy.
Ask someone in the class when they last cried.

Which pronoun, *you* or *they*, do we often use to refer to:
a) people in general, including the speaker and listener?
b) a single, but unspecified, person?

Past Continuous + Past Simple + Past Simple; key word: *make*; environmental noises; comparatives/superlatives; *so* + adjective

3 Grammar: Past Continuous vs Past Simple

While the people inside *were preparing* the party, James *arrived* home and *opened* the door with his key.

1 Look at the sentence above from the story you heard.

1 Which action started first? Is this expressed in the Past Simple or the Past Continuous form?
2 Which action interrupted it? Which form is this in?
3 What happened next? Which form is this in?

2 Tell the complete story you heard in the order it happened. Use your list of noises and Past Simple and Continuous forms.

3 Listen to the tape again and check your stories. What made the man say 'Oh no!' at the end?

4 Key word: *make*

MAKE

a) food/drink/meals ......
b) to cause ......
c) with unpleasant result ......
d) a type ......
e) to create/produce ......
f) other expressions ......

1 Put each sentence below into one of the groups above. Then add other expressions you know to the last group.

1 e. That? Yeah. **Who made the jar?** Did you take the o
2 hank you ... **Can I make an appointment, please?** ...
3 got Ray? ... **What make is it? A Sony? Yeah, it is.**
4 ... **Do you have to make such a disgusting noise?** Mu
5 make me laugh. **She makes me laugh.** ... she makes me
6 t rent it. **Are you making a cup of tea?** Yeah I'm go

From the *British National Corpus* (Spoken)

2 Do this quiz. How many questions can you answer correctly?

1 What make is the most expensive car of all time?
2 What two colours make green?
3 Which vegetable do they say makes you see in the dark?
4 How do you make fire with two sticks?
5 Which makes the most noise, a female or a male cricket?
6 What is the sun made of: fire, gas or solid matter?

SOURCES OF NOISE

5 Grammar: comparison

1 Look at the noise chart above and each pair of words below. In each case, which is: a) noisier b) less pleasant?

heavy traffic/pop music
office equipment/low planes
family life/the countryside

2 What do you think? What is:

a) the best/worst sound in the world?
b) the nicest/nastiest sound first thing in the morning?
c) the most exciting sound in a new town or country?

3 Make rules for forming comparatives and superlatives using the examples in the questions above.

4 Tell another student:

a) the nicest place you've been to. What made it so nice?
b) the nastiest person you've ever met. What made them so nasty?
c) the most interesting experience you've ever had. What made it so interesting?

1

Couple sent to jail for arguing too much

THE NOISIEST couple in Britain were jailed yesterday – for arguing too loudly. Squabbling Bill and Elizabeth Greechan argued so much they terrified neighbours up to 600 yards away. Former miner William, 60, and ex-waitress Elizabeth screamed and swore at each other from 12.10 pm until early next morning. Their latest row went on for over 12 hours. It only ended when husband William called the police, claiming he had been hit by his 56 year-old wife.

The row was the last straw for tenants in the tower block at Great Yarmouth, Norfolk, where the Scottish couple had lived and argued for two years.

The couple had a blazing two hour row the day they moved into their flat two years ago. Twice this year, they were taken to court and in March they were told: 'Once more and you go to jail.' They managed to keep the peace by going into separate rooms when they felt an argument coming on, but, finally, they started again. Yesterday the couple were stunned into silence when a judge jailed them for 14 days because of their noise. He told them: 'The end of the road has been reached.' And last night they were starting their sentences – in prisons 100 miles apart.

From *The Daily Mirror*

2

£12,500 fine for noise pest

A TEENAGE GIRL who made life a misery for neighbours was fined a record £12,500 yesterday. Dianne, of Beaumont Leys, Leicester, angered neighbours by playing her stereo system at full volume all hours of the day and night, Leicester magistrates heard. The noise level was recorded at 44 decibels in a neighbour's bedroom – and could be heard above other residents' televisions.

Dianne ignored warnings from anti-noise officials and was even recorded playing her radio when she should have been in court answering earlier charges.

The fine is thought to be the largest ever under the controversial 'pay as you earn' system introduced in October. Jobless Dianne gets just £70 a week from Social Security and lives in a rented flat – but failed to fill in a form saying how much she earns. She said: 'There's no way I can pay that much. It's a joke.'

Council spokesman Roger Webster said he hoped the size of the fine would be a warning to others. Noise Abatement Society chairman John Connell said: 'This fine is high, especially for the level of noise. But I welcome anything which leads to the reduction of noise suffered by people.'

6 Reading

1 Before you read, which of these things would neighbours in your country generally complain about?

a) noise after 10 pm
b) loud music
c) children playing
d) a noisy party
e) dogs barking
f) family arguments
g) anything else?

2 Work in two groups. Each group, read one of the articles opposite and answer these questions.

1 Which of the noises above caused the problem between neighbours?
2 What was the noisy neighbour's punishment?
3 How did she/he react?

3 Check your answers with a student who read the same article. Then find reasons why the punishment was so heavy.

4 Tell a student in the other group about the story you read and find out about their story. What do you think?

1 Was the punishment fair in both cases?
2 What would happen in the same situations in your country?

7 Writing

1 Look at this picture from a Fougasse cartoon with another student.

Why is the man buying such a large radio? Suggest as many reasons as possible.

2 **Look at the rest of the cartoon above. Where does the picture you looked at opposite go in the story? Number the pictures 1-7.**

3 **Now work with another student and tell the story as it happened last week.**

Grammar: Past Continuous (other uses)

a) Alphonso	*was studying* for exams last week.
b) While he	*was studying*, his neighbour *was listening* to the radio.
c) The music *was playing* louder than ever	when Alphonso had an idea.

1 **Look at the sentences above and answer.**

1 Which cartoon picture/s, 1–7, is each sentence describing?
2 In which sentence is the Past Continuous used:
- to describe an interrupted action?
- to describe the scene?
- to describe two actions happening at the same time?

3 Which word, *when* or *while*, can go in both sentences b) and c)?

2 **Now, write the story based on the cartoon. Begin like this:**

Last week, Alphonso was trying to study for his accountancy exams ...

8 Function: complaints

1 **Listen to three conversations between neighbours.**

1 What is each complaint about?
2 Which complaint is expressed:
a) most aggressively b) least aggressively?

2 **Work with another student. Complete the gaps in these complaints from the conversations.**

1 I . . . to complain . . . your bonfire is filling our garden with smoke.
2 I'm . . . it's the . . . again.
3 It . . . carry . . . like this, I'm afraid.
4 This . . . isn't good . . . .
5 I'm sorry . . . this isn't the . . . time.

3 **Listen, check your answers and repeat the complaints with feeling.**

4 **Have short conversations with your partner. Take it in turn to complain about these situations.**

1 She/he hasn't returned something you lent her/him.
2 She/he didn't meet you as promised yesterday.
3 She/he forgot to give the teacher an important message.

english in action

YOU ARE GOING TO COMPLAIN IN A VARIETY OF SITUATIONS.

1
First, use some of these expressions to say what is wrong with the things on this page.

It is broken/cracked/missing.
There's something wrong with it.
It doesn't work properly.

2
Listen to the first part of a conversation in a shop and answer these questions.

1 What is the complaint about?
2 How sympathetic is the sales person?
3 What do you think the customer should say next?

3
Listen to the next part of the conversation.

1 What did the customer say? Was it successful?
2 What made her hesitate again?
3 What should she say next?

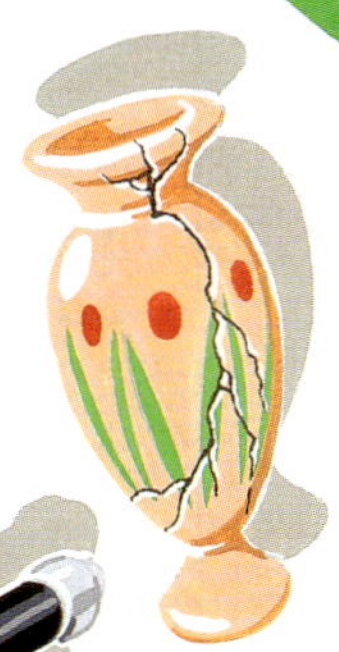

4
Choose one of the objects on the page to complain about.

NOW GO TO THE SHOP TO MAKE YOUR COMPLAINT.

5
Read these instructions. Then, as a class, choose a student to be 'the customer'. (Your teacher is the salesperson.)

a) If the customer isn't sure how to answer the salesperson at any time, stop the conversation and discuss possible answers together.
b) Start the same conversation from the beginning, with a different student as customer. Include the answer you all agreed on.
c) Repeat a) and b) until you finish the conversation in a satisfactory way.

6
Change the situation and customer. Complain about something else!

Language review 6

1 Verbs: Past Continuous vs Past Simple

- **Past Continuous + Past Simple + Past Simple**

Use the Past Continuous to show an action in progress when another action interrupted it.
He was reading when the phone rang.
While/when he was reading the phone rang.

Use the Past Simple to interrupt the action in progress and to say what happened next.
When the phone rang he answered it.

He was reading.
He began reading. The phone rang. He answered it.
(past)

- **Past Continuous**

Use the Past Continuous to:
a) describe a scene in the past.
The family were having dinner.
b) show an action in progress before an interruption.
They were eating when he told them the news.
c) show actions in progress at the same time.
They were eating while the children were playing.

A

B

C

D

a **Use the Past Continuous and the Past Simple to describe each picture. Then write what you think happened next.**

b **Put the verbs in brackets in this story in the Past Continuous or Past Simple form.**
The other day I (sit) in my garden, (read) a book. It (be) a beautiful day and so I (decide) to hang some washing out to dry. While I (do) this, I (notice) my next door neighbour who (build) a bonfire in his garden. I (finish) hanging my washing and (say) hello. He (smile) and (light) his fire. We don't talk any more.

2 Comparative and superlative adjectives

Comparatives compare individual things or people.
Superlatives compare one member of a group with the whole group.
Elena is *nicer* than her sister Sue.
She is *the nicest* of the three sisters.

Adjective	Comparative	Superlative
cheap beautiful	cheaper (than) more/less beautiful (than)	the cheapest the most/least beautiful
good bad	better (than) worse (than)	the best the worst

c **Use the adjectives in brackets to compare each group of words below twice.**
Example: A cat is bigger than a mouse. A cow is the biggest.

1 mouse, cat, cow (big)
2 kilometre, centimetre, millimetre (long)
3 a house, a block of flats, a bungalow (high)
4 silver, gold, copper (expensive)
5 car, bicycle, plane (fast)
6 a feather, a stone, a brick (heavy)
7 armchair, chair, stool (comfortable)

3 Making complaints

Use *I'm afraid* and *I'm sorry, but …* in complaints to make them less aggressive. Generally in English this makes the person you are talking to more sympathetic.

A: I'*m sorry* to bother you *but I'm afraid* you're making too much noise. The children just can't sleep.
B: Oh, *I'm terribly sorry*. I'll turn the music down.
A: Thanks very much.

d **Write short dialogues between you and a shop assistant when you go to complain about:**
a) a watch which loses five minutes every hour.
b) a new dishwasher which doesn't get dishes clean.
c) a new car. The brakes failed yesterday and nearly caused a serious accident.
d) an expensive new dinner service with two broken cups and three chipped plates.

7 *Let's do it...abroad!*

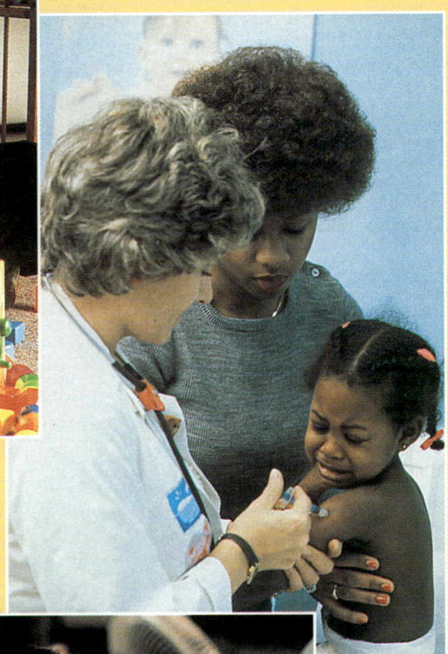

1 Diagnosis

Present Simple/Continuous

1 Close your eyes and listen to noises outside. What is happening?

2 Now, look outside and around you. What more can you *see* happening?

3 Work with another student. Describe the people in the photographs.

1 What is the name of their job?
2 What is each person doing?
3 What other things do they do at work?
4 What personal qualities do you think people in these jobs should have?

4 Find out what people in your class do.

1 How many are full-time students? What are they studying? What do the others do?
2 What things do they typically do each day?
3 How many hours a week do they have to work/study?
4 What do they like most/least about what they do?

5 What do you think? Which job in the photos would you most/least like to do? Why?

> **NB** ***like* vs *would like***
>
> a) I *like* work*ing here.*
>
> b) I'*d like to* work here.
>
> Which sentence means *I work here and I like it?*
>
> Which means *I don't work here but I want to?*

There is a Revision exercise for Present Simple/Continuous on page 128.

2 Listening

1 Listen to someone talking on a radio programme.

1 Who is speaking?
2 Who is she speaking to?
3 What and who is she speaking about?

2 Listen again and number these things in the order the woman mentions them:

a) the cost of living in Sweden
b) her daughter's daily routine
c) the pay
d) the cost of living in London
e) the au pair's housework
f) the hours of work *(1)*

3 Listen again. Which five of these things does the woman say the au pair has to do?

look after the child
do the shopping
make the beds
do the washing
tidy up
do homework
do babysitting
do the sweeping
do the ironing
do the washing up
do the vacuuming
wash the floor

Speaking

1 Tell another student how you feel about the things on the au pair's list above, like this:

I *quite like* I *don't mind* I *can't stand*	do*ing* the ironing.

2 What do you think? How should au pairs be treated? Consider:

pay/hours
duties
time off
relationship to family
free-time activities

3 Grammar: *to be/get used to*

Q: *Are* you *used to having* pocket money . . .?
A: Yes, I am.

1 Read the question to the au pair above. Is the idea of receiving pocket money strange to her? Has she had pocket money before?

2 Look at the examples of *be* and *get used to* in the sentences below.

1 Which ones refer to a) a new situation, and b) a familiar situation?
2 Which verb form follows both *be used to* and *get used to*?

1 g me crackers. I 'm used to working day and night. I
2 [A] Yeah, well I 'm used to it. [B] No, you're not.
3 Now he's got to get used to another dog. Do you kno
4 You'll have to get used to signing your name on ch

From the *British National Corpus* (Spoken)

3 With another student, imagine a situation for each sentence above. Who said the words? What were they talking about?

4 Read about some visitors to Britain below. Write sentences with *be* and *get used to* for each person, like this:

Example: Toshi came to Britain from Japan where she ate a lot of rice. In Britain they eat a lot of potatoes.

a) At first she found it strange. She *wasn't used to* eat*ing* so many potatoes.
b) But after a while she began to *get used to* it.
c) Now she finds it normal. She *is used to* eat*ing* a lot of potatoes.

1 Anna came to Britain from Poland. In Poland they drive on the right. In Britain they drive on the left.
2 Carlos came to Britain from Spain. In Spain he had dinner after 9 pm. In Britain dinner was at 6 pm.
3 Ali came to Britain from the Sudan where the weather was hot. But in Britain he had to walk to school in the snow.
4 Janey came to Britain from the USA. In America they use dollars to buy things. In Britain they use pounds.
5 Joelle came to Britain from France. In France they drink their beer cold. In Britain it's often quite warm.

5 Talk to other students about the situations above and compare Britain to your country.

Writing

Write part of a travel guide for British tourists to your country.

- What are *you* used to that they might find strange?
- What will they have to get used to, to enjoy their stay?

Present Simple vs Present Continuous;
key word: *do*

4 Reading

1 Before you read, answer the questions below.

1 When did you last face changes in these things?

accommodation   food   weather   transport

2 Which things did you have to get used to?
3 Which things couldn't/can't you get used to?

2 Read this letter from Jo to her family and answer the questions above for her.

International Language Institute
P.O. Box 13
Embaba
Cairo
15th November

Dear Mum and Dad,

Well, I've been here for more than a month now and everything is fine. I'm living with two other teachers who are really nice. And work is okay too.

I'm sitting on the balcony of the flat, watching the sun go down behind the mosque in front of the building and eating water melon. I think I'm really lucky!

When I arrived everything seemed so different – the language, the food, and the lifestyle in general. Now I feel quite at home... though I'll never get used to the crowds of people wherever you go!

I take Arabic lessons every day so I'm beginning to understand a few simple expressions. I do basic shopping most days now with no problem.

The weather is fantastic - beautifully sunny - but it is still strange to be wearing summer clothes in the middle of winter!

Oh yes, I'm learning to ride... at the Pyramids ... horses not camels, I hasten to add! I go horseriding every Saturday in the desert - I love it!

I hope everyone is well at home.

Come and visit me soon (before it starts getting really hot). How about going for a cruise on the Nile?!

Lots of love,
Jo

5 Pronunciation: /iː/ vs /ɪ/

1 Listen. Which sentence do you hear, a) or b)?

a) I'm leaving with other teachers.
b) I'm living with other teachers.

a) I saw a sheep in the Nile.
b) I saw a ship in the Nile.

a) How do you say 'eat' in Arabic?
b) How do you say 'it' in Arabic?

2 Listen and repeat each sentence. Then, say sentences above and test your partner.

6 Grammar: present time

Jo *lives* in London. She *is living* in Cairo.

1 Look at the sentences above. Where is Jo's a) permanent, and b) temporary home?

2 Reread Jo's letter. Find three examples each of:

1 Present Continuous: to say what she is doing
  a) at the moment of writing.
  b) generally, around the present time.

2 Present Simple: to talk about her
  a) routine.
  b) thoughts/feelings at the moment of writing.

3 Make questions and ask another student about:

a) the place they live/are living in.
b) a book they are reading and their opinion of it.
c) their feelings about something in the news.
d) what they do on an ideal weekend.

Key word: *do*

What *do*(1) you *do*(2) on an ideal weekend?

1 Look at examples of *do* above. Which is used as:

a) a main verb to indicate activity, 1 or 2?
b) an auxiliary verb to make questions/negatives?

2 Put these words under the verb they go with. Find out when your partner last did each thing.

homework   a favour   a phone call
a decision   a cake   the shopping
your hair   a mistake   (a lot of) money

Do	Make

Fish; nationalities; survival equipment; holidays; suggestions + *-ing* form/infinitive

7 Listening

1 Before you listen to the musical hit *Let's do it*, find things in group a) in the picture below.

a) Things that live in the sea — clams, eels, jellyfish, oysters, soles, shad, goldfish, sponges

b) Things that fly

c) Nationalities

2 Complete groups b) and c) above with these words. Which three don't go in either group?

Spain	fleas	bees	Siamese
birds	Lithuanians	Dutch	Finns
Letts	English	beans	Argentines

3 Listen and number the words in exercises 1 and 2 above in the order they are sung.

4 Listen again and sing the words on page 132.

Function: suggestions

1 Let's go for a nice meal somewhere.
2 Do you fancy going down there? ... C
3 What about showing Daddy it? ... Wha
4 Shall we go to the Job Centre? ... I
5 Well, why don't we call her Sam? ...
6 How about ringing George up? Well, r

From the *British National Corpus* (Spoken)

1 Divide the suggestions above into two groups:

a) expressions followed by verb + *-ing*.
b) expressions followed by verb only.

2 Complete and practise this dialogue in pairs.

A: What shall we do tonight? Do you fancy . . . ?
B: Oh, I don't know. Why don't we . . . ?
A: Oh, no. I don't fancy that. How about . . . ?
B: No, definitely not. But what about . . . ?
A: For goodness sake! Let's stay at home and . . .

3 Read the disaster situation below. Then, in groups, choose eight things to help you survive.

You were on a cruise in the sun when your ship began to sink, fifty kilometres north of land. Your group has to escape in a lifeboat. You can only take eight things from the ship before it sinks.

matches	a blanket each
oars	a telescope
a compass	string and fishhooks
signal flares	an oil lamp and oil
a lifebelt each	a can of water each

8 Vocabulary: holidays

1 Check the differences in meaning between the words in these pairs in your mini-dictionary.

cruise/flight	beach/sea
travel/journey	package tour/trip
all-inclusive/a supplement	customs/duty-free
full-board/self-catering	sunbathe/sunburn

2 Explain some of the words to another student. How soon can she/he guess the word?

3 Use some of the words above to tell other students about your most disastrous holiday.

english in action

HAMMAMET, TUNISIA

HOTEL - CLUB EL FELL		AAA
Half Board		Holiday no. MR105
Departures on or between	7 nights per person	14 nights per person
1 NOV - 9 NOV	£219	£259
10 NOV - 24 NOV	£179	£219

SPECIAL OFFER

Free tennis, windsurfing, pedaloes, table tennis, volleyball, bowls and sailing. Free entrance to disco. Free quarter bottle of wine and half bottle of water per guest per day.

ZELL AM SEC, AUSTRIA

HOTEL HEITZMANN	AAAA
Half Board	Holiday no. SZ109
Departures on or between	7 nights
8 JAN - 15 JAN	£329
15 JAN - 22 JAN	£339

SPECIAL OFFER

Free children. Groups: 1 in 8 travel free. Honeymoon suite on request. Ski packs offering boots, skis, lift passes and ski school lessons available for a supplement.

OCHO RIOS, JAMAICA

FISHERMAN'S POINT		AAAA
Self Catering - 14 nights		Holiday no. MB116
Departures on or between	3 share per person	2 share per person
1 NOV - 9 NOV	£499	£549
10 NOV - 24 NOV	£499	£549

SPECIAL OFFER

Free starter pack includes tea, coffee, bread, jam, milk, sugar, butter and fruit juice. Manager's rum punch party once weekly.

KISSIMMEE, DISNEYLAND

HAWAIIAN MAINGATE	AAA		
Room Only - 14 nights	Holiday no. MC251		
Departures on or between	4 share per person	3 share per person	2 share per person
1 NOV - 15 NOV	£399	£449	£499
16 NOV - 26 NOV	£399	£429	£489
27 NOV - 11 DEC	£409	£439	£499

SPECIAL OFFER

One child (10 years and under) eats free per paying adult at the hotel restaurant.

YOU ARE GOING ON A WINTER HOLIDAY WITH OTHER STUDENTS.

1

First work with another student and match these people to the holidays advertised. Use each holiday once only. Who doesn't get a holiday?

1 A comfortably-off retired couple who can go when and for as long as they like, but want something 'different'.
2 A newly-married couple who want a honeymoon to remember.
3 A group of sporty friends in their 20s.
4 A family including a six and a thirteen year-old who haven't got much money.
5 A single woman who wants a relaxing reasonably-priced holiday.

DECIDE ON THE BEST HOLIDAY FOR YOUR GROUP.

2

Work with other students and make suggestions:

- When/where will you go?
- How much will it cost?
- What clothes will you take?
- What accommodation will you need?
- What things will you do when you get there?

HAVE GOOD HOLIDAY!

Language review 7

1 *to be/get used to*

Use these forms to talk about things you are/aren't familiar with.
In my country we drive on the right, so *I'm not used to* driv*ing* on the left. (*I'm used to* driv*ing* on the right.)

am/are/is *was/were* *will be*	*used to*	something
get/gets *got* *will get*		do*ing* something

be used to = *be accustomed* to something already
get used to = *become accustomed* over time

a Which of these sentences have mistakes in them? Correct the mistakes you find.

1 I used to getting up early. I've been doing it for months.
2 I can't get used to the weather here. It's always raining.
3 She used to be much friendlier than she is now.
4 I am not used to have bacon and eggs for breakfast.
5 Are the children used to go to their new school yet?
6 We're slowly getting used to the pace of life here but it takes time.
7 They used to living in London but not any more.
8 I am get used to my new car but it was hard.

2 Present Continuous vs Present Simple

Use the Present Continuous to say what is happening:
a) at the present moment.
I am reading about English grammar.
b) at the time around the present moment (often of a temporary nature).
I come from Italy but I'm living in Japan at the moment.

Use the Present Simple:
a) to talk about present routines and habits.
I always get up at six o'clock.
b) with state verbs (e.g. thoughts/feelings) which are not generally used in a continuous form.
She hates him because she thinks he's cruel.

b Put the verbs in brackets in the correct present tense.

Dear Simon,
We arrived in Montevideo on Sunday. We (stay) in this wonderful hotel overlooking the beach. At this moment I (sit) on the balcony and (drink) a long, cool drink! We (begin) to relax and forget all the problems of the last few months. I (think) that everything will be better when we come home after the holiday. Mike (practise) his volleyball on the beach every day. It's great, everyone is so friendly and we (have) such a good time! We (love) everything: the people, the place and of course the food! You really should come out for a holiday, I (know) you would love it . . . it's your sort of place!
Love, Ruth

3 Making suggestions

Use these expressions to offer ideas which generally include the speaker.

Let's *Why don't we* *Shall we*	*go out(?)*
What about *How about* *Do you fancy*	*going out?*

c Make at least two suggestions for each of these people. Try and use all the forms opposite.

1 A bored 11 year-old boy you are looking after in the middle of the school holidays.
2 Your colleagues/school friends who want to get a leaving present for another friend.
3 A friend who wants to expand her social circle and make lots of new friends.
4 The students in your class would like to make the place you learn in more environmentally-friendly.

8 *Under the weather*

Imperatives; reported commands; reporting verbs

1 Diagnosis: giving instructions

1 Work as a class and play the game 'statues'.

- One student stands in an interesting position outside the room.
- Another student looks and gives instructions for everyone to stand in the same position.

2 Listen and follow the instructions on the cassette.

There is a Revision exercise for positive and negative imperatives on page 128.

2 Grammar: reported commands

1 Complete this sentence, reporting what the instructor said in the last exercise.

She . . . us . . . stand up straight.

2 Listen, check your answer and repeat the sentence.

1 Which words are stressed?
2 How is *to* pronounced?
3 Which type of word comes immediately after the verb *tell*?

3 Check the instructor's other commands with another student. Begin each example like this:

She told us . . .

4 What do you think? How do you report a negative command?

Example: Don't bend your knees.
She told us . . . . . . bend our knees.

3 Vocabulary: reporting verbs

1 Match each of these verbs to the sentences below. Use each verb once only.

to warn · to remind · to persuade · to ask
to invite · to advise · to encourage

1 'Be careful! Don't sit down, that paint is wet.'
2 'Can you do me a favour? Don't lend him any money.'
3 'Come for dinner and don't bring anything.'
4 'Get some chocolates. Don't forget it's Bruno's birthday.'
5 'Buy it. Don't even hesitate. You look wonderful in it.'
6 'Please come shopping, it won't take long. Don't make me go on my own.'
7 'You should speak to her about it. Don't turn it into a misunderstanding.'

2 Now write a sentence for each example, using the correct verb, and other reporting verbs, as necessary.

Example: 1 He warned me to be careful and not to sit down because the paint was wet.

4 Listening

1 Listen to a conversation between two friends, Anita and Chris about his future trip to India. Each time there is a pause in the conversation, use a different reporting verb to tell your partner what has just happened.

Example: 1 She has persuaded him to go to Calcutta.

2 Before you listen again, what do you remember?

1 Where is Chris going?
2 Why is Anita so interested?
3 Where is he going to stay?
4 What medicine is he going to take?
5 What is he going to do at midday?
6 What is he going to learn before he goes?

3 Listen again and check your answers.

NB Present Perfect for recent past

She's *just* persuaded him to go to Calcutta.
She hasn't been there *recently*.

The Present Perfect is often used to talk about the recent past. Which of these expressions is it used with: a) *a minute ago*, b) *lately*?

5 Grammar

Going to vs *will* (predictions 2)

a) 'Come on. It's going to rain.'
b) 'I know, I'll teach you some Bengali.'
c) 'I think you'll be really good at it.'
d) 'I'm going to stay with Anita's family in India.'

1 Look at each sentence above. Which one shows:

- a decision made at the time of speaking?
- a decision made before speaking?
- a prediction based on personal opinion?
- a prediction based on present evidence?

2 With another student, look at the lines from a variety of conversations below. For each one:

a) decide what the situation is, and
b) predict what the speaker is going to do next.

1 Can I have the bill, please?
2 It fits beautifully, I'll take it.
3 I've had enough. I can't take any more.
4 Well, it was lovely speaking to you.
5 I feel terrible. Can I have a glass of water?

Pronunciation

1 Listen and count the number of words in each sentence you hear. Count contracted forms as two words, e.g. *I'm* = two words, *I am*.

2 Listen again and repeat the sentences.

3 Complete this conversation with the correct form of *going to* or *will*.

A: What have you decided? . . . (you) see Jo?
B: I don't know. I've got a terrible headache.
A: Oh, look sit down. I . . . get you an aspirin.
B: Thanks. I feel awful. I think I . . . be sick.
A: Look, why don't you phone Jo and say you can't go? I'm sure she . . . understand.

4 Practise the conversation with another student, contracting *am/are/is going to* and *will* if possible.

A

B

C

D

6 Vocabulary: weather and illnesses

1 Look at the photographs above. What do you think is going to happen to the weather?

2 Look at the weather map below and answer these questions with other students.

1 Which types of weather are represented?
2 Which type of weather do you usually have in your country in a) January b) April c) July?
3 What weather makes you feel most irritable?
4 What weather makes you feel most energetic?
5 What weather/seasons do you associate with a) coughs/colds b) sore throats/runny eyes?

3 Check the meaning and pronunciation of these illnesses in your mini-dictionary on page 138.

depression asthma a heart attack a stroke
rheumatism migraine skin cancer

4 What do you think? What types of weather can cause these problems to health? Put each word above in a gap beside the weather map. Some words go in more than one place.

5 Read the article quickly and check your answers. What is SAD and where would it go on your map?

WHY YOU FEEL
under the weather

Most of us casually tune in to the weather forecast to find out whether we should take an umbrella to work or if we should go to the football match. But perhaps we should listen more carefully, because the day's weather could seriously affect how we feel.

Of course, we mostly feel better when the sun shines and worse when it rains. But scientists and doctors are starting to realise that ordinary cold weather can bring depression, severe headaches and asthma. Growing numbers of people are being diagnosed as weather-sensitive.

The hazards of hot climates are well-known, particularly the danger of the sun's rays leading to skin cancer. But did you know that high temperatures can lead to strokes and heart attacks?

Of course, sufferers from rheumatism and asthma have long complained of feeling worse when it rains, but more dangerously, a very cold period can bring on fatal heart attacks and strokes in the elderly.

It may come as a surprise to learn that even temperate climates present a health risk. 500,000 people in Britain are said to suffer from Seasonal Affective Disorder (SAD), brought on by low cloud and the long dark nights of winter. People with SAD become extremely depressed due to changes in their brain biochemistry. They sleep for many hours but never feel rested. They are irritable and feel incapable of work or socialising. But they feel better as soon as the days start to get longer and 80% of sufferers are helped in the winter months if they spend two hours a day under artificial lights.

From *The World in Focus*

7 Reading

1 Read the article in detail. Is a), b) or c) correct in each statement below?

1 The article advises us to listen more carefully to the weather forecast to find out
a) if it's going to rain
b) if it's a good day for sport
c) if we're going to feel well.

2 We usually feel depressed if
a) it's too hot
b) it's cold and wet
c) it snows.

3 The writer thinks that for hot weather people understand
a) all the health problems
b) some of the health problems
c) none of the health problems.

4 The most serious problem for old people in the cold is
a) their rheumatism
b) their asthma
c) their heart.

5 SAD sufferers are thought
a) to have a real illness
b) to be pretending because they don't like work
c) to be afraid of sunlight.

6 SAD sufferers are helped by
a) sleeping for many hours
b) staying up longer
c) spending time under lamps.

2 Check your answers with another student. Did anything surprise you?

3 What do you think?

1 How far does the weather influence how you feel?
2 Which of these things help you feel better in weather you don't like?

- having a bath
- having a good meal
- having a holiday
- having a drink
- having a haircut
- having a talk with a friend
- other?

8 Key word: *have*

HAVE

- a) illnesses ......
- b) food/drink/meals ......
- c) possessions ......
- d) family relationships ......
- e) money ......
- f) + washing ......
- g) in physical descriptions ......
- h) in other expressions ......

1 Match each of these sentences to one of the groups above.

1 ow him well. But **he's got dark hair.** ... Ah yes ...
2 rs on me **I mean she's got two children** to dump on m
3 any, sore throat. **I've got a sore throat** too. ... I
4 ced. Yeah I was. **I had a shower.** Well, perhaps the
5 . **What time did he have dinner then?** ... Ba ba boom
6 ma your new shoes? **Have you got new shoes?** Didn't s
7 's made. **He didn't have very many friends.** Did he,
8 got some money? **I haven't got any money** ... uncle

From the *British National Corpus* (Spoken)

2 Look again at the groups and sentences above.

1 In which groups do we generally use a) *have*, and b) *have got*?
2 How do you make the negative and question form of each verb?
3 What is the Past Simple of both *have* and *have got*?

3 Ask your partner questions to find out:

a) what she/he had for breakfast this morning.
b) if she/he has got her/his own car.
c) if she/he has ever had a serious illness.
d) what she/he has got in her/his pocket.
e) how often she/he has colds.
f) how often she/he needs to have a break when studying.

english in action

YOU ARE GOING TO PLAN A DAY OUT.

1
Read about the different things you can do in Edinburgh. Write down the names of the film, the place to eat and the place of interest you would most like to go to.

2
Work in groups and decide what to do. Use these advertisements, or advertisements for local places. You have enough money for a complete day out.

- Tell other students in your group what you know about the different places and why you want to go there.
- Plan what time you'll go to each place and how long you will spend there.
- Find a date when everyone is free and arrange how you'll get there.
- Think of alternative plans in case of bad weather.

3
Tell the class what your group has decided.

1 Where/when are you going?
2 How are you going to travel?
3 What are you going to see/do?
4 How long will you spend in each place?

4
Listen to other groups. If for some reason, you couldn't go with your group, which group would you join?

HAVE A GREAT TIME!

THE CAMEO 1 2 3

Home Street Tollcross
Tel 0131-228 4141

FROM FRIDAY FOR 2 WEEKS

Like Water for Chocolate (15)
1.35, 4.05, 6.35, 9.05pm
(Late Nights Thur, Fri, Sat 11.45pm)

The Piano (15)
1.05, 3.40, 6.15, 8.50pm
(Late Nights Thur, Fri, Sat 11.55pm)

Batman 2 (pg)
2.30, 5.35 (both not Sun), 8.30pm

See listings for late nights and matinees

THE CAMEO BAR

What's on?

in Edinburgh

WAVERLEY SHOPPING CENTRE
Princes Street, Edinburgh EH1 1BQ
Tel: 0131-557 3759
Fax: 0131-557 9179
Open seven days with over 80 shops, food court, café bar and themed restaurant bar.

HERITAGE TOURS OF EDINBURGH
18 Restalrig Drive, Edinburgh EH7 6JS
Tel: 0131-659 5134
Informative and entertaining historical and themed walking tours of the Royal Mile. £4.00 for 1 1/2 hours.

EDINBURGH CASTLE
Castlehill, Edinburgh
Tel: 0131-225 9846
Scotland's most famous castle, home of Crown Jewels and Mons Meg. Open 7 days.

SCOTTISH EXPERIENCE & LIVING CRAFT CENTRE
12 High Street, Royal Mile Edinburgh EH1 1TB
Tel: 0131-557 9350
Fax: 0131-556 0615
Experience the crafts, history, culture, music, food of Scotland all under one roof. Daily 10 am - 6 pm

EDINBURGH ZOO
Corstorphine Road, Edinburgh EH12 6TS
Tel: 0131-334 9171/7730
Fax: 0131-316 4050
Scotland's largest zoological park with over 1,000 animals. World's largest penguin enclosure and daily Penguin Parade (April-September). Play Area, Cafeteria and Gift Shop. Open daily.

PRINCE CHARLIE'S EXTRAVAGANZA
12 High Street, Royal Mile Edinburgh EH1 1TB
Tel: 0131-557 9350
Fax: 0131-556 0615
Scottish evening of entertainment which includes 4-course banquet, music, song & dance. Held every evening at 7 pm.

From Edinburgh Holidays

Language review 8

1 Reported commands

Requests, instructions and commands are reported with verbs like:
tell ask warn remind invite persuade encourage

The sentence pattern is usually like this:

Subject	+ reporting verb	+ indirect object	(+ not)	+ infinitive
I	told	him	(not)	to go.
You	asked	her	(not)	to phone.
She	warned	you	(not)	to try.
He	reminded	the people	(not)	to drink.
It	persuaded	me	(not)	to write.
We	invited	them	(not)	to come.
They	encouraged	us	(not)	to leave.

a Look at the words in the letter above. What did Pete ask the young woman to do? Make as many sentences as possible using the verbs opposite.

b Change from reported speech to direct speech.

1 He invited me to go to dinner with him.
2 They warned me not to be home late.
3 She advised me to lie down and have an aspirin.
4 She asked me to bring the book back.
5 We reminded them to ask their parents.
6 She tried to persuade me to go to the party.
7 She encouraged them to talk to each other more.

2 *going to* vs *will* (predictions 2)

You can often use *going to* or *will* for predictions (see Unit 3). However:

a) we usually use *going to* for predictions based on present evidence.
It's so cold, I'm sure it's going to snow.

b) we often use *will* to stress personal opinion.
I'm sure she won't mind.

c In this conversation change *will* to *going to* where it is more appropriate.

A: What will you do at the weekend?
B: I'm so tired, I will sleep all day Saturday. Then, maybe I will go with Carlos and Yumi to Cambridge on Sunday. And what about you? What will you do?
A: Oh that's easy. It's all arranged. I'll go to see Marisa. She's living by the sea in Brighton.
B: Well, take your raincoat. By the look of these clouds, it will rain!

3 *have got/have*

Use *have (– got)* before words to do with food/drink/meals, free time, washing and other set expressions. Use auxiliary *do* for negative and question forms.
Do you *have* dinner late? No we *don't* (*have* dinner late).

Use *have got* in British English to talk about possessions, relationships, illnesses, appearance.
Have you *got* any brothers or sisters? No, I *haven't*.

NB
a) *Have* can be used instead of *have got* but generally sounds more formal.
b) We do not usually use *got* forms to talk about the past. Use *had* and *didn't have*.
c) We can use contractions with *have got* but not with *have*.
She's got a car.
She has a car. (*not* She's a car.)

d Complete these sentences using the verb *have*. Use *got* and contracted forms if possible.

1 I . . . a letter from my sister yesterday.
2 . . . (you ever) an operation?
3 What . . . (he) for breakfast this morning?
4 They . . . big blue eyes like their mother's.
5 She . . . a beautiful baby girl at six o'clock last night.
6 . . . (you) a shower or a bath each morning?
7 They . . . a large family.
8 . . . a house in the country?
9 I . . . a terrible headache.
10 I think we should . . . a break now!

9 *The caged bird*

UNITED STATES PENITENTIARY: ALCATRAZ, CALIFORNIA

INSTITUTION RULES AND REGULATIONS
Revised 1956
PAUL J. MADIGAN, WARDEN

1 PRIVILEGES
You are entitled to food, clothing, shelter and medical attention. Anything else that you get is a privilege. You earn your privileges with good conduct.

2 THREATENING, RIDICULING, OR ATTEMPTING TO INTIMIDATE OR ASSAULT OFFICERS, OFFICIALS OR VISITORS is a very serious offence.

3 WORK and RECREATION
You are required to work at whatever you are told to do. As a general rule, you will work eight hours a day, five days a week, with Saturdays, Sundays and holidays devoted to recreation. Movies are shown twice each month. Exercise Yard activities include baseball, handball and various table games.

1 Diagnosis: obligation

1 Tell other students what you know about Alcatraz. Where is it? Why is it famous?

2 What do you think? Give two or three ideas for each question below.

1 What unpleasant things do prisoners typically have to do?
2 What mustn't they do?
3 What everyday things can't they do?

3 Complete the sentences below with your own ideas.

Example: Something I often have to do which I hate is walk to class in the rain.

1 Something I often have to do which I hate is . . .
2 Something I don't have to do but which I occasionally do is . . .
3 Something I'd love to do more but I can't do except on holiday is . . .
4 Something I can do now without permission but couldn't do as a child is . . .
5 Something I should do but rarely do is . . .
6 Something I shouldn't do but I sometimes find myself doing is . . .
7 Something I really mustn't do is . . .
8 Something I must remember to do tomorrow is . . .

There is a Revision exercise for *don't have to/mustn't/shouldn't* on page 128.

2 Reading

Read the rules for prisoners in Alcatraz. Match each sentence below to one of the rules. Which part in the text does it refer to exactly?

1 You must be prepared to do any work you are asked to do.
2 You mustn't hit or abuse an officer.
3 You are not allowed to keep money on you.
4 You have to save part of the money you earn.
5 New prisoners can't do sport during their first month.
6 You don't have to get up until 7.15 am at the weekend.
7 Prisoners don't need to have special permission to write letters to prison officials.
8 You need to behave very well to earn special privileges.
9 You can always have the clothes and food you need.
10 You are allowed to buy books for study.

Newly arrived inmates are kept in Quarantine Status for 30 days and are not allowed recreation during that period.

4 MONEY
You cannot have money of any kind in your possession while in this institution. Use of cigarettes or other items as 'jail money' is forbidden. You are required to save a part of what you earn, and may contribute part of your earnings to dependents. You may withdraw funds from your account in order to purchase text books and educational material.

5 THE PRISONER'S MAIL BOX
This is designed to provide any inmate with the opportunity to write directly, without inspection by institutional authorities, to various prison officials.

6 DAILY ROUTINE
7.00 am weekdays ... 7.15 am Saturdays, Sundays and holidays. Morning wake-up bell.

3 Grammar

Prohibition/obligation/permission

1 Put the underlined words from Exercise 2 Reading in the correct group below.

prohibition	
obligation	*must*
no obligation	
permission	

2 Now put each rule opposite into the past.

Example: 1 They had to be prepared to do any work they were asked to do.

3 Tell other students if you have ever been in a 'caged' situation. Think about: boarding school, an organised holiday, the army, etc.

1 What were/weren't you allowed to do?
2 What did you have to do which you really enjoyed/disliked?

4 Vocabulary: furniture/possessions

1 Look at the photograph of a cell at Alcatraz. Answer these questions with another student.

1 What furniture did each prisoner have?
2 What do you think? Which of these possessions were prisoners allowed to have in their cell? Where were they supposed to keep them?

a musical instrument	books
cigarettes and an ashtray	a brush
personal papers	food and drink
a wastepaper bin	a small cooker
a knife, fork and spoon	radio headphones
shaving things	a calendar

2 Now check your answers.

STUDENT A: Ask questions about the things above, like this:
Were they allowed to have a musical instrument? Where were they supposed to keep it?

STUDENT B: Turn to page 124 and answer Student A's questions.

3 Draw a plan of your favourite room at home. Label the furniture and some of your possessions.

4 Describe your room to your partner. Then, listen and draw the room, furniture and possessions she/he describes.

english in action

DRACULA

Set in Transylvania, this is a story of Count Dracula and vampires. The Englishman, Jonathan Harker, becomes Dracula's prisoner, and across the sea, Jonathan's fiancée Mina is soon caught up in the story with terrifying results.

BRAVE NEW WORLD

Imagine a world in which all human values have changed; a world where family life has disappeared and peoples' thoughts and lives are planned for them from start to finish. This is the Brave New World. Is it so different from life today?

OLIVER TWIST

This well-loved tale of 19th century England begins as the orphan, Oliver Twist, asks for more food! For this offence, Oliver is sold for £5. A miserable life follows as he meets one cruel person after another. But there are kind people too.

SHERLOCK HOLMES

As a detective, Sherlock Holmes has unusual powers of reasoning and deduction. His friend, Watson, is often able to help him in moments of danger. As Watson tells us the stories, we begin to understand the way Holmes' mind works.

THE GREAT GATSBY

Jay Gatsby holds huge parties.The young, rich and beautiful come from New York, but few of them seem to know their host. But Gatsby is there for a reason. He is following a dream – a dream of love for the girl Daisy he knew long ago.

YOU ARE GOING TO BUILD UP A LIBRARY OF BOOKS TO READ IN ENGLISH.

1

Read about the books above and match a title to each type below.

Type	Example
a/an (auto)biography	*'I Know Why The Caged Bird Sings'*
science fiction	
a thriller/detective story	
a horror story	
a classic	
a love story	

2

Do a class survey and find out which types of book your class prefer.

3

Listen to three extracts from book cassettes.

1 Which book above does each one come from?
2 Which one would you most like to read?

4

With another student, put this information for a book review in a logical order.

COMMENTS:	What did you think of it?
TITLE:	What is it called? *(1)*
TYPE:	Is it a thriller/love story, etc.?
CHARACTERS:	Who are the main people in it?
AUTHOR:	Who wrote it?
SETTING:	When and where does it take place?
SUBJECT:	What is it about? Don't tell the whole story, but enough to interest people!

5

Ask your partner about an English book she/he has read and enjoyed recently.

6

Use the reorganised information above and write a review for the class of a book you've read.

READ THE CLASS BOOK REVIEWS AND DECIDE WHAT TO READ NEXT.

Language review 9

1 Prohibition/obligation/permission

The modal verbs *can/should/must/have to/need to/ be supposed to/be allowed to* and their negative forms can be used to express these functions.

Prohibition	Obligation	No obligation	Permission
not supposed to	supposed to		
shouldn't	should		
	need to	don't need to	
	have to	don't have to	
can't			can
mustn't	must		
not allowed to			allowed to

NB

***Not allowed to* is used to talk about a definite rule.**
***Not supposed to* is often used to talk about a rule which people sometimes break.**

You are not allowed to copy in exams.
You are not supposed to speak your own language in English classes!

HOUSE RULES

- No smoking in rooms
- No visitors after 11.30 pm
- Rooms will be cleaned between 10 am - 2 pm
- Please keep your rooms tidy
- Washing machine to be used before 10 pm
- Breakfast is between 7 am and 9 am
- Don't stick posters on the walls
- No loud music after 10 pm
- Self-catering kitchen facilities available
- Rent to be paid every Friday

a Look at the house rules for a student hostel above. Put them into complete sentences using the language opposite.

Example: You aren't allowed to smoke in your room.

b Write sentences to describe your work/school/ home life in the past and in the present, using the following words:

must (not) *am (not) allowed to* *(don't) have to*
can (not) *am (not) supposed to* *(don't) need to*

Example: When I was younger I had to go to bed by 10 pm but now I can stay up as late as I like.

2 *So . . . that* vs *such . . . that*

***So* and *such* give extra emphasis to an idea.**

***So* is used before adjectives (without nouns).**

She is *so* kind.

***Such* is used before nouns (with or without adjectives).**

She's *such* a kind person.

***So* and *such* can be followed by a clause of result or consequence beginning with *that*. Sometimes, *that* is omitted.**

It was *so* hot (*that*) I went swimming.
It was *such* a hot day (*that*) I went swimming.

c Make one sentence from these pairs of sentences using *so . . . that* or *such . . . that*.

Example: It was a very hot day. They decided to go swimming.
It was such a hot day that they decided to go swimming.

1 The film was extremely boring. They left the cinema.
2 She was a very clever student. She passed all her exams first time.
3 He did his work very quickly. It was finished by lunchtime.
4 The service was really good. They gave the waiter a large tip.
5 He was a very nice person. She agreed to marry him.
6 She was very pleased with his work. She bought him a drink.

ESCAPE FROM ALCATRAZ

RULES

1 Use a dice, counters and game cards of the escape items.
2 Start in the cell and move clockwise round the board.
3 Collect cards of escape items by correctly doing the language tasks on the squares you land on.
4 When you have collected $30 you can bribe a guard and get an escape item you need.
5 Just before your turn, you can exchange escape items with another player or buy one from them if they agree.
6 To escape finally, you must have a dummy to put in your bed and the two other items for the escape route you choose.
7 The winner is the first player with the items they need to throw the exact number and land on the correct escape square.

In one sentence, use adjectives of material, colour and size to describe something you can see.
Tell the person on your right what you'll do unless they are nicer to you!
Lucky find! You have an extra $10.
Miss two turns.
ESCAPE!
ESCAPE ROUTE 3
THROUGH THE FENCE
gun
wirecutters
dummy
Tell the group about a past habit you no longer have.
Say what another player was doing when you rolled the dice and what they did next.
ESCAPE ROUTE 2
THROUGH A TUNNEL
keys
tools
dummy
THEFT
Lose one of your escape items. You say which one.
Say what material your shoes are made of and which country they were made in.
Do what another player tells you to do and then report what they said.
Say something which you a) are used to doing and b) can't get used to doing in your present routine.
ESCAPE!
Predict the weather tomorrow. What makes you think this?

10 *Consolidation*

1 Language in context: *Dock of the Bay*

Revises
Vocabulary: describing people
Grammar: Past, Present, Future forms

1 Find the odd word out in each group below. Use your mini-dictionary on page 138.

a) tide, sun, moon
b) stay, remain, watch
c) dock, bone, ship
d) walk, roam, roll
e) loneliness, happiness, sadness
f) Georgia, San Francisco (Frisco) Bay, Canada

2 Listen. Put one of the words above in the correct form in each gap in the song.

Sitting in the morning (1) . . .
I'll be sitting when the evening comes
Watching the (2) . . . roll in
Then I'll watch them roll away again.

I'm just sitting on the dock of the bay
Watching the (3) . . . roll away
I'm sitting on the dock of the bay
Wasting time.

I left my home in (4) . . .
And I headed for the (5) . . .
'Cos I've got nothing to live for
And looks like nothing's going to come my way.

So I'm just gonna sit on the dock of the bay
Watching the tide roll away
I'm sitting on the (6) . . . of the bay
Wasting time.

Looks like nothing's going to change
Everything seems to stay the same
I can't do what ten people tell me to do
So I guess I'll (7) . . . the same.

Sitting here resting my (8) . . .
And this (9) . . . won't leave me alone
It's two thousand miles I (10) . . .
Just to make this dock my home.

Now, I'm just sitting on the dock of the bay
(11) . . . the tide (12) . . . away
Sitting on the dock of the bay
I'm wasting time.

3 Listen again. In pairs, imagine the singer.

1 What is he like?
2 What does he do on a typical day?
3 What does he think about as he sits on the dock of the bay?

2 Thinking about learning: grammar patterns

Revises
Vocabulary: Everyday actions; times
Grammar: Continuous forms; likes/dislikes; suggestions

1 Finish each sentence with one of the phrases below.

1 I *was sitting* watching the ships . . .
2 I*'m sitting* watching the ships . . .
3 I*'ll be sitting* watching the ships . . .

a) at the moment b) yesterday at 9 am c) at this time tomorrow

2 Now match each of these time lines to each completed sentence above and answer the questions below.

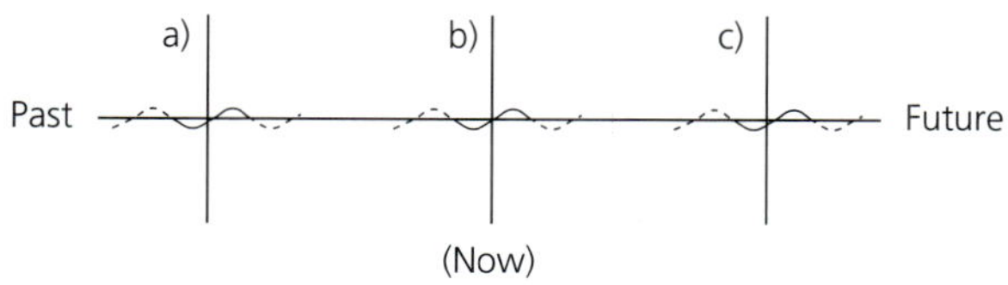

1 Is this usual/unusual behaviour for the singer?
2 Did each action begin before or at the time referred to?
3 What is similar about the form of the three sentences?

3 Work with another student. Look at the photographs of people going about their daily routine. Take it in turns to say what:

a) each person is doing now in each photograph.
b) each person was doing yesterday at the times given.
c) each person will probably be doing at the same time tomorrow.

4 Tell your partner what you were doing at each of those times yesterday, and what you will probably be doing at the same times tomorrow.

5 Talk about activities you do regularly which you: a) like doing b) don't mind doing c) can't stand doing.

6 Now write six sentences to say what you'd like to do this weekend.

7 Look at your sentences and write suggestions. What could you and your partner do together? Use *Let's. . . / How about . . .?* etc.

8 Tell your partner your suggestions. Decide on a plan together. Then tell the class what you are going to do this weekend.

9 Now think about the grammar patterns you used.

1 Which of the suggestions on your list followed the pattern:
a) expression + infinitive? b) expression + *-ing* form?
2 Which of these patterns did you use when you talked about your likes and dislikes in a) exercise 5 and b) exercise 6 above?

9.30 am

11.45 am

3.10 pm

7.50 pm

3 Across cultures: health and exercise

Revises
Vocabulary: Sports; the body; weather; health
Grammar: Direct/reported commands; Present Continuous (now); *going to* (future)

1 Tell the class which sports/exercises are most popular in your country. Which do you enjoy doing most?

2 Look at the pictures on these two pages and answer these questions with another student.

1 Which pictures represent someone doing a) T'ai Chi, b) Yoga, c) Shiatsu?
2 What do you know about these techniques?
3 Which country do you associate with each one?
4 What are they good for?

3 Now work in three groups, A, B and C. Each group, read about one of the techniques above.

- Read the introduction and find out what each technique is good for.
- Check this with another student in your group. Then read and follow the exercise instructions together.
- Decide what you need to remember to instruct a student who hasn't read the article.

T'AI CHI, popular in China, is based on a series of slow, dance-like movements, usually performed in the open air. It is good for those recovering from physical or emotional problems. It aids blood circulation, posture and co-ordination, and helps to improve muscle tone. Here is one basic exercise:

1 Stand with your legs apart and breathe normally. Let your arms hang by your sides and, with your hands open, gently press your thumbs and first fingers of each hand against your thighs – so that your palms are facing down.

2 Slowly lift up your arms in front of you, with your hands drooping down, until your arms are at chin level. Bend your knees slightly.

3 Keeping your hands in the same position, drop your arms to chest level and let your elbows fall so they are pointing towards the floor.

4 Bring your fingers up so that they are pointing towards the ceiling.

5 Slowly and gently, move your hands away from your body, as though you are pushing, until your arms are almost straight. Hold this position for as long as is comfortable, then drop your arms and shake them out.

YOGA, originating in India, is simply a series of gently stretching exercises based on different 'postures', which are practised while you breathe in a controlled way. It is good for loosening stiff joints, back or muscle aches and pains, and strengthening weak muscles. The 'triangle' position is also good for the digestive system. Try not to bend your knees and keep your hips facing the front.

1 Stand with your feet well apart. Point your right foot to the right and your left foot a little to the right.

2 Stretch your right arm out to the side at shoulder level and bring your left arm straight up against your left ear.

3 Breathe in.

4 As you breathe out, bend to the right, without bending forward. Slide your right hand as far down your right leg as it will go.

5 Look at your left hand and take a few deep breaths.

6 Repeat, bending to the left.

SHIATSU is a Japanese healing art. It uses finger pressure to re-energise the body and relieve a variety of health problems, tension and pain. Try these simple exercises.

1 First, with the thumbs of both hands, find the indentations at the bottom of your skull (at the top of your neck, on either side of your backbone). Spread your fingers out at the sides of your head as you apply pressure with your thumbs for about 15 seconds. Stay relaxed and repeat.

2 Find the indentation at the top of your head. Apply gentle pressure to this point, with one of your thumbs, for about 15 seconds, resting your fingers on your forehead. Stay relaxed and repeat.

3 Place the little finger of your left hand on the hairline in the middle of your forehead. Spread your fingers about a centimetre apart along a middle 'parting', resting your thumb on the side of your head. Apply pressure first with your little finger, then your ring finger, then your middle finger and then your index finger. Repeat the whole thing three times, without lifting your fingers.

MIND OVER MATTER

It is surprisingly easy to achieve a relaxed state almost instantly, once you know how.

Techniques of visualisation – controlled day-dreaming – can relax you and help you learn by opening channels to the creative, right-hand side of your brain. This side of the brain is said to be more open to suggestion than your brain's logical left-hand side.

4 Now work in new groups of three, with one student from Group A, one student from Group B and one student from Group C. Take it in turns to instruct the other students.

5 Tell other students what you think about these techniques and other medical practices.

1 Which did you enjoy most and why?
2 Do you consider them to be:
  a) important medical practices?
  b) alternative/complementary medical practices?
  c) not medical practices at all?
3 What type of medicine is generally practised in your country?
4 What happens when someone is ill in your country? What type of health care is there?

6 Now read the last section of the magazine article *Mind over matter* above.

1 Which side of the brain does it say creative visualisation works with?
2 How do the two halves of the brain complement each other?

7 Use a visualisation technique to help you revise language you have learned recently.

- Relax.
- Take three deep breaths.
- Listen and follow the instructions on the cassette with your eyes closed.

8 Now tell another student what you remember about the walk and the house. What did the speaker tell you to do/not to do?

Check What You Know!
Test what you have learned in Units 6–10 by completing Check What You Know 2.
(See Teacher's Book.)

From *Best*

11 *Sweet revenge*

1 Diagnosis: reported statements

1 Read these quotes from the real-life drama of Ruth Ellis and David Blakely. Who do you think said each quote, the man or the woman?

A 'I'm sorry, darling. I do love you. I'll prove it. I want to marry you.'

B 'I am obviously jealous of him, now...'

C 'I can't stand it any longer. I want to get away from her.'

D 'I was very, very upset when he didn't come back.'

E 'Arrest me – I have just shot this man .'

2 Make up a story with another student. Include the information in the quotes. Begin like this:

When Ruth Ellis met David Blakely in 1953 . . .

3 Tell the class how each quote fits into your story.

Example: She said that she was jealous when she saw him with another woman.

There is a Revision exercise for reported statements on page 128.

2 Vocabulary: crime

1 Work in groups of four. Check the meaning and pronunciation of these words in your mini-dictionary on page 138.

STUDENT A:	a murder	a trial
	a judge	to sentence
STUDENT B:	to hang	to accuse
	to be guilty	to charge
STUDENT C:	a jury	a verdict
	the defence	the law
STUDENT D:	an appeal	an execution
	a witness	a suspect

2 Put each word in a sentence to explain its meaning to the group. Can they say it correctly?

3 Work together and complete the gaps in the story below. Use each word above once only.

4 Read the completed story. Write three questions you would now like answered.

The last woman to be hanged

Ruth Ellis met David Blakely in 1953. On April 2nd 1955, she shot him in front of numerous (1) ... and was immediately (2) ... with his murder; there were no other (3) ... . Reports of her (4) ... were in every newspaper. The prosecution (5) ... her of premeditated (6) ... . The (7) ... said Blakely had provoked her. The (8) ..., Mr Justice Havers, told the people of the (9) ... that there was no case for changing any possible (10) ... from murder to manslaughter. By English (11) ..., if they found Ruth Ellis (12) ..., this could only mean one thing. She would be (13) ... to death and (14) ... . At this point, only an (15) ... to the Home Secretary could possibly stop the (16) ... .

APRIL 28 Ex-model Ruth Ellis was today sent for trial at the Old Bailey. She is accused of the murder of racing driver David Blakely. The 28 year-old platinum blonde is said to have shot him outside a pub in Hampstead, North London, on Easter Sunday. His death – from two bullet wounds in the back – marked the violent end to a stormy relationship which began two years ago when the couple met at the London club where Ellis was manageress. On the day of his death Ellis believed Blakely was leaving her for another woman. She begged him not to go.

1

JUNE 21 Femme fatale Ruth Ellis was today found guilty of the murder of the man she adored. She was immediately sentenced to hang. Her trial had lasted only two days. The jury of ten men and two women took just 25 minutes to reach their verdict, after hearing that jealousy was no defence in English law.

Ellis shot David Blakely with a Smith and Wesson. She claimed it was given to her three years before as security for a debt at one of her bars. The ex-model and mother of two showed no emotion as she was sentenced. She will appeal.

2

JULY 13 Ruth Ellis was up early on the last morning of her life at about half past six. The bravery of her final hours was almost inhuman. There were no tears, no regrets. She calmly wrote her final letters. Her parents were not outside the prison. They were at home, drinking endless cups of tea, hoping the Home Secretary would respond to the appeal. He didn't.

Ruth was given a glass of brandy and with complete courage walked to the execution room. A moment later she was hanged.

3

3 Reading

1 Work in three groups. Each group, read *one* article above only.

1 How many of your questions are answered in your article?
2 What other new information did you learn?

2 Now work in groups of three with one student who read article 1, one who read article 2 and one who read article 3. Tell the other two students what you found out.

3 Retell the story by putting the verbs in brackets in the Past Simple passive or active form.

1 Ruth Ellis and David Blakely (be) . . . lovers.
2 He (drink) . . . heavily and often (beat) . . . her in fits of jealousy.
3 Eventually, he (decide) . . . to leave her. She (think) . . . it (be) . . . for another woman.
4 So one evening she (wait) . . . for him with a gun and he (killed) . . . as he (leave) . . . his local pub.
5 Ruth (arrest) . . . and (take) . . . to the police station where she (confess) . . . to her crime.
6 She (accuse) . . . of murder and (sent) . . . for trial.
7 The jury (find) . . . her guilty and she (sentence) . . . to death.
8 She (hang) . . . in 1955, the last woman in England to receive the death penalty.

4 Speaking

1 What do you think? Was Ruth's punishment fair?

2 Put these crimes in order of seriousness. What punishment does each one deserve?

- a bank robbery where no-one was hurt
- tax evasion by an individual
- drunken driving
- shoplifting of a few small items
- vandalism of a telephone box
- (football) hooliganism
- looting during a riot
- a revenge killing

5 Listening

1 Listen to people talking about revenge. Does each one now feel satisfied or ashamed?

2 Listen again and complete the chart.

	Who against?	How?	Result?
PERSON 1			
PERSON 2			
PERSON 3			

6 Grammar: Past Perfect

a) He *left* when I arrived.
b) He *had left* when I arrived.

1 Look at the sentences above. Which one means:

- He left before I arrived?
- He left at the time I arrived ?

How do you form the Past Perfect?

2 Use information from the listening and put these verbs in the Past Simple or Past Perfect.

1 When the man (spray) paint on the windows, the shopkeeper (be) already unpleasant.
2 When the police (arrive) he (spray) the window.
3 Her boss just (bought) another beer when the woman (throw) it at him.
4 By the time she (leave) the pub, he (sack) her.
5 When he (phone) the USA , she already (leave) the flat and (go) on holiday.

7 Writing

1 Work with another student. Match each of these past forms to an example sentence below.

1 Past Simple + Past Perfect for describing the main action and what happened before it
2 Past Simple + Past Simple for describing past events in the order they happened
3 Past Simple + Past Continuous for describing what interrupted an action in progress
4 Past Continuous for describing the scene
5 Past Continuous + Past Continuous for describing actions going on at the same time

Example sentences

a) She opened the door and a stranger pushed past her into the house.
b) She was reading and he was preparing supper.
c) They were eating when the doorbell rang.
d) She turned and looked for her husband but he had gone.
e) They were spending a quiet evening at home.

2 Reorder the sentences above to make a story.

3 Now put the pictures below in a possible order. Check the story with other students.

4 In groups, write the story. Each group:

a) choose a different picture and start the story at that point in time.
b) include earlier and later information, by using different past forms.

5 Listen to each story. What do you think? Which starting point begins the most dramatic story?

Reported statements + Past Perfect; key word: *would; would/could/might +/– if*

A LADY'S REVENGE

SIR PETER WILFRED GILLES GRAHAM-MOON, 5th Baronet, spoke out yesterday against his wife Sarah's much publicised jealous acts, 'She doesn't need any more public exposure – she needs a psychiatrist.'

Act One: of this melodrama was when Lady Sarah drove from their home at 3 am to a village six miles away and saw Sir Peter's BMW parked in the driveway of 42 year-old Amanda Asheson's cottage. She promptly poured a can of white paint over his car. It was Amanda who saw the car first and told Sir Peter that his blue BMW was now two-tone.

Act Two: began ten days later when Sarah phoned and told him she would meet him at the house that afternoon. 'By the time I arrived there she had pulled out the drawers of my chest and attacked 16 hand-made shirts with scissors.' She had also cut the arms off four cashmere sweaters. Sir Peter phoned his lawyer, 'Sarah seems to have gone mad,' he said. 'She has stamped on a box of 25 Havanas and thrown six boxes of them out of the window.'

Act Three: came a week later. A friend phoned Sir Peter at Amanda's and said she had noticed five or six jackets with the sleeves cut off lying in the drive to the house. She had also seen three bottles of wine on the roof of his BMW. 'In fact,' Sir Peter said, 'she has cut an arm off each of 32 tailor-made suits, jackets and overcoats'. He also claimed she had delivered two cases of his best vintage wine to village doorsteps.

Lady Sarah said that this three act melodrama of revenge on a cheating husband had given her 'a real buzz'.

From *The Daily Mail*

8 Reading

Read the newspaper version of the story.

1 Who are the three main people in the story?
2 What had the man's wife done when he found his:
   a) car b) shirts c) sweaters
   d) cigars e) jackets f) wine?
3 Why had she behaved like this?

Grammar: reported statements

1 Read the article again. Who said these words: Sir Peter, his wife, Amanda or his friend?

a) 'Your blue BMW is now two-tone.'
b) 'I'll meet you at the house this afternoon.'
c) 'I have noticed five or six jackets with their sleeves cut off lying in your drive.'
d) 'She has delivered two cases of my best vintage wine to village doorsteps.'
e) 'It gave me a real buzz.'

2 Find the reported version of the words above in the article.

1 In reported speech, which words change and how?
2 Which two forms change to the Past Perfect?

3 Report what Sir Peter said about:

a) Lady Sarah's sanity (paragraphs 1 and 3).
b) his cigars (paragraph 3).
c) his jackets, suits and coats (paragraph 4).

4 What do you think of Sarah's behaviour? What would you advise a) her, b) her husband to do?

9 Key word: *would*

Complete these examples to show different uses of *would*. Use contracted forms if possible.

a) Advice, e.g. *If I were you, . . .*
b) Invitation, e.g. *Would you (like) . . . ?*
c) Request, e.g. *Would . . . ?*
d) Past of *will*, e.g. *I asked him to phone; he said . . .*
e) Unreal condition, e.g. *If I had £1,000,000, . . .*
f) Speculation, e.g. *In Sarah's position, I . . .*

Function: speculation

1 **I'd tell someone about it,** if I were
2 **I couldn't do that anyway.** I'd have
3 **I might try and do that.** I'll do it
4 **I wouldn't know what to do** because .

From the *British National Corpus* (Spoken)

1 Look at the sentences above. Then use the highlighted language to tell other students what you would do if you saw:

- a mugging in the street
- a mother repeatedly hitting her child
- someone throwing stones at a dog in the street
- a policeman treating a homeless person roughly
- someone hurting a member of your family

2 Write a sentence using *if* for each situation above. What comes after *if*, a past or future form?

english in action

YOU ARE GOING TO CONDUCT A SURVEY TO FIND OUT PEOPLE'S VIEWS ON CRIME.

1
First work with other students and decide which things to ask about. Use these controversial statements to give you ideas.

- Crime is increasing because of violence on television.
- Capital punishment should be brought back/used more.
- The police should be more heavily armed.
- Everybody is a potential murderer.
- Prisons are 'schools of crime'.

2
Make a questionnaire. Add other questions to the one below.

3
Decide how to get your information.

1 Each person in your group should interview an agreed number of people.
2 Try to interview and record one English-speaking person per group on cassette.

CONDUCT YOUR SURVEY.

4
Tell people in your group what you found out.

a) Look at the results of the questionnaires.
b) Listen to the recorded interview and take notes of this person's views.

5
Decide how to present your information to the class. Give everyone responsibility for part of the presentation.

- One person could introduce the subject and say how you carried out the survey.
- Another person could present the survey questionnaire.
- Another person could report what people said.
- Another person could summarise the recorded interview and play the most interesting section.
- Another person could finish the presentation by saying what surprised or interested you most.

GIVE YOUR PRESENTATION.

SURVEY ON CRIME AND PUNISHMENT

Which of these statements do you agree with?

1 The main cause of crime is:

a) violence on TV ○
b) poverty ○
c) a lack of discipline at home/at school ○

Language review 11

1 Verbs: Past Perfect vs Past Simple

The Past Simple is used to talk about past actions.
I arrived at the party.

The Past Perfect can be used to talk about actions before that time.
He had (already) left when I arrived.

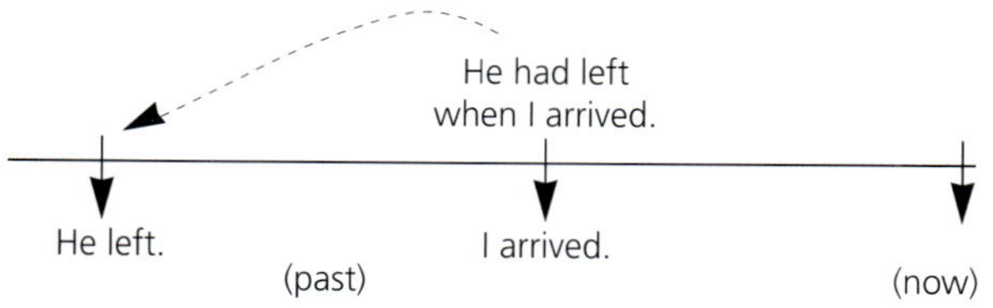

a Five of the verbs in the following story need to be in the Past Perfect. Rewrite the sentences concerned correctly.

The other day I got home to find someone broke into my house. One of the bedroom windows was broken and I could see that someone climbed in. I soon realised that the thief moved lots of things around but only took a few things. I found out from the police that there were a number of crimes like this in my area recently and so I made a decision to get new locks for the windows so this wouldn't happen again.

2 Past Perfect in reported statements

In reported statements, verbs generally move back one tense.

The Past Perfect can be used in this way for both the Past Simple and the Present Perfect.

Direct speech	Reported speech
'I saw her there.'	He told me/said (that) he *had seen* her there.
'I've been to the shops.'	She told me/said (that) she *had been* to the shops.

b Put the following dialogue into reported speech.

Example: A asked B what she was going to do that evening . . .

A: What are you going to do this evening?
B: I haven't decided yet but I think I'll go to that party at Mary's.
A: Oh I don't feel like going to a party. I went to a party last weekend and it was awful. I didn't know anyone and it was really crowded and noisy.
B: But Mary's got a lovely house and you'll know most of the people there.
A: I'm not sure. I might just stay at home and watch a video.

3 *Would/could/might* (speculation and second conditional)

We use *would/could/might* + main verb when we imagine, often improbable, present or future situations.

Positive

I/you/we/they She/he/(it)	*'d (would)* *could* *might*	go and live abroad.

Negative

I/you/we/they She/he/(it)	*would* *could* *might*	*not* go and live abroad.

Question

Would/could/might	they	go and live abroad?

• ***If* + past + *would/could/might* (second conditional)**

This expresses an improbable or impossible condition and its result.

***NB Were* is often used instead of *was* after *if*.**

(+) *I'd* be rich if I *were* a film star.
(–) He *couldn't* stop *if* he wanted to.
(?) What *might* you do *if* you *won* the lottery?

c Write five sentences to say what you *might/could/would/wouldn't* do if you won £500,000 in a national lottery.

Example: If I won £500,000, first of all, I'd buy a new car.

"And if you fixed the roof you wouldn't have to stay in every time it rained."

12 *Acting politician*

1 Diagnosis: Present Perfect Simple + *for/since*

1 Talk to other students and complete this chart. What questions will you ask each student?

Who has done these things for	the shortest /	longest time?
	(name/time)	(name/time)
Been in this town/country		
Known their best friend/partner		
Had their own room/house		
Been able to drive		
Played their favourite sport		

2 Read about Glenda Jackson in the extract from *Hello* magazine below.

1 What major change has she made in her career?
2 What did she use to do which made her famous?
3 Which career does she seem to value most?

3 What do you think? Do you agree with her opinions?

There is a Revision exercise for Present Perfect Simple + *for* and *since* on page 128.

Glenda Jackson – the Oscar-winning actress, tells *Hello!* how satisfying her new life is.

The spotlight has shifted from Glenda Jackson, double Oscar-winning actress to Glenda Jackson, Labour Member of Parliament. Instead of Hollywood she has chosen Hampstead and Highgate in London as the centre of her working world.

Do you feel your popularity as an actress helped you get elected?
'I really don't think so. For all those who might like the idea of an actress in Parliament, there are many more who don't. And it's my conviction that people are far more concerned with serious political issues than personalities.'

Do you miss acting at all?
'Not at all. It's only valid when you're actually doing it.'

If you could wish for one great change in society what would it be?
'Greater equality ... Of course people can't all be born equal, but I'd like to see more being done to equalise educational and economic chances early in life.'

From *Hello*

2 Listening

1 Before you listen to an interview with Ms Jackson, which words below apply to:

a) the British political system?
b) the American system?
c) your country's system?

Labour	Conservative
Republican	Democrat
Prime Minister	President
Monarchy	Republic
House of Commons	
Member of Parliament (MP)	
House of Representatives	

2 Listen to the first part of the interview and complete this chart with dates.

. . . born
. . . began drama school
. . . left drama school
. . . first voted Labour
. . . acted in her first film
. . . stopped acting
. . . became an MP

3 Listen to the next part of the interview and answer these questions.

1 Which things below did she:
  a) receive from Parliament?
  b) have to provide herself?
  - an office
  - a desk
  - a fax
  - filing cabinets
  - a telephone
  - a word processor
  - office staff

2 Which two political issues concern her most at present?
3 What does she think of work as an MP?

4 Now look at the completed chart above and say how long Ms Jackson:

a) was at drama school.
b) has been a Labour voter.
c) has been working as an MP.

3 Grammar: Present Perfect Simple vs Continuous

She *has worked* as an actress.
She *has been working* as an MP since 1992.

1 Look at the sentences above. Which job is she still doing? Which sentence is in the Present Perfect a) Simple, b) Continuous?

2 Read each pair of sentences below. In which pair/s is the meaning of the two sentences a) the same/similar, b) different?

1 How long have you lived here?
How long have you been living here?
2 She has painted the office.
She has been painting the office.
3 He has typed all the letters.
He has been typing letters all day.
4 I haven't worked here for long.
I haven't been working here for long.

3 Read the sentences in 2 and 3 again. Which form, the Present Perfect Simple or Continuous, describes something which:

a) is completed and emphasises the result?
b) may be unfinished and emphasises the activity?

4 Ask another student for detailed answers to these questions.

1 How many of each of these things have you done recently?
letters (write) films (see)
book (read) places/people (visit)
2 How long have you been a) studying English, b) working today?

5 Add a verb from each of these examples to its category below.

1 **How long has he had his car?** ... Er he had a, had a
2 ... **I've never liked him** ... They were handy for t
3 ou. **I've always loved you, you know** and I'll be he
4 ape. **We haven't seen him for years** ... That Kenny F
5 ... **Well, I've known Derek since I was six** weeks c

From the *British National Corpus* (Spoken)

Verbs not generally used in the continuous form = verbs of:			
a) emotion e.g. *hate* .../...	b) possession e.g. *own* ...	c) the mind e.g. *think* ...	d) the five senses e.g. *hear* ...

6 Make questions to ask your partner about their life so far. Use these prompts and the Present Perfect Continuous where possible.

1 Where/born? How long/be married? How many children/had?
2 How many places/lived in? How long/live in your present home?
3 How many jobs/done or schools/been to?
4 How long/do present job or course? How long/know/teacher?

4 Key word: *for*

1 Look at these sentences written by students of English.

a) Which are correct/incorrect?
b) Correct the incorrect ones.

1 They've been here *since* 11 hours.
2 She's been waiting *for* ages.
3 How long have you been in England *for*?
4 I haven't seen him *since* two years.
5 She lived there *for* ten years.
6 She's been crying *since* a long time.
7 I'm going to stay at this hotel *for* two weeks.

2 Now listen and repeat the correct sentences.

1 In each sentence, is *for* stressed or unstressed?
2 How is *for* pronounced:
a) before a consonant?
b) before a vowel sound?
c) at the end of a sentence?

3 Look at the correct sentences. Which of these explanations are true?

1 *For* is used to talk about:
a) a period of time.
b) an exact point in time.
2 *For* can be used to talk about:
a) past time.
b) present time.
c) future time.

4 Ask another student:

a) how long she/he was/has been in full-time education.
b) if she/he has ever been in hospital and for how long.
c) how long she/he has been using this book.
d) how long she/he is going to have a break for after class.

5 Vocabulary: the cinema/theatre

1 Work with other students and check you know the difference between the words in the groups below. Use your mini-dictionary on page 138, if necessary.

a) a play, a game, a match
b) a scene, scenery, a curtain
c) an audition, a rehearsal, a performance
d) an actor (actress), an artist, a comedian
e) a script, a review, a critic
f) a director, a producer

2 Complete these sentences with a word from each group above. Choose from groups a)–f), in that order.

1 The children had a new . . . for Christmas.
2 At the end of the play the safety . . . came down.
3 The tickets were expensive but the . . . was worth it.
4 The . . . sold her paintings at the exhibition.
5 The . . . in the local newspaper was wonderful.
6 The . . . inspired the actors and his instructions resulted in a very polished performance.

Speaking

Ask your partner about a film or a play she/he has enjoyed recently. Find out:

- where it was on (TV or the name of the cinema/theatre)
- what type of film/play it was
- who was in it
- who directed it
- where it was set
- who the main characters were
- what the plot/story was about
- what she/he thought about it
- if she/he would recommend it to the class

It's really worth seeing.

Don't bother! It's not worth going.

I recommend getting really good seats.

I don't recommend spending too much on them.

6 Reading

1 Look at the poster for Glenda Jackson's Oscar-winning film *A Touch of Class*. Which information from the last exercise does it give?

2 Read the film script opposite. What is the relationship between a) Vicky and Steve, and b) Gloria and Steve? What makes you think this?

3 Reread the script and answer these questions.

1 What had Steve arranged with Vicky before this scene?
2 What upset these plans? How does she feel about this?
3 What had Steve arranged with Gloria?
4 What upset these plans? How does she feel about this?
5 What is Steve's solution? What will he have to do:
a) before 7.30 pm?
b) at 7.30 pm?
c) at 10.30 pm?
d) at 11 pm?
e) before tomorrow morning?

4 Tell other students what you think will happen next.

1 How far will Steve's evening go to plan?
2 What could the consequences be?

7 Writing

1 Find words and expressions in the script which suggest informality and that the speakers know each other well.

2 Work in groups and write the script for a scene later in the play.

a) First, discuss the type of people you think Steve, Vicky and Gloria are. Who is the most organised, easy-going, quick-tempered, forgetful, caring, understanding, etc?
b) Decide when and where the scene you have chosen will take place. What has happened since the telephone calls?
c) Discuss the new scene in detail.
d) Choose a secretary to write the first draft of the scene as you say the words.
e) Reread and change things in your script. Include words/expressions to keep the language natural and informal.

(The telephone rings in Vicky's office.)

VICKY: Hello.
STEVE: Hi! Did I catch you?
VICKY: Hm. I'm just this minute going out the door.
STEVE: Don't hurry.
VICKY: What?
STEVE: A call just came in. I have to get a prospectus out to New York and Oslo immediately.
VICKY: ... God!
STEVE: If I work straight through I can be there by eleven. Is that OK?
VICKY: Listen, why don't we just forget tonight? I mean, if you've got to work, then work.
STEVE: Don't blow a fuse[1], please *(phone 2 rings in Steve's office)*. Can you ...? Hold on just a second ... *(He picks up and talks into phone 2)* ... Hello. Could you wait just one second, please ...? *(He returns to phone 1)* Vicky, don't be ridiculous. I will be there by eleven, no matter what happens, and if my work isn't done, I'll come back and finish it later. Is that OK?
VICKY: Perfectly.
STEVE: You're sure?
VICKY: Absolutely. I'm sorry I sounded like such a twit[2].

[1] *don't blow a fuse* = don't be angry
[2] *a twit* = an idiot

STEVE: Forget it. I'll see you at eleven. *(He puts phone 1 down and picks up phone 2)* Hello?
GLORIA: Hello, Steve?
STEVE: Oh, hello Gloria.
GLORIA: Where are you?
STEVE: What do you mean, where am I? I'm here at the office. You called me, didn't you?
GLORIA: You're supposed to be home, getting ready. The curtain goes up at 7.30.
STEVE: What curtain?
GLORIA: The preview of the new Pinter play – UNICEF benefit[3] – I'm on the committee.
STEVE: Oh God! I forgot. Gloria, I've got to get a report out to Oslo and New York tomorrow. It's going to take me hours.
GLORIA: Then go back and finish it after the play but come home now. I am not walking into that theatre alone.
STEVE: OK. OK. OK. OK. Now, what time does the play finish?
GLORIA: Ten thirty.
STEVE: Alright, but I'm going to have to work later, Gloria, much later.
GLORIA: Right, but come home now.
STEVE: Bye. *(He puts down phone 2)*

[3] *UNICEF benefit* = the money from this performance goes to the United Nations children's charity

From *A Touch of Class*

english in action

YOU ARE GOING TO AUDITION FOR A PART IN A THEATRE VERSION OF GLENDA JACKSON'S OSCAR-WINNING FILM 'A TOUCH OF CLASS'.

1
In groups of three, work with the script on page 75. Before you practise reading the play out loud, make sure:

a) you agree which words give important information and are stressed in each sentence.
b) you understand how each character is feeling as they say each line.

2
Take one part each and read the script out loud. Then discuss if you need to change the way you say anything.

3
Practise the scene again a few more times. By the last rehearsal, look up between lines to make the reading more natural.

HAVE THE AUDITION.

4
Take it in turns to read the scene to the other groups.

5
Take a vote. Which group should get the parts?

6
Now listen to actors performing the scene.

1 How is it different from the way you acted it?
2 How does each person feel at a) the beginning, and b) the end of the conversation?
3 Who is British? Who is American?

Language review 12

1 Verbs: Present Perfect Continuous vs Simple

Present Perfect Continuous

+	I	*have*	*been working*.
–	She	*hasn't*	
?	*Have*	you	

• Similar to Present Perfect Simple

Both forms are used to refer to situations which started in the past but continue in the present. Continuous forms can be used to emphasise temporary situations.

I*'ve* always *lived* here.

I*'ve been living* here for three years.

***NB* 'Stative' verbs aren't generally used in the continuous form. These include *be*, and:**

• Different from Present Perfect Simple

Present Perfect Simple emphasises result (a completed action).

A: How many times *have* you *read* that book?

B: I*'ve read* it three times.

Present Perfect Continuous emphasises activity (an unfinished action).

A: How long *have* you *been reading* this morning?

B: For three hours.

a Complete this dialogue with the Present Perfect Simple or Continuous. Use the Continuous form where possible.

A: you (see) Charles today?
B: Yes, he was in his office earlier.
A: Well, he (not be) there since lunch.
B: I think he (work) on the dog food publicity material.
A: Good. Mike (wait) for it for the last week and he isn't very pleased.
B: Actually, I (hear) that Mike's going to get the sack.
A: I think he knows.
B: Really?
A: Yes. He (look) at advertisements for other jobs for the last few weeks.

b Make possible questions for these answers.

1 . . . ? No, not for ages. I must give her a ring.
2 . . . ? Yes. Isn't the acting great!
3 . . . ? Nothing much. Just watching TV.
4 . . . ? No, I'll finish them this afternoon.
5 . . . ? Yes. That's why I'm covered in mud.
6 . . . ? Since January. My father gave it to me.

"How's he been?"

2 *For* (preposition of time)

***For* refers to a period of time (*not* a point in time.)**

This period can be at any time in the past, present or future, and any tense is possible.

We lived there *for* three years.
We have been here *for* seven weeks.
We're only here *for* a few days.
We'll stay there *for* a month.

c Put these words in order to make questions. Then answer the questions yourself.

1 friend long have how known best you your?
2 school how for you were primary long at?
3 doing have exercise how you been long this?
4 on year how will long go holiday next you for?
5 doing for you tonight long are homework how?

3 Recommendations

Use these expressions to say something is good/not good, in your opinion.

It is (not) *worth*	it.
I (don't) *recommend*	*going*.

d Complete each example below with one of the expressions opposite. Use a different *-ing* form with each expression.

1 It was a great film. It . . .
2 The food in that restaurant is awful. I . . .
3 Don't bother buying that book. It . . .
4 Edinburgh is a beautiful town. I . . .

13 *Food, glorious food*

TESCO MILK
PACK OF 6 X 1
LITRE CARTONS
~~£2.65~~
£2.19

ST HUBERTUS HOCK
75cl BOTTLE
£1.89

TESCO CHIPS
4lb PACK
~~£1.59~~
79P

BOLD 3 AUTOMATIC
WASHING POWDER
~~£1.69~~
£1.59

TESCO BEANS
4 X 439g CANS
~~98p~~
79P

GILLETTE BLUE 2
DISPOSABLE RAZORS
PACK OF 10
~~£2.30~~
£1.75

SLICED WHITE LOAF
800g SIZE
~~61p~~
53p

ONIONS PER lb
~~25p~~
15p

CARLING BLACK LABEL
4 X 440ml CANS
~~£2.99~~
£2.49

MCVITIES DIGESTIVE
BISCUITS 500g PACK
~~63p~~
55p

APPLES (LOOSE)
PER lb
~~42p~~
27p

COOKED MEAT
(LOOSE) PER 1/4lb
~~73p~~
55p

CROSSED OUT PRICES
WERE PREVIOUSLY
CHARGED AT MOST
TESCO STORES.

The price is dropping on your weekly shopping

TESCO

1 Diagnosis: quantity

1 Look at the advertisement. What does it say is the advantage of shopping at Tesco supermarket? Give examples.

2 Work with another student and check the shopping against the price list. What has the customer bought?

Example:

A: He's bought a packet of oven chips.
B: Yes, here it is. It cost 79p.

3 Read the transcript of the customer's conversation when he got home. Find and correct eight grammatical mistakes.

A: Hi. I'm home. Can you help me unpack the shopping?
B: Yeah. Oh good, you got some chips for lunch. But why did you get so few bread? And you've bought so little biscuits.
A: They're fattening and there weren't some chocolate ones which are the only ones I really like. I've bought much milk – you said we needed some.
B: Good. But why have you bought so much razors?
A: We didn't have some left and we haven't got many washing powder either, so I decided to get some more.
B: I hate it when you go shopping. You never get some chocolate.
A: Listen, *you* go next time.

4 Listen to what they actually said and check your answers.

There is a Revision exercise for *some/any/much/many/a lot of* on page 128.

2 Grammar: *some/any; much/many; a few/a little*

1 get; hungry. **Make a few chips.** ... yes darling. Oh
2 ... **Would you like a little lemon on your fish?** Mir
3 What? **Have we got any apples?** ... Has she got any
4 s ... **There aren't any crisps.** ... Can you pass the
5 ... **Would you like some chicken for dinner?** ... Sha
6 You? **There aren't many other nice puddings.** You'll
7 **I can't really put much salad in them** there, becaus

From the *British National Corpus* (Spoken)

1 Choose the correct alternative in each of these explanations and find an example sentence for each one above.

a) *Some/any* is generally used in questions to find out if something exists.
b) *Some/any* is generally used in offers and requests if we think the answer is 'yes'.
c) *Some/any* is generally used in sentences with a negative meaning.
d) *Much/many* is generally used with countable nouns.
e) *A few/a little* is generally used with countable nouns.
f) *Much/many* is generally used with uncountable nouns.
g) *A few/a little* is generally used with uncountable nouns.

2 Now use the highlighted words in the examples above to tell another student what you had for each meal yesterday.

Example: For breakfast, I had *some* coffee and *a few* pieces of toast, but I didn't have *any* jam.

3 Vocabulary: food and ways of cooking

1 Reorder these jumbled words and put one in each column below.

Example: eta = tea

eta mabl crie sheeec rrtcoa lepap lomsna

meat	fish	vegetable	fruit	dairy produce	drink	other?

2 With another student, list other food in the columns above.

3 Play a memory game, saying why you went to the supermarket. Each person remembers what went before and adds to the list alphabetically, like this:

A: I went to the supermarket to get an apple.
B: I went to the supermarket to get an apple and some beef.
C: I went to the supermarket to get an apple, some beef and a few ...

4 Use your mini-dictionary to check the meaning and pronunciation of these verbs. Which adjective describes food cooked each way?

to fry to bake to scramble
to boil to grill to roast

5 Work with another student. In which ways above can you cook each of these types of food?

eggs bread potatoes
fish beef

Pronunciation

1 Listen and repeat the names of food with adjectives, like this:

t
baked apple grilled tomato
fried potato roast beef
scrambled egg boiled rice

2 Tell another student about your favourite food. Which ways do you prefer to eat it?

4 Writing

1 Close your eyes and imagine a house just before a party.

2 Write a list of things you can see, hear and smell.

3 In groups, write a poem called 'Before the party'. Use patterns like these:

A lot of people running
Some baked potatoes
A few packets of crisps
Not much time

english in action

YOU ARE GOING TO HAVE AN INTERNATIONAL/NATIONAL DINNER PARTY.

1
Decide who to invite to the party.

1 When and where will it be?
2 How many people can you invite?
3 What should people wear?
4 What do you want your guests to bring, e.g. drink?

2
Write invitations to send to your guests.

You are cordially invited to dinner

at the home of ....

on ....

at ....

Dress: ....

Please bring: ....

RSVP

WORK IN GROUPS AND PLAN THE MENU.

3
Choose which type of party to have:

a) an international dinner party with a variety of dishes from different countries, *or*
b) a national dinner party with a variety of dishes from one country.

4
Decide who will contribute things you need.

- Which dish can you cook/bring?
- What music/decorations would add to the national/international flavour?

USE YOUR TIME TO COLLECT/WRITE YOUR RECIPES IN ENGLISH.

5
Tell another student about your dish. Explain what ingredients you need and how you are going to prepare it.

6
Talk in your group again and check:

a) what you need to buy.
b) what responsibilities each person has.

ENJOY YOUR DINNER PARTY.

Language review 13

1 Quantity: *some/any; much/many; a lot of; a few/a little*

Use *some/any* with uncountable and plural countable nouns.

	some	***any***
Questions	expecting the answer yes e.g. Can I have *some* sugar?	asking about existence e.g. Have you got *any* sugar?
Positive	expressing existence e.g. We've got *some* sugar.	meaning the exact person/thing isn't important e.g. *Any* sugar is better than no sugar!
Negative		sentences with negative meaning e.g. We never have *any* sugar!

Use *much/a little* with uncountable nouns.

Use *many/a few* with plural countable nouns.

***NB Much/many* is generally used in negative sentences and questions. Otherwise use *a lot of*.**

a Describe the picture below using the expressions of quantity opposite.

2 The definite article: *the*

***The* is used when:**

a) there is only one of something.

the moon

b) it is clear in a particular situation which one the speaker means.

Where's *the* bathroom?

c) something has already been identified.

I had an egg and a sausage. *The* egg was bad.

d) a superlative adjective is used.

It's *the* best sound in the world.

b Change *a* to *the* if necessary in these sentences.

1 She boiled some eggs in a large saucepan.
2 Where's Dad? He's in a kitchen.
3 He is a most attractive man I've ever seen.
4 I'd like a sandwich and an orange juice please.
5 A President of Chile arrived this morning.
6 I've got two children. A girl is called Maria.

3 Present Continuous vs *going to* and *will (future)*

(See also Units 3 and 8.)

The Present Continuous is used for arrangements which often involve other people and/or advance organisation.

We're meeting José tonight.

The *going to* future is used for plans. It can show determination.

I'm going to work really hard next term.

***Will* is used for predictions and spontaneous decisions.**

I think José will be late. I know, I'll phone him.

c Write sentences in the Present Continuous about Carey's day tomorrow.

8.45 Children to school
11.00 Visit Sarah in hospital
1.00 Lunch in town with Mum
2.00 Shopping
3.30 Pick up children. Take them swimming
7.30 Mike, Julie and Derek for dinner

d Use the Present Continuous (future) *going to* or *will* once only to complete these dialogues.

1 A: Why are you filling that bucket with water?
B: Because I . . . (wash) the car in a minute.

2 A: Are you going to phone Tom now?
B: No. Maybe I . . . (see) him in the morning.

3 A: Are you going to the station to meet her?
B: No, I can't. I . . . (work) tomorrow evening.

14 *Positively disabled*

Christy Brown was born in 1932 with a severe physical handicap. The fifth of 22 children, he was the victim of cerebral palsy, but inside a helpless body was a brilliantly imaginative and sensitive mind. Here was a writer who would become one of the great men of Irish literature.

This is Christy Brown's own story. He describes how, as a child, he learned to read, write, paint and finally type with the toe of his left foot.

My Left Foot is now a major and critically acclaimed film starring Daniel Day Lewis as Christy Brown.

I remember the first thing I learned to write was my initials: 'C.B.' ... Soon afterwards I learned to write my full name ... I was tremendously proud of myself when I could do this. I felt quite important.

I was now going on six and soon I got tired of just writing my own name. I wanted to do something else - something bigger. But I couldn't, because I couldn't read. I didn't exactly know what being able to read meant. I just knew that Jim could do it, Tony could do it, that Mona and Peter could do it and that made me want to do it too. I think I was jealous.

Knowing the alphabet was half the battle won, for I was soon able to put letters together and to form little words. After a while I began to know how to put words together and form sentences ...

Although I couldn't talk very much at seven years old, I was now able to sit alone and crawl from place to place on my bottom without breaking any bones or smashing any of mother's china.

I was now just ten, a boy who couldn't walk, speak, feed or dress himself. I was helpless, but only now did I begin to realise how helpless I really was. I still didn't know anything about myself: I knew nothing beyond the fact that I was 'different' from others.

People always thought that it was marvellous that I could paint with my toes and told me I was lucky, yes, quite a remarkable boy ... I only wanted to be ordinary like everybody else ...

Then suddenly I had an idea. I had always been fond of writing letters ... But now I decided to try something more ambitious, not just letters, but stories ...

I had first learned to write with my toes when I was five years old, but I had to wait till I was almost seventeen before I realised that it could give me the key to a new sort of life ... , a grand new world of thought and ideas. From then on writing became my only real interest ... a pencil was seldom out of my foot.

1 Diagnosis: ability

1 Find someone in the class who can do each thing below. How well can they do them?

- act
- draw
- sing
- cook
- dance
- do a sport
- do DIY
- use a computer
- play an instrument
- speak another foreign language

2 Read the back cover of the book *My Left Foot* by Christy Brown.

1 What does it say he can do? Why is this remarkable?
2 Write one sentence to say what the book is about.

3 Now read the extracts from the book.

1 Which of these things does Christy say he could do by the age of a) six, b) seven, c) seventeen?
2 Which couldn't he do by the age of ten?

write the complete alphabet
write sentences
write words
feed himself
write stories
dress himself
write his name
sit up by himself
speak clearly
walk
crawl

4 Check your answers with another student, like this:

By the time he was six, he could . . .

There is a Revision exercise for *can/can't* + levels of ability on page 129.

2 Grammar: *can/could/be able to*

a) I *could* paint with my toes.
b) I *couldn't* read.
c) I *was able to* crawl.

1 Look at Christy's sentences above and answer these questions.

1 Are these sentences about Christy's past, present or future ability?
2 Which two expressions in italics have the same meaning?

2 Complete this chart showing ways to express ability.

	Positive	Negative	Question
Present	. . . am/are/is able to	can't (cannot) am not/isn't able to	Can you/she? Are you/Is she . . . ?
Past	could was/. . . able to	. . . . . . /weren't able to	. . . ? Were you/Was she . . . ?
Future	will be able to	. . .	. . . ?

3 Correct seven mistakes in this letter from a friend who has invited you to the cinema. They are mistakes in the forms above.

Dear . . .,

Great news! I wasn't able to get tickets for *My Left Foot* on Saturday at 6 pm, so we'll definitely able to see it. Unfortunately, I couldn't to get anything later but this means we'll be able eat afterwards and I can to give you a lift home now that I could drive!
If for any reason you can't able to come, please let me know. Otherwise I'll see you on Saturday.

Love,
. . .

4 Reply to the letter. Where will you put your address/the date?

Pronunciation: weak forms of *can/be able to*

1 Put sentences a), b) and c) above into present and future forms.

2 Listen and check your answers. Then repeat the sentences.

1 Which verb is stressed in each sentence?
2 Which words are pronounced with the weak sound /ə/?

3 Complete this chart for yourself. Tick (✓) the things *you* can do.

	You	Your partner
Make quick decisions Adapt quickly to new things Get on well with most people Organise work/social events efficiently Work well in a team		

4 Now tell your partner what you can/can't do. Say each thing once only. Listen to her/him and tick her/his part of your chart.

5 Check the answers in your chart with your partner's chart. Did you hear correctly?

6 Tell the class some of the main strengths/qualities of your partner.

Example: She is able to get on well with most people, and she can . . .

7 Now ask your partner about their childhood or about a child they know well. By what age were they able to do some of these things?

write their name   talk   walk
tell the time   read   swim
ride a bicycle

8 Tell the class one thing you can't do now, but will be able to do when you can speak fluent English.

NB ***Can*** **(present and future)**

I can drive so I can give you a lift to the station.
(1 = first *can*, 2 = second *can*)

Which *can* refers to present ability, 1 or 2?
Which *can* refers to future possibility?

Uses of *can*; verbs of size/position; *too/enough*; passive infinitive; Present Perfect passive

3 Key word: *can*

CAN

a) permission ......
b) an offer ......
c) a request ......
d) an invitation ......
e) a suggestion ......
f) ability ......

1 Match each use of *can* to an example below.

1 **[A] Can you see it? [B] I can.** There
2 ok. **Can you bring me the book?** Postm
3 **[A] Can I wear this then? [B] Er no.**
4 **You can always leave it** if you think
5 , **I can get you hot water.** Hm, yeah,
6 **You can come with me.** Okay, lovely,

From the *British National Corpus* (Spoken)

2 Rephrase each sentence above, but keep the same meaning. Which word/s can replace *can* in each case: *could, be allowed to* or *be able to*?

3 Play 'I spy'. Can other students guess what you can see in the classroom in ten guesses?

Example: 'I spy with my little eye something beginning with X. What can I see?'

4 Vocabulary: changing size/position

1 Look at the verbs in the first column. Which one means *to make something*: a) smaller b) bigger c) shorter d) longer e) wider f) higher g) lower?

Verb	Past Simple	Past participle
to shorten	shortened	shortened
to enlarge		
to reduce (in size)		
to widen		
to lower		
to raise		
to lengthen		

2 Complete the chart above. What do you notice about the form of the Past Simple and past participle of these verbs?

3 Look at the picture of the kitchen. What problems could the things below cause a disabled person in a wheelchair?

Example: The entrance is too narrow. *or*
It isn't wide enough.

the entrance	the electric socket
the light cord	the shelves
the cord for the blinds	the cooking surface
the space in front of the kitchen units	

Grammar: passives (2)

The entrance is too narrow.
It needs *to be widened.*

1 Look at the sentences above and answer these questions.

1 What is the active form of *to be widened*?
2 What is the passive infinitive of the other verbs listed opposite?

2 Talk to another student. How could the kitchen be adapted to suit a disabled person? What needs to be done?

3 Now look at an adapted kitchen on page 124. Say what *has been done*. Which of these things did you think of?

5 Listening

1 Before you listen, describe the photographs.

2 Listen to Celeste Dandeker talking about dance since an accident put her in a wheelchair.

1 Who do you think Darshan Singh Bhuller is:
a) a doctor, or b) a film director?

2 What kind of person do you imagine Celeste is:
a) optimistic, b) fatalistic, or c) pessimistic?

3 Listen to the first part of this interview again. Is each of these sentences true (T) or false (F)?

1 Darshan Singh Bhuller had the idea for the film.
2 He had forgotten she couldn't walk.
3 It sounded like a depressing film.
4 She really didn't think she should do it.
5 It helped her find new ways of moving.
6 She only dances in her wheelchair now.

4 Listen to the last part of the interview again.

1 What does she think makes 'good dance':
a) a dancer's body, or b) the feelings inside?

2 What parts of the body does she refer to?

5 Tell other students how far you agree with her view of 'good dance'.

1 How many other parts of the body can you name?
2 Which can you dance with?

6 Grammar: *although/in spite of*, etc.

1 Complete this sentence for Celeste Dandeker.

Although parts of my body don't work any more . . .

2 Look where these words go in the sentences below. What parts of speech can follow each pair?

a) *although/even though* b) *in spite of/despite*

1 She can dance *although* she had an accident.
2 *Even though* she had an accident she can dance.
3 *In spite of* the accident she can dance.
4 She can dance *despite* having an accident.

3 Choose the correct alternative in each example.

1 Darshan Singh Bhuller asked her to dance in his film *in spite of/even though* she couldn't walk.
2 *In spite of/although* her disability, she was prepared to take part in the film.
3 She danced to the music *even though/despite* her wheelchair.
4 *Although/despite* she had to lie on the floor, she danced out of her wheelchair.
5 She enjoyed the experience *in spite of/although* not being able to move her whole body.

4 Read the information below in groups. Discuss who is the best candidate for the job.

Example: Although Thomas is inexperienced . . .

WANTED
10th July – 31st August
SOCIAL ACTIVITIES/SPORTS ORGANISER
for international residential centre

Requirements: age 20+. Good all-round sports ability. Experience of working with teenagers and/or foreign students. 24 hour availability.

Conditions: free accommodation plus competitive

CANDIDATES

Name: Thomas Westphal	**Name:** Rachel Taylor	**Name:** Clive Shepherd
Age: 19	**Age:** 25	**Age:** 60
• going to college to train as a sports teacher • has organised social activities for teenagers at his local church • can begin July 15th	• a primary school teacher on holiday • has been a tour guide • enjoys dancing and swimming but has no other sports	• retired • was a professional football coach and played rugby and cricket • has lived abroad for a number of years

english in action

She has sold more paintings than Van Gogh. She is also disabled.

If it's so much trouble and strife, how come married people live five years longer?

If you're thinking of taking the plunge, you need to have and to hold Options March edition on marriage. OPTIONS

YOU ARE GOING TO DESIGN ADVERTISEMENTS.

1
Look at the advertisements and answer these questions with another student.

1 What are they trying to do?
2 What do you think? Are they effective? Why/why not?

2
Now follow the instructions below. Plan an advertisement with other students. Show the contribution to society of a subject which is often considered negatively.

1 Think of as many advantages for each subject below as possible:
   a) the over 70s
   b) high taxation
   c) traffic wardens
   d) commercials on TV
   e) something else?
2 Decide which advertisement your group would prefer to make.
3 Decide what image you want to give to your subject. Decide on the exact picture and write the caption.
4 Finally, show your advertisement to other groups. Explain how you came to your final idea.

3
Listen to other students and look at their advertisements. Which do you think is most effective? Why?

Language review 14

1 *Can/could/be able to*

Can, could **and *be able to* all express ability.**
Can **is used most often and has only present and past forms. *Be able to* is used for all other forms.**

Present	She *can*	
Past	She *could*	swim.
Future	She'*ll be able to*	

Could **and *was/were able to* are often interchangeable but we must use *was/were able to* if talking about past success as well as ability.**
She swam well and was able to (*not* could) reach the beach.

a Complete the following sentences with possible forms of *can/be able to* from the table opposite. How many different ways can you complete each gap?

1 Mike . . . swim until he was 14 and he still . . . swim very well.
2 I don't think I . . . be at the restaurant until 8 pm.
3 He . . . to open the door by breaking the lock with an axe.
4 They . . . come to Jon's birthday party next Saturday, . . . they?
5 She . . . go to university if she doesn't do well in her exams.

2 Passives: infinitive and Present Perfect

All passives move the focus from the subject to the object of the sentence and are formed with *be* + past participle. (See Unit 2.)

Subject	+ *be*	+ past participle
It	*is* *was* *has been*	taken.
They	*are* *were* *have been*	

- **Passive infinitive (*be* + past participle)**

The passive infinitive is used with modal verbs, e.g. *can, could, need, may, might, must,* etc.
It needs *to be done*. = Someone needs to do it.

- **Present Perfect passive (*has/have been* + past participle)**

It has *been done* = Someone has done it.

b Look at the picture of the house and use each verb below to say what *needs to be done* to it.

fix paint mend cut put in replace

c Look at the picture on page 124 of the same house a few months later and say what *has been done*.

3 *Although/even though; in spite of/despite*

These words link opposing ideas but each pair has different sentence patterns.

Clause 1		Clause 2
Although *Even though*	she cried,	she was happy.
In spite of	crying,	
Despite	the tears,	

NB **Clause 1 and 2 can change position.**
She was happy although she cried.

d Make each sentence grammatically complete and put the words in a logical order.

1 raining/although/went to park
2 in spite of/I like John/bad temper
3 all of the film/I watched/very boring/even though
4 not have the qualifications/despite/I got the job
5 although/some progress/been very slow/we make
6 all night/work hard/I wasn't tired/in spite of

15 *Consolidation*

1 Across cultures: good manners

Revises
Vocabulary: Food, behaviour
Grammar: Quantity; passives; *although/in spite of*, etc.; future time; *should/shouldn't*

1 Describe the picture of people at a dinner party.

1 What have they been doing since the party began?
2 What have they eaten/drunk?
3 What is left on the table?

Example: There is a little . . .

2 Tell other students what you think of the guests' behaviour. What should/shouldn't they do?

3 Now look at the guidelines for acceptable behaviour at meals in Britain on page 125. How is British opinion different from opinion in your country?

4 Write sentences using *although/even though, in spite of/despite* to describe some of the people's behaviour at the party.

Example: In spite of knowing you shouldn't put your elbows on the table, one person has both elbows on it.

5 Tell other students about the next party/social event you are going to.

1 What's the occasion?
2 Who is going?
3 What food/entertainment will there be?
4 What will need to be done beforehand?
5 What has already been organised?

6 Now look at the cartoon below and answer these questions.

1 What did the first snake do that was wrong? Why was it wrong?
2 Why was the giraffe surprised by the second snake's reaction?

From *Hello*

2 Thinking about learning: conversation patterns

Revises
Vocabulary: Cinema; travel; everyday actions
Grammar: Present Continuous (future); Present Perfect Simple and Continuous; reported speech

1 Listen to two conversations between friends and complete the chart below.

	1	2
Where does the conversation take place?		
What is the main topic of conversation?		
What has been decided by the end of the conversation?		

2 Listen to the start of each conversation again.

1 Which question do both people ask in:
a) conversation 1? b) conversation 2?

2 Which word has main stress in:
a) the first question in each conversation?
b) the second question in each conversation?

3 Ask and answer questions with another student. Answer in detail, then return the question. Ask:

a) if she/he's seen any good films lately.
b) if she/he's done her homework.
c) if she/he likes Indian food.
d) if she/he's been to America.
e) if she/he's doing anything special tonight.

4 Now listen to the complete conversations again. Which of the words below are used to:

a) start the conversation?
b) introduce new information?
c) finish the conversation?

OK, fine . . .	Right, well, . . .	Oh, hello . . .
Listen, . . .	Hi! . . .	Anyway, . . .
You see, . . .		

5 Read the situations below and make phone calls to other students. Begin like this:

A: Oh hello. Is that (+ her/his name)?
B: Yes.
A: Hi! This is (+ your name).

Student A: Phone and invite Student B to come and stay with your family some time soon. Explain some of the things you'll be able to do together.

Student B: Answer the phone. Find out what Student A has been doing lately and tell her/him about your own activities. Accept her/his invitation and find out as much as possible about the suggested visit.

6 Tell the class some of the things you discussed.

Example: X phoned and asked me to visit her family. I said I would love to and she told me . . .

INSIDE INFO

If you could have three wishes ...

What would you fancy? A big tub of chocolate ice-cream? A hunky boyfriend? No more rain? We've been playing fairy godmother ...

Vanessa 21
Dancer
'Oh, I can't think of three wishes! Let's see ... I'd like to get in touch with this guy I met 'cos I've lost his phone number ... I'd like to dance in shows and pantomimes ... oh, and I wish it would stop raining!'

Ruxandra 15
Student
'One wish would be that I could have the whole of Marks and Spencer's foodstore all to myself ... I'd like a big tub of chocolate ice-cream, and I wish that school would be over ...'

Hattie 15, Student
'If I had three wishes, I'd like to live in a French chateau, and I'd like to live with my boyfriend Con. I'd really like a green Volkswagen Beetle too.'

Sally 14, Student
'I'd wish for a million trillion pounds, for school to be over and to pass my exams.'

Ben 16, Student
'I'd wish for the most expensive car in the world, I want to be a millionaire. Er ... oh yeah! Eternal happiness.'

Louise 17, Dancer
'I'd wish for loads of money, to have a really hunky boyfriend and to travel around the world dancing.'

Greg 18, Clerk
'If I had three wishes, I'd like everyone in the world to be really happy. I'd like to own a Ferrari and live in New York.'

Matthew 17, Student
'Ooh, that's a tough one off the top of your head ... Money, success and a holiday, I think.'

From *Mizz*

3 Language in context: wishes

Revises
Vocabulary: Possessions; *some/any/no/everybody*, etc.
Grammar: *Can/could/able to*; *would* (second conditional)

1 Look at the magazine article. What do you think?

1 What question was asked?
2 Were the people interviewed or did they write their answers? What language in the texts makes you think this?

2 Read the texts and find out how many of the people have wishes connected with:

a) money and possessions?
b) personal relationships?
c) their home?
d) travel?
e) school/work success?
f) happiness?
g) other?

3 Tell other students *your* answer to the question in the article.

1 If you could have three wishes what would they be?
2 Which of the things above do you think are most important?
3 Which other things do you think are important?

4 Listen to a rock song made famous by Freddie Mercury and Queen. What does the singer wish for?

5 Read the verses of the song. Put one word in each gap.

6 Listen again and check your answers. Then write the question the singer asks in the chorus. Does he suggest he has ***somebody, anybody, everybody*** or ***nobody*** to love?

7 Complete each gap below with one of these words:

some/any/every/nobody
some/any/every/nowhere, or
some/any/every/nothing

1 I've looked . . . but I can't find my glasses . . . .
2 He says there's . . . wrong but . . . is worrying him.
3 She's terribly secretive. She never tells . . . .
4 They can't be in. . . . is answering the door and . . . is so quiet.
5 Does . . . mind if I smoke?

8 Read the story below about four people called Everybody, Somebody, Anybody and Nobody. Choose the best of these titles for the story.

a) A job well done
b) A difficult job
c) An unfinished job

There was an important job to be done and Everybody was asked to do it. Everybody was sure Somebody would do it. Anybody could have done it but Nobody did it. Somebody got angry about that because it was Everybody's job. Everybody thought Anybody could do it but Nobody realised that Everybody wouldn't do it. In the end, Everybody blamed Somebody when Nobody did what Anybody could have done.

Each (1) ... I get up I die a little, can't barely stand on my (2) ...
Take a look in the (3) ... and (4) .... Lord, what you're doing to me.
I have spent all my (5) ... in believing you,
but I just can't (6) ... no relief.

I work hard every day of my (7) .... I (8) ... till I ache my bones.
At the end, I take (9) ... my hard-earned pay all on my (10) ....
I get down on my (11) ... and I start to pray
till the (12) ... run down from my eyes.

Every day I try and I try and I (13) ...
But everybody (14) ... to put me down. They say I'm going (15) ...
They say I have a lot of water in my brain.
I've got no common (16) ... , he's got nobody left to believe.

Got no feel. I got (17) ... rhythm. I just keep losing my beat.
I'm OK. I'm (18) ... Ain't gonna face no defeat.
I've just gotta get (19) ... of this prison cell
one day I'm gonna be (20) ...

Check What You Know!

Test what you have learned in Units 11–15 by completing Check What You Know 3. (See Teacher's Book.)

16 *All in the mind*

"Of course you're depressed. I'm very expensive."

1 Diagnosis: advice

1 **Listen to people talking about their problems on a radio phone-in. What is each caller's problem?**

2 **Check your answers with another student. What advice would you give each caller?**

3 **Write a sentence to include in a letter to each caller, giving your main piece of advice. Begin differently each time, like this:**

I think you should . . .
If I were you, . . .
Why don't you . . . ?

There is a Revision exercise for ways of giving advice on page 129.

2 Reading

1 **Before you answer the questionnaire, look at the cartoon above:**

a) who is the psychotherapist?
b) what does she/he do?

2 **Answer the questionnaire below. For each question, decide if a), b) or c) best represents your feelings.**

3 **Vote on each question and find out how your class feel about psychotherapy. Write the number of people who voted for each question.**

4 **Now turn to page 125 and read what a survey of British people found. Which opinions are similar/very different from your class?**

Psychotherapy no longer happens only in California. More and more people in more and more countries are in therapy. How do you feel about it?

1 Do you like talking about your problems? If so, who to?
a) a good friend or partner ☐
b) a member of your family ☐
c) a professional person like a doctor or a religious adviser ☐

2 Do you know what having therapy is like?
a) Yes, I've heard about it from friends. ☐
b) Yes, I've read about it in books/magazines, etc. ☐
c) No, I've no idea. I don't know anybody who has had therapy. ☐

3 Do you think therapy is good for:
a) people with serious depression? ☐
b) anybody; people like you and me? ☐
c) no-one at all? ☐

4 Who do you think might need therapy more in their lives?
a) men ☐
b) women ☐
c) no difference ☐

5 Would you like to have therapy?
a) if I was very depressed ☐
b) if I could afford it ☐
c) under no circumstances at all ☐

6 Would you expect therapy to help you:
a) solve problems ? ☐
b) develop your creativity? ☐
c) understand your feelings? ☐

7 Which age group do you think has therapy most?
a) 16–26 ☐
b) 30–40 ☐
c) 55–65 ☐

8 What makes people need therapy most? Are they things like:
a) divorce, death, etc.? ☐
b) general stress, anxiety, etc.? ☐
c) unemployment, etc.? ☐

9 How would you describe people who have regular therapy?
a) weak ☐
b) strong ☐
c) self-indulgent ☐

3 Key word: *like*

LIKE

a) to introduce examples ......

b) to mean something is enjoyed ......

c) to offer/wish for something ......

d) to ask for a description/opinion ......

e) to express similarity in character/appearance ......

1 Look at the uses of *like* above. Find one example for each use in a) the questionnaire, and b) these sentences.

1	incess and **she looks like her mum. ... Yeah** that l
2	.. Oh oh! ... Yeah **I like living round here,** it's n
3	**It just means things like painting and decorating** .
4	ular. **What would you like to do today?** ... well I'm
5	**Well, what are they like ?** ... I've done some that

From the *British National Corpus* (Spoken)

2 Write questions using *like* and ask another student:

a) about the weather last time she/he went on holiday.
b) if she/he has hobbies of the types you name, e.g. sports, music.
c) if she/he wants to have a coffee after class.
d) what she/he enjoys doing at the weekends.
e) about the appearance or character of someone in her/his family.

4 Vocabulary: families

Look at the pairs of words below with another student.

1 What's the difference in meaning between the words in each pair?
2 What three spellings for the sound /ʌ/, as in uncle, can you find?

a parent/a relative	a stepmother/a mother-in-law
a cousin/an uncle	an only child/an orphan
a son/a child	a nephew/a niece

Pronunciation: /ʌ/ vs /æ/

1 Listen to the difference between a) *uncle* and b) *ankle*. Decide which word you hear in each sentence on the cassette.

2 Listen and decide which of these words you hear.

1 Goodness me! That's a large cup/cap.
2 Put that rug/rag back in the cupboard.
3 Isn't that hut/hat awful!
4 It isn't a very good truck/track, I'm afraid.

3 Read and answer these questions with a partner. Who can solve each puzzle most quickly?

Example:
STUDENT A: Who is married to your father?
STUDENT B: Your mother.

1 Who is married to your uncle?
2 Who is married to your mother-in-law?
3 Who is your cousin's mother?
4 Who is your brother's sister?
5 Who is your husband's brother?
6 Who is your mother's son by a previous marriage?

4 Tell your partner about your family. Show photos if possible or draw a family tree.

1 Who are you most like?
2 Who do you look like?

Adjectives describing character; selected multi-word verbs; *should have done*

5 Listening

1 Before you listen, match each expression in column A to one of similar meaning in column B.

A	B
1 look after somebody	a) not give in to somebody
2 stand up to somebody	b) agree with somebody
3 back somebody up	c) take care of somebody
4 go along with somebody	d) be on somebody's side

2 Listen to Virginia Ironside, a newspaper Agony Aunt, talking about her family relationships.

1 How many brothers and sisters does she have?
2 Which of her parents is she most like?
3 Who does she look like?
4 What was family life like for her as a child?

3 Listen again. Which of these adjectives describe a) her father, b) her mother, c) herself?

rational	helpless	sensible
controlled	(not) self-confident	temperamental
vulnerable	artistic	

4 Listen to the next part of the interview. How did Virginia's mother's job in fashion cause her problems?

5 What do you think? What advice would you give a child in Virginia's position?

6 Listen to Virginia's own advice. Do you agree?

7 Discuss the advantages/disadvantages of having a parent who works in fashion. What problems over clothes, if any, have you had with your parents?

NB ***sensible*** **vs** ***sensitive***

a) I often cry at sad films.
b) It might rain. I'll take my umbrella.

Who is *sensible*, a) or b)?
Who is *sensitive*?

Virginia Ironside, Agony Aunt and columnist for *Today* and *The Independent* newspapers

6 Grammar: *should have done*

I *should have stood* up to my mother.
I *shouldn't have gone* along with all her requests.

1 Look at Virginia's words in the box above which say how she now views her past behaviour.

1 Did she stand up to her mother? Does she regret it?
2 Did she go along with all her mother's requests? Does she regret it?

2 Listen and repeat the sentences in the box.

1 Which words are stressed?
2 How do you pronounce *should have/shouldn't have*?

3 Write sentences to say what Virginia now thinks she *should/shouldn't have* done as a child.

- talk to another adult
- be frightened
- agree to everything
- say no

4 Talk to other students about difficult family situations you have heard of.

1 What happened?
2 What do you think the people involved should/shouldn't have done?

5 Write one true sentence about something you regret. Show it to another student and explain the situation.

7 Reading

1 Find out about your own personality. Read this story and complete the gaps with the first thing that comes to mind.

Once upon a time, I was walking through a forest. It was ... *(what was the forest like?)* and all the trees were ... *(what were the trees like?)*. The weather was ... and ... *(what was the weather like?)*. I was feeling *(describe your state of mind)* when, all of a sudden, I saw a bear. I stopped. The bear I had seen was ... *(what was the bear like?)*. When it saw me, it ... *(describe what it did)*.

After I had passed the bear, I came to a bridge. The water below was ... *(say whether it was the sea, a stream, a river, a lake, etc.)* and ... *(what did it look like?)*.

After walking a little further, I came to a field. In the middle of the field, I found a cup. It was ... *(describe the cup in detail)*. It had started to get dark, so I decided to go home by the quickest route possible. On the way back, I saw a cave. It was .... *(what was the cave like?)* and made me feel ... *(say how you felt)* so I ... *(what did you do as a result?)*.

After that I went home and lived happily ever after.

2 Now read the analysis of your story on page 125.

3 Tell other students what you found out about your personality. How true do you think it is? How true do *they* think it is?

Grammar: *after/before* + verb

First action	Second action
After I (had) passed the bear,	I came to a bridge.
After walking a little further,	I came to a field.
I left the cave.	*After that* I went home.

1 Look at the examples of *after* and *after that* in sentences from the story above. Which can be followed by the:

a) Past Simple? b) Past Perfect? c) *-ing* form?

2 Rephrase the sentences in the box above. Use *before* + *ing* form and keep the original meaning.

3 Write a list of things you did yesterday, in the wrong order. Ask questions and put another student's list in the right order.

Example: STUDENT A: When did you go shopping?
STUDENT B: Before going to the hairdresser's.

8 Writing

1 Look at the story about the walk in the forest again. Find an example of the:

a) Past Continuous to describe the scene.
b) Past Simple to interrupt a state or action in progress.
c) Past Perfect to refer back to an earlier event.
d) Past Simple to say what happened next.

2 Look at the picture below of the forest before a storm. Continue this paragraph and describe the scene.

It was a typical Sunday in the forest. Visitors from the town were picnicking peacefully. Some people . . .

3 Write the rest of the story. Use *before* and *after* (*that*) to show the order of events when it began to rain.

4 Tell your story to other students. Then rewrite any parts they didn't find clear.

english in action

Cognitive psychologists, like Jerome Bruner, think how we tell our life story could be as interesting as what we say. They think our choice of language shows how we see the world today.

- Are the sentences in the active or passive voice? Does the speaker make things happen or do they happen to her/him?
- What and how much is presented positively/negatively?
- Does the speaker regret much?
- Does she/he talk more about events or feelings?
- What other ways could the same story be told?

YOU ARE GOING TO ANALYSE LIFE STORIES.

1

Read the article above. Does it suggest that when analysing life stories:

a) the content is the most important part?
b) the language is the most important part?
c) the language and content are equally important?

2

Listen to someone talking about her life. Which of these things does she mention?

a) pre-school primary school secondary school higher education work
b) family life social life marriage political views religious views

3

Look at the tapescript on page 136 and answer the questions in the article with another student. What sort of person do you think the speaker is?

4

Prepare to tell your own life story. Which of the topics from the listening exercise above will you mention?

5

Tell your life story into a tape recorder or write it as if you were speaking, for about three minutes.

NOW ANALYSE YOUR ENGLISH.

6

Look at the pronunciation categories below. Then play or tell another student your story. What do you think?

1 Is there anything which makes her/him difficult to understand?
2 What would *you* most like to improve in your pronunciation?

- *Stress*: Is the important information clearly stressed?
- *Intonation*: Do you sound friendly and interested or unfriendly and bored?
- *Sounds*: Do you make enough difference between the underlined sounds in these words?

cap/cup	leave/live	thing/sing	right/light
hair/air	work/walk	had/head	pat/bat

7

Listen to or read your story again. Note and correct any mistakes you find. Are there any things you want to correct/reword but don't know how to?

8

Work as a class and suggest how to say things better.

Language review 16

1 Verbs: *should have/shouldn't have*

Use *should have/shouldn't have* + past participle to criticise past actions.

+	She	*should*	*have* done it (?)	(but she didn't).
–		*shouldn't*		(but she did).
?	*Should*	she		(Yes, she *should*.)

tidy vacuum shave get dressed empty put away make comb

a Look at the picture and use the words above to say what Tom should/shouldn't have done. He promised his mother he'd tidy his room for his grandmother's arrival at 11 am.

2 *Like*

- **Verb**

like + noun	I *like* tea.
like + *-ing* form	I *like* ski*ing*.
would + *like* + noun	I'*d like* a coffee.
would + *like* + *to* infinitive	I'*d like* to go.

- **Preposition**

asking for description	What is she *like*?
meaning *similar to*	She looks *like* her mother.
meaning *for example*	I do things *like* cooking and washing up.

b Put these words in order and make questions. Then answer the questions in complete sentences.

1 evenings doing do like on what Friday you?
2 is like weather the today what?
3 on sort doing you things do like of holiday what?
4 friend what best your look does like?
5 would what afternoon like do to you tomorrow?
6 for you tea like coffee do breakfast or?
7 meet like famous would to which person you?
8 like like do dancing doing you things swimming and?

3 *Before/after (that)*

Use these words to describe the order events happened in.

Before / *After*	phoning her / he (had) phoned	he went home.
He phoned her.		*Before that/ After that* he went home.

***NB Before/After + -ing* form can be used only if the subject in both clauses is the same.**
After arriving, they went straight to bed.
After he (had) arrived, they went straight to bed.
Although grammatically correct, the Past Perfect is often not used with *before/after* as the meaning is clear without it.

c Read Julie's diary and then put the events in a paragraph to describe what she did today. Use *before/after (that)* and each of the forms in the box opposite.

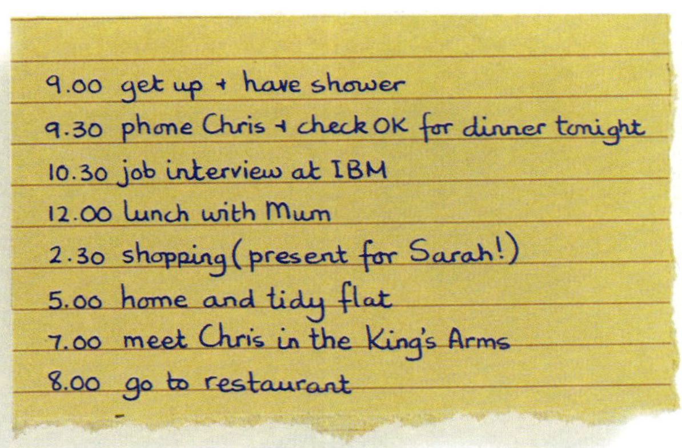
9.00 get up + have shower
9.30 phone Chris + check OK for dinner tonight
10.30 job interview at IBM
12.00 lunch with Mum
2.30 shopping (present for Sarah!)
5.00 home and tidy flat
7.00 meet Chris in the King's Arms
8.00 go to restaurant

THE UNICORN IN THE GARDEN

A complete story by James Thurber, read on cassette by Nigel Anthony

Once upon a sunny morning a man who sat in a breakfast nook looked up from his scrambled eggs to see a white unicorn with a gold horn quietly cropping the roses in the garden. The man went up to the bedroom where his wife was still asleep and woke her. 'There's a unicorn in the garden,' he said. 'Eating roses.' She opened one unfriendly eye and looked at him. 'The unicorn is a mythical beast,' she said, and turned her back on him. The man walked slowly downstairs and out into the garden. The unicorn was still there; he was now browsing among the tulips. 'Here, unicorn,' said the man, and pulled up a lily and gave it to him. The unicorn ate it gravely. With a high heart, because there was a unicorn in his garden, the man went upstairs and roused his wife again. 'The unicorn,' he said, 'ate a lily.' His wife sat up in bed and looked at him, coldly. 'You are a booby[1],' she said, 'and I am going to have you put in the booby-hatch[2].' The man, who had never liked the words 'booby' and 'booby-hatch', and who liked them even less on a shining morning when there was a unicorn in the garden, thought for a moment. 'We'll see about that,' he said. He walked over to the door. 'He has a golden horn in the middle of his forehead,' he told her. Then he

went back to the garden to watch the unicorn; but the unicorn had gone away. The man sat down among the roses and went to sleep.

As soon as the husband had gone out of the house, the wife got up and dressed as fast as she could. She was very excited and there was a gloat in her eye. She telephoned the police and she telephoned a psychiatrist; she told them to hurry to her house and bring a strait-jacket. When the police and the psychiatrist arrived they sat down in chairs and looked at her, with great interest. 'My husband,' she said, 'saw a unicorn this morning.' The police looked at the psychiatrist and the psychiatrist looked at the police. 'He told me it ate a lily,' she said. The psychiatrist looked at the police and the police looked at the psychiatrist. 'He told me it had a golden horn in the middle of its forehead,' she said. At a solemn signal from the psychiatrist, the police leaped from their chairs and seized the wife. They had a hard time subduing her, for she put up a terrific struggle, but they finally subdued her. Just as they got her into the strait-jacket, the husband came back into the house.

'Did you tell your wife you saw a unicorn?' asked the police. 'Of course not,' said the husband. 'The unicorn is a mythical beast.' 'That's all I wanted to know,' said the psychiatrist. 'Take her away. I'm sorry, sir, but your wife is as crazy as a jay bird.' So they took her away, cursing and screaming, and shut her up in an institution. The husband lived happily ever after.

Glossary

[1] *booby* – a crazy person (old-fashioned American slang)

[2] *booby-hatch* – a mental institution

17 *Cries of freedom*

1 Diagnosis: likes/dislikes

Find out about pets kept by people in the class.

Pet owners

Answer these questions and tell the other students about your pet/s.

1 Why do you like having a pet?
2 If you have more than one, which do you prefer?
3 What things do you enjoy doing with or for it?
4 What about the more unpleasant things? Which do you a) hate? b) not mind? c) quite like?

Non-pet owners

Ask the people with animals what they like/don't like about having a pet.

1 What is the biggest advantage/disadvantage of each animal?
2 Which pet would you prefer to have and why?

There is a Revision exercise for likes/dislikes on page 129.

2 Vocabulary: animals

1 Tell another student which animals below are used in your country for:

- food
- work
- clothes/jewellery
- hunting/sport
- research (e.g. medicine/cosmetics)
- entertainment (e.g. circuses/zoos)

budgerigars	chickens	rabbits	dogs	cows
guinea pigs	elephants	horses	foxes	rats
crocodiles	monkeys	camels	pigs	

2 Talk to other students about your attitude to animals. How far do you agree/disagree with these opinions?

1 It is cruel to keep animals in cages and zoos.
2 It is unnecessary and immoral to eat meat.
3 All animal sports are cruel and should be banned.
4 It is necessary to use animals for scientific/medical research.
5 Animal rights are irrelevant until we have full human rights.

"I think it's cruel the way they keep them in those little cages."

3 Reading

1 Read Tanya and Mark's stories opposite and answer these questions for each person.

1 When did she/he first have contact with animals?
2 What was her/his first act on behalf of animals?
3 What action does she/he think people should take?

2 Check your answers with another student and discuss these questions.

1 What is the main difference in the opinions of the two people?
2 Which person do you have most sympathy with?

3 Look at Mark's story with your partner. Are these sentences true (T) or false (F)?

1 Mark's mother didn't mind keeping birds in cages.
2 Mark only started getting interested in animal rights by reading about the ALF.
3 Mark was still a teenager when he decided to commit his first 'crime'.
4 Mark admits being quite scared about breaking the law at first.
5 One place stopped cutting up animals as a direct result of action by Mark's group.
6 Mark admits burning down places where they experiment on animals.
7 Mark is learning to make bombs to use in high security laboratories.
8 Mark denies ever hurting innocent people.
9 Mark says the ALF wants to get as much publicity as possible.

TANYA'S STORY

I've always loved animals. I lived on a farm when I was young and there were always animals inside and outside the house – cats, dogs, chickens, goats ... you name it, we had it!

I became a vegetarian very early on. I just couldn't bring myself to eat meat – it just seemed so disgusting. My friends at school always thought I was a bit strange but I think they respected my views.

I feel quite strongly that it's wrong to hurt animals in scientific experiments and I think that if anything is really going to change, it must be by peaceful protest, writing letters and so on. We must convince the government to change the law – breaking into scientific laboratories, setting places on fire – doesn't help anyone.

In fact I really disapprove of violence of any sort. I don't understand how people against violence to animals can then justify doing violent things themselves. Violence is wrong, full stop, whether it is used against people or animals. There must be other ways to fight for what you believe in.

MARK'S STORY

I don't think I was particularly close to animals as a child. My mother had pets – dogs, budgerigars and she was against cruelty to animals. But it was really through reading Animal Liberation Front (ALF) newsletters that I got involved in animal rights.

My first action was to break a window of a butcher's shop. I was 20 at the time. There were three of us. We just decided to do it. ... my job was to throw in a pot of paint after the window was smashed. I was very nervous at first – but things got easier.

The most immediately successful raid I was involved in was on a school which kept animals for dissection. A group of us broke in, rescued the animals – a few rats and guinea pigs. The next day the school announced that they would no longer use animals for dissection.

Sometimes we set fire to places – but not if there are people or animals in there. ... I don't approve of using bombs though. They are too dangerous and inaccurate. We have never harmed anyone not directly involved in mutilating animals.

I would say there are about 50 ALF groups – of about three to four people – active in Britain. Our aim is to destroy property and force laboratories to close – publicity is not the most important thing.

From *New Internationalist*

4 Grammar: verb + *-ing*/infinitive

1 Put each underlined verb in the last exercise in one of these columns.

Verbs + infinitive	Verbs + *-ing* form

2 With another student, retell Mark's story using as many of the verbs above as possible.

3 Complete these sentences with information about yourself. Use infinitive or *-ing* forms.

1 I hate . . . , but I don't mind . . .
2 Before I get much older, I want . . .
3 Next year I'm going to learn . . .
4 I'm definitely going to stop . . .

5 Key word: *to*

Look at the sentences below and translate these uses of *to* into your own language.

1 **When did you go back to the cinema?**
2 when **he's old enough to understand.**
3 your foot. **I'm glad to hear it.** I c
4 ... **Can you give it to me?** I'll get
5 . Do you? ... **Listen to me!** Well, it
6 Mm. **It was about ten to eight,** when
7 er **I went to Bromley to get that** ...

From the *British National Corpus* (Spoken)

Grammar: *to/so that* (purpose)

1 Complete sentence b) below to mean the same as sentence a).

a) She went to the butcher's *so (that)* she could buy some meat.
b) She went to the butcher's *to* . . .

2 Use *to* and *so that* to answer these questions in as many ways as possible with your partner.

1 Why do most people learn English?
2 Why do people get married?
3 Why do people want to be rich?
4 Why do people do sports?
5 Why do people go on public demonstrations?

6 Listening

1 Listen to people talking about strong views they hold and complete the chart.

	Belief	Suggested action	Purpose
Person 1			
Person 2			
Person 3			

2 Listen again. Which person refers to each of these things? What do they say about them?

the countryside factories smoking
the south-east a petition roads
three hours a day

King of reggae

At the time of his death in 1981, Bob Marley was not only the world's most commercially successful reggae artist but also an influential leader in the world of Jamaican and pan-African politics. Through his music he told poor people in Jamaica and black people everywhere to fight injustice.

He combined vast international success with an outspoken commitment to Rastafarianism. Reggae music and the Rastafarian religion have always gone hand in hand. Rastafarians (Rastas) say their faith is based around a peaceful and loving way of life. They believe that God is not a spirit in the sky, but lives on earth and that God is black. For this reason black is one of the Rastafarian colours. The others are red, gold and green: red represents the blood of the martyrs and African slaves, gold represents the Rastas' faith and the richness of life and green is the grass of Ethiopia, the spiritual home and resting place of all Rastafarians.

7 Grammar: preposition + -*ing*

1 Look at these sentences from the listening above. Which preposition goes in each gap?

1 I *believe* . . . giving girls the best education they can get.
2 Girls can be as *good* as boys . . . studying sciences.
3 I *agree* . . . mixing the sexes outside lessons.
4 It was beautiful but now I'm *thinking* . . . moving.
5 They *insist* . . . making the roads bigger.
6 They are not *interested* . . . giving us a pleasant environment to live in.
7 The baby won't be *punished* . . . having a stressed or anxious mother.
8 Mothers-to-be are always *accused* . . . doing the wrong thing.

2 Check your answers with another student.

1 Which verb form follows the preposition?
2 What do you think? Which word is stressed, the preposition or the word before it?

3 Complete these gaps with a verb. Then ask your partner the questions.

1 What's your main reason for . . . English?
2 What film/play are you most interested in . . . ?
3 Are you good at . . . ?
4 Do you think you could live without . . . ?
5 In your country, how much do you get paid for . . . ?

4 Tell the class your partner's most interesting answer. What did you ask her/him?

8 Reading

1 Before you read about reggae music, what do you know about this type of music?

1 What do most reggae musicians believe in?
2 Where did reggae originate?
3 What other music influenced reggae?
4 Which famous reggae singer was also considered a leader of pan-African politics?
5 What (other) famous reggae singers/songs are there?
6 How has the music changed with time?
7 What is the significance of the colours: red, gold, green and black?

2 Work in two groups and read different articles. Which questions above does your article answer?

Group 1: Read 'King of reggae' above.
Group 2: Read 'Reggae music' on page 126.

3 Talk to a student who read the other article. Check the answers to all the questions above and tell each other any extra information you remember.

NB Reported questions

a) I asked her *if* she had a reason.
b) I asked her *what* her reason was.

What were the direct questions?

Listening

1 Listen to the reggae song *Three little birds* by Bob Marley. The lines in column A are in the correct order. Join each line in column A to a line in column B.

A	B
Don't worry	beside my doorstep,
'cos every little thing's	of melodies pure and true.
Rise up this morning,	about a thing,
Three little birds,	gonna be alright.
Singing sweet songs	'this is my message to you'.
Saying,	smile with the rising sun.

2 Listen again and answer these questions.

1 What is the message of this song?
2 Is the singer optimistic or pessimistic? Which words suggest this?

3 Sing or follow the words. The first two lines are repeated.

9 Writing

1 Put these words from a poem into three groups. Tell another student why you put the words together.

colours crying scratches laughing violins music grey
singing trying humming thinking loving drums doing

2 Read the poem *When . . .* by the West Indian poet, Mustapha Matura. Put each word below into one of the gaps in the poem.

humming violins half thinking two
crying tomorrow scratches grey trying

3 Read the completed poem. What do you think? Is the writer feeling happy or sad? Why?

4 Read the poem to your partner. Make sure:

a) you stress the underlined and gapped words.
b) your voice rises in the middle of each sentence and falls at the end.

5 Listen to the poem. How did your version compare?

6 Write your own verses for the poem. Use the poet's structure but change the underlined and gapped words.

When...

When will I stop hearing ...
and hear only <u>drums</u>
When will I stop seeing ...
and see only <u>colours</u>
When will I stop hearing ...
and hear only <u>music</u>
When will I stop being ...
and be only <u>one</u>
When will I stop feeling ...
and start feeling <u>whole</u>
When will I stop saying ...
and start saying <u>now</u>
When will I stop ...
and start <u>doing</u>
When will I stop ...
and start <u>laughing</u>
When will I stop ...
and start <u>singing</u>
When will I stop ...
and start <u>loving.</u>
When will I be free, when,
when?

english in action

Bretecher

YOU ARE GOING TO GIVE A SHORT TALK ABOUT SOMETHING IMPORTANT TO YOU.

1

First, read the cartoon above. What does the mother believe in?

2

Choose one of these subjects, or something else that interests you, and prepare your talk.

- the environment
- violence on television
- pre-school education
- public transport

a) Make notes about what you want to say.
b) Check you know the necessary vocabulary.
c) Collect pictures or statistics for your talk.

3

Organise your ideas on this subject.

- Why is it important to you?
- What do you think people who agree into you should do?

4

Prepare a poster or leaflet to help other students follow your ideas.

GIVE YOUR TALK.

5

Listen to other students. Ask them questions to get more information.

Language review 17

1 Verb + *-ing* form or infinitive

• Some verbs are usually followed by the *-ing* form. As well as verbs expressing likes/dislikes, these include:
admit deny keep (don't) mind start stop
She admits stealing a bag but denies taking money.

• Some verbs are usually followed by the infinitive (with *to*). The action of the verb in the infinitive is usually later than the first verb. These include:
decide hope learn plan refuse want
He decided to go but refused to stay late.

a Put the following verbs in the spaces in the correct form. Use each word once only.

cough write stay get smoke play go build

1 We plan . . . a small house in France.
2 She doesn't mind . . . up early in the morning.
3 I don't think they know where they want . . . on holiday yet.
4 They like . . . tennis in the summer.
5 Why do you keep . . . him letters when he never replies?
6 I've decided . . . at home this summer.
7 He stopped . . . after he started . . . badly.

2 *To/so that* (purpose)

To say why somebody does something you can use:
a) *to* + verb, or b) *so that* + subject + (modal) verb.

I phoned *to* say I love you.
I phoned *so (that)* I could say I love you.

b Write sentences using *to* and *so that* to say why you went to these places.

the police station the hospital the bank the pub
the passport office the dentist's the shop
the post-office the tourist information centre

3 Preposition + *-ing* form

The *-ing* form is used after all prepositions. Certain verbs and adjectives take certain prepositions.

Verb + prep. + *-ing* form	Adjective + prep. + *-ing* form
to *agree with, believe in insist on, think of* to be *arrested for, accused of*	to be *good/bad at, interested in, proud/ashamed/afraid of bored/fed up with*

I *agree with* doing that. I *am good* at doing that.

c Complete the gap with the correct preposition and an appropriate verb.

1 You talk to the French farmer. I thought you were good . . . French.
2 That's the man who was arrested . . . chickens.
3 He was so ashamed . . . his brother that he bought him some sweets.
4 What are you thinking . . . when you finish this course?
5 If he insists . . . I'll tell the police.
6 I'm bored . . . housework. Let's go out.

4 Reported questions

In reported questions the word order of the question changes. If there is no question word (e.g. *who, when, how*, etc.) use *if* instead.

Direct question	Reported question
'*Where* are *you* going?'	She asked him *where he was* going.
'*Are you* English?'	I asked *if you were* English.

d Report these questions.

1 'Do you like going swimming?' she asked him.
2 'How old are you?' I asked her.
3 'Do you have a large house?' he asked them.
4 'When did you see Paul?' they asked us.
5 'Why aren't you doing your homework?' she asked me.
6 'How long does it take to get to your house?' he asked her.

18 *Changing your genes*

At the annual plastic surgeons' dinner the wives look *(young)* but they're not. For, as soon as they begin to look *(old)* to be a good advertisement they know they can speak to a sympathetic doctor - their husband. If their nose isn't *(straight)* and their ears are *(pointed)* then these can be changed. If their legs are *(fat)* for comfort and their arms aren't *(fat)* then the fat can be transferred. And why not? After all, a stranger can walk in off the street and tell a doctor their nose sticks out *(far)* and their face isn't *(smooth)*. And just because they are *(rich)*, they can have an immediate operation or a face-lift. So why shouldn't doctors extend the privilege to their wives?!

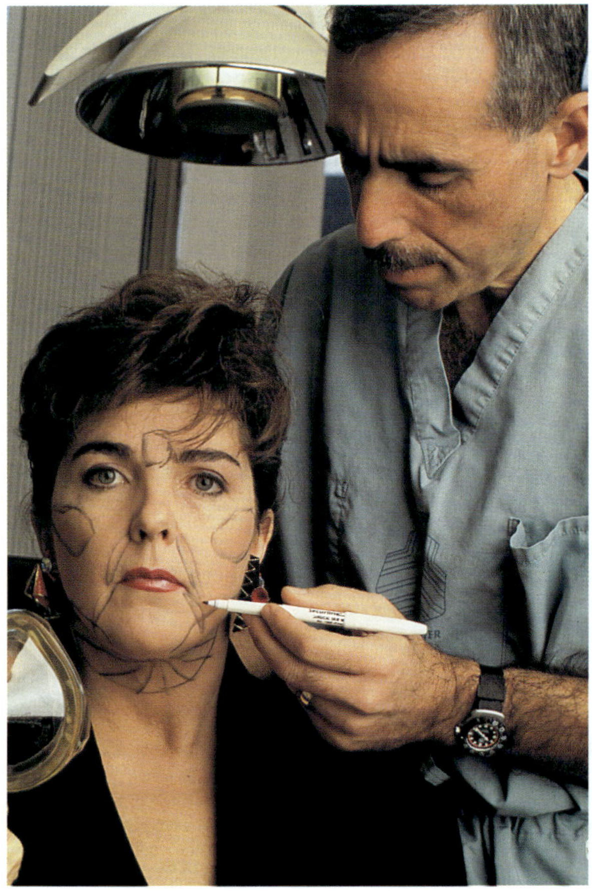

1 Diagnosis: *very/too/enough*

1 What do you think? Answer these questions and make up a story to explain the photograph above.

1 What is the relationship between these two people?
2 Why is he marking her face?
3 What is going to happen next?

2 Now read the article which explains the photograph.

1 What are the answers to the questions above?
2 What things surprise or shock you?

3 Read the article again and add *very, too* or *enough* to the words in brackets.

There is a Revision exercise for *very/too/enough* on page 129.

2 Vocabulary: describing faces

1 Work with another student. Point to these parts of the body in the photograph above. Which one *can't* you see?

cheeks eyebrows chin ears nose lips
eyelashes forehead waist jaw neck

2 Match a definition to a part of the face.

1 You smell with it.
2 They go red when you are embarrassed.
3 You raise them when you are surprised.
4 You kiss with them.
5 You move it when you eat.
6 You grow a beard on it.
7 You hear with them.

3 Match these words to the parts of the face they can go with.

large pointed long straight
small sticking out short flat

4 Someone you know is missing. Write a description of their face for a police artist.

3 Listening

1 Listen to people who have had cosmetic surgery. Are they happy with the results?

2 Listen again and complete this chart.

	1	2	3
1 What part of the body was operated on?			
2 Why did they want the operation?			
3 How do they feel about cosmetic surgery now?			

4 Grammar: *to have something done*

1 Listen to sentences spoken by the people above and complete these gaps.

1 I . . . . . . a nose job . . . .
2 I . . . . some fat . . . from my waist to my cheek.
3 Why don't you . . . it . . . ?

2 Listen and repeat the sentences. Is *to have something done* used when a) the speaker does the work herself, or b) somebody else does it?

3 What do you think? Is cosmetic surgery a good idea? Would you like to have something done?

4 Discuss services in your country.

1 Where do people generally go to have:
a) their passport renewed?
b) their television repaired?
c) their blood pressure taken?
d) their keys cut?
e) their teeth filled?

2 Why do people go to the following places:
a) the hairdresser's?
b) the shoe mender's?
c) the carwash?
d) the dry cleaner's?

3 When did you last have any of the things above done?

5 Speaking

1 Talk to other students about what makes people behave as they do. What do you think?

1 How important are appearances? In what ways can how we look affect our lives?
2 Which influences our development most: family, friends, school or work?
3 How fixed are our personalities? Can our childhood or way of life change our nature or is it all in our genes?

2 Read the extract below from an article on genetic engineering.

1 What can scientists now do to our genes?
2 What do you think? What good or bad uses could be made of this development?
3 Which predictions surprise you?
4 Which illnesses are the biggest problem to health in your country?

Why life will never be the same again

Nature was the last frontier. But now scientists can take 'nature' apart and put it back together again. In plants, animals and potentially humans, it will be possible to change genetic characteristics. Genetically engineered drugs will fight disease, and most major illnesses will be curable by the time this baby is out of her teens.

COMMON COLD *Cure expected within ten years*

HEART ATTACK *Controllable now. Preventable in 10-20 years*

CANCER *Cures for most cancers in 10-20 years*

DIABETES *Cure expected within ten years*

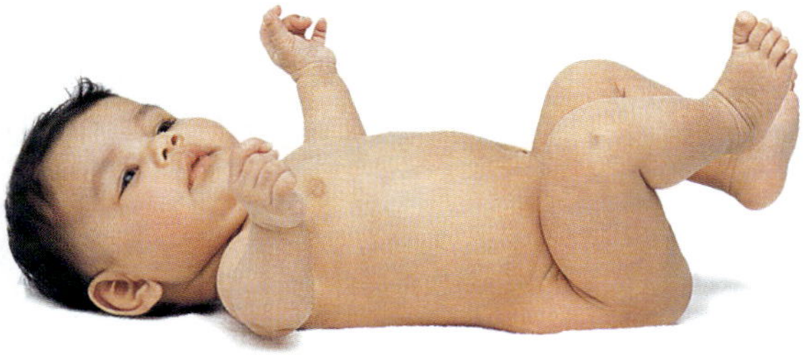

AIDS *Symptoms controllable within five years*

INJURY *Rapid healing products available within ten years*

From *The Sunday Times Magazine*

6 Reading

1 Work in two groups. Group A, read Article 1 and Group B, read Article 2. Answer these questions with information from your article.

1 What new scientific developments does it report?
2 What problems might this bring? Find examples in the text.

2 Work with a student who read the other article. Compare your answers to the questions above.

3 Together, find a word in Article 1 that means:

a) near. (*adj.*)
b) shocked. (*adj.*)
c) a feeling of comfort and happiness after some unpleasant feeling. (*n.*)
d) the practice of killing incurably ill people in a painless way. (*n.*)
e) people aged 100 years old or more. (*n.*)

4 Find a word in Article 2 that means:

a) a person who no longer works and who gets money to live on from the government. (*n.*)
b) angry and bitter. (*adj.*)
c) a written document after an investigation. (*n.*)
d) to stop work, usually because of your age. (*v.*)
e) completely necessary. (*adj.*)

5 Read both articles again. What predictions or facts are given using the numbers below?

Example: They say we will soon live to be 400.

ARTICLE 1: 400 60 80 395 22 75 266,000
ARTICLE 2: 2031 £1,000,000 50–74 20—30

Speaking

Answer these questions and tell other students what you think about the 'Third Age'.

1 How are 'Third Agers' (50–74 year olds) viewed in your country?
2 How do they make a living?
3 What different things do/can they contribute to society?
4 Is there age discrimination? Should anti-ageist laws be introduced?
5 What would be *your* ideal situation after you retire? Where would you live? Who with?
6 What would be your daily routine? How would you fill your time?

1

Cheer up, you could live until you're 400

from GEORGE GORDON in New York

SCIENTISTS claim they are close to discovering how people could live to be 400.

They believe they are near to producing drugs which would almost stop the ageing process. But horrified experts last night were describing a nightmare of Earth as an 'overcrowded zoo of ancient mutants'. They said that stopping ageing would result in millions of smooth-faced individuals waiting for death as the only relief from boredom. People wouldn't marry until they were 60. Women would be giving birth at 80.

Laws would have to be passed to stop them having more than two children. At the age of 395, most people's memory banks would be full. They would have to be extended by hormone treatment. And by the time they reached 400, millions would be pleading for legalised euthanasia.

In the era of the Roman Empire life expectancy was 22 years. Today the average age is 75 and people over 85 make up the fastest-growing part of the population. There are now over 36,000 centenarians in the US. In 30 years there will be 266,000. Dr William Regelson of the Medical College of Virginia says 'As we learn to control the genes involved in ageing, the possibility of lengthening life appears practically unlimited'.

2

Generations at War

By SEAN POULTER

A BATTLE OF THE GENERATIONS is being predicted which could bring misery to young and old.

Medical advances are lengthening lives and by the year 2031 there will be 46 pensioners for every 100 people of working age, a study says today. It warns that, unless action is taken, tens of thousands of old people could become isolated, bored and poverty-stricken. At the same time, an increasingly resentful younger working population would find it almost impossible to create the wealth necessary for health services and pensions.

The forecast comes in the report of the three-year £1 million Carnegie Inquiry into the 'Third Age', from 50 to 74. The inquiry was prompted by the fact that people are now retiring from full-time work with 20 or 30 active years ahead of them. The report says 'Third agers are a substantial and growing proportion of the active, independent adult population and it is essential they contribute to society through paid work or in other ways'. It also calls for early action to stop ageism by employers and others, possibly with the help of anti-age discrimination laws.

From *The Daily Mail*

7 Grammar: future time + modals

The government	*will*	help the elderly.
	might well	
	might	
	should	

1 Look at the four ways the sentence above can be expressed and answer these questions.

1 Which one suggests that this idea is:

a) possible?
b) very possible?
c) a moral obligation?
d) certain to happen?

2 What is the negative form of these sentences?

2 Think of scientific, political or personal developments which could happen in the next ten years. Make a list of at least one thing:

a) you feel sure *will* happen.
b) you think *might well* happen.
c) you think *might* happen.
d) you think *should* happen.

3 Show your list to another student. Are any of your predictions the same?

4 Work with your partner and put these ideas into group a), b), c) or d) above. Are there any you think definitely won't happen?

- People can choose the sex of their babies.
- Most people are not in full-time work.
- America is no longer a 'superpower'.
- Men and women are equal in the workplace.
- Starvation no longer exists on a major scale.
- The weather is generally hotter and drier.
- Cars are not the main form of transport.

5 Now, change each idea so it reflects what *you* both think about the future. If you can't agree, write separate sentences.

8 Writing

1 List reasons you think one idea you discussed either will *or* won't happen.

2 Look at the expressions below for linking points in an argument. Which expressions can:

a) begin b) continue c) end an argument?

Lastly, . . .
In the first place, . . .
To begin with, . . .
As well as this, . . .
Added to this, . . .
Furthermore, . . .
Finally, . . .

3 Use some of the words above to link the ideas you listed in a paragraph. Begin like this:

In my opinion, . . .

9 Key word: *will*

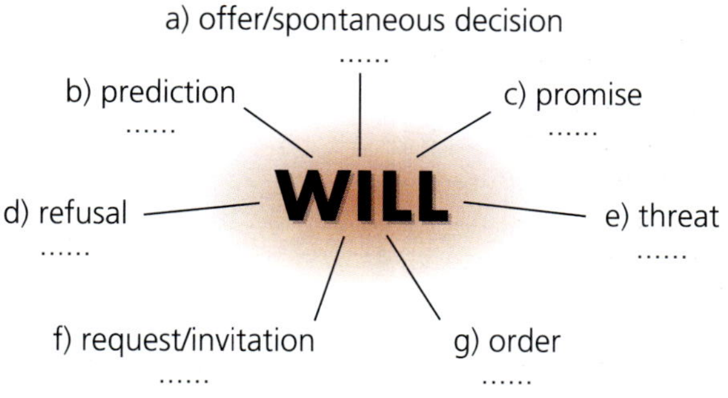

1 Match each sentence below to one of the uses of *will* above.

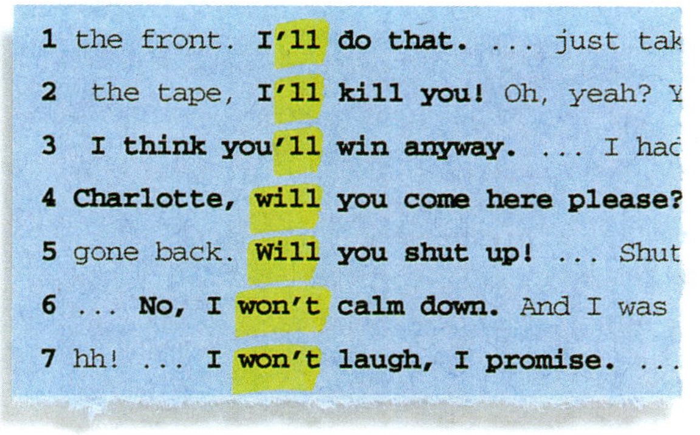
1 the front. I'll do that. ... just tak
2 the tape, I'll kill you! Oh, yeah? Y
3 I think you'll win anyway. ... I had
4 Charlotte, will you come here please?
5 gone back. Will you shut up! ... Shut
6 ... No, I won't calm down. And I was
7 hh! ... I won't laugh, I promise. ...

From the *British National Corpus* (Spoken)

2 Listen and repeat the sentences. Make sure your tone of voice reflects the meaning.

3 Act this situation out with a partner. How many uses of *will* can you include?

A student's final school exams begin next week. She/he wants to go to a party this weekend and would like her/his parent's permission.

english in action

YOU ARE GOING TO TAKE CONTROL OF THE FUTURE BY DOING SOME LIFE-PLANNING.

1 **First, list all your wildest ideas for the future. What might you do next – travel, study, marriage, etc.?**

2 **Now decide what kind of person you are: the SWOT test should help. Take a large sheet of paper and list your:**

SWOT = **S**trengths
Weaknesses
Opportunities
Threats

- **Strengths:** What are you good at? (for example, getting on with people, etc.)
- **Weaknesses:** Be honest, even cruel, if you can.
- **Opportunities:** What advantages do you have or could you look out for?
- **Threats:** What problems can you identify?

3 **Next, decide what success means to you. Put these in order of priority on the large sheet of paper:**

- achieving your own personal goals
- getting good results at school/work
- making a lot of money
- creating new ideas
- being popular
- becoming a leader

4 **Decide which of the following are the most important to you. Put these in order on the large sheet of paper:**

- relationships: partners, parents, children
- work
- friendships
- home life
- sport
- creative hobbies: painting, writing, etc.
- spiritual/personal growth: religion, therapy, etc.
- travel
- cultural interests: theatre, opera, cinema, etc.
- study

You now have a check list of your present needs, as well as clues to your future ones.

5 **Work with another person and look at both life-plans in turn. Check each person's ideas for the future against the list of Strengths, Weaknesses, Opportunities and Threats. Help your partner discover which things might well be a) rewarding, or b) disappointing.**

From *New Woman*

USE YOUR LIFE-PLANS WHEN YOU HAVE IMPORTANT DECISIONS TO MAKE.

Language review 18

1 Verbs: *to have something done*

Use *have* + object + past participle when the subject of the sentence doesn't do the action her/himself but gets someone else to do it.

<table>
<tr><td>I/you/we/they</td><td>have</td><td rowspan="2">the car serviced at the garage.</td></tr>
<tr><td>She/he (it)</td><td>has</td></tr>
</table>

NB *To have something done* can be used in other forms.

Past Simple
She *had* the car servic*ed* yesterday.

Present Perfect
She *has* just *had* the car servic*ed*.

Future Simple
She*'ll* probably *have* the car servic*ed* tomorrow.

a Look at the picture and write four sentences. What has Sophie just had done?

2 Future time + modals

Use modals + main verb to show attitude to predictions of future events.

<table>
<tr><td>certainty</td><td>I will/won't</td><td rowspan="4">go.</td></tr>
<tr><td>good possibility</td><td>She might well (not)</td></tr>
<tr><td>possibility</td><td>We might (not)</td></tr>
<tr><td>moral obligation</td><td>They should (not)</td></tr>
</table>

b Make predictions from these prompts using the language opposite.

1 Taxes/go up this year.
2 Visit/my parents at the weekend.
3 Do two hours of English homework tonight.
4 Get a (new) job this year.
5 Move house in the next five years.
6 Go on holiday this year.
7 Go to bed early tonight.

3 Uses of *will/won't*

***Will* can refer to present or future time.**

a) a spontaneous decision
I know, I'll buy her a watch.

b) a prediction
I think he'll arrive late.

c) a request
Will you open the window, please?

d) an order
Will you be quiet.

e) an invitation
Will you dance?

f) a refusal
I won't phone him.

g) an offer
I'll carry your bags.

h) a promise
I won't tell anyone your secret.

i) a threat
I'll hit you!

c Put the following into direct speech. Use *will/won't*, and do not repeat the underlined verb.

Example: 'I'll definitely give you the money on Friday.'

1 He promised to give me the money on Friday.
2 They refused to come to the wedding.
3 He threatened to blow up the plane if they didn't give him the money.
4 She offered to give him a lift home if he wanted one.
5 They asked him to open the building at the weekend.
6 She invited me to go to the cinema with her.
7 He suddenly decided not to go to the party.
8 They ordered us to stand up and face the wall.
9 She predicted that I would be sorry in the morning.

19 A magical mystery tour

Hotel facilities; transport + *catch*, *get on/off*, *get into/out of*, *miss*, *take*; *rather than* + noun

1 Diagnosis: *must/might/can't* + verb

1 Look at the advertisement for Superlative Travel. What are Concorde, The Princess and The Orient Express? In what ways are they 'superlative'?

2 With another student, complete the chart below. Which of these facilities do you imagine the train/ship/plane has?

first-class food	a swimming pool	a casino
a health club	a business centre	a bar
a theatre	a disco	shops
private bathrooms	telephones	TV/films

	definitely	perhaps	definitely not
The Orient Express			
The Princess			
Concorde			

3 Check your ideas on page 126. Were you right?

There is a Revision exercise for *must/might/can't* + verb on page 129.

2 Vocabulary: transport

1 The types of transport below are referred to in the advertisement. Do you use them to travel by air, land or sea?

a helicopter	a coach	a train	a ship
a supersonic plane	a 747	a yacht	

2 Read the advertisement. Which type/s of transport above is/are *not* included in the:

a) trip to New York?
b) six-night stay in Toronto and Niagara?
c) £999 five-night stay in Toronto and Niagara?

3 Name other types of transport with other students. Then answer these questions.

1 Where do you *catch* the different types of transport, e.g. train/station?
2 Which do you a) *get on/off*, b) *get into/out of*?
3 Which can you easily *get* later if you *miss* them?
4 What are the advantages/disadvantages if you *take*:

a) a taxi rather than a bus?
b) a train rather than a plane?
c) your own car rather than public transport?

CONCORDE THE PRINCESS AND THE ORIENT~EXPRESS

Now you can travel on the ultimate train, ship and plane.

Journey on the Orient-Express Pullman from Victoria to Tilbury on 31 August. Cruise for eight nights on the Royal Princess to New York. Sightsee by coach, yacht and helicopter during your three night stay. Return supersonic on Concorde. The holiday is priced from £1,999.

You could fly to Toronto and spend six nights at the Sheraton before your Concorde return. Dine overlooking Niagara Falls, at the CN Tower and at Harbour Castle Hotel. Enjoy the city tour and the harbour yacht cruise. View the spectacular falls on your helicopter excursion. See the Phantom of the Opera. The additional cost is £500.

TORONTO AND NIAGARA

Fly supersonic on Concorde and stay five nights at the deluxe Sheraton. After the guided coach tour you will cruise around the harbour before your Castle Hotel luncheon. See the Phantom of the Opera, and dine at the CN Tower. In Niagara experience the helicopter excursion after lunching overlooking the mighty falls.

Departures are on 23 June, 13, 20 August, 17, 25 September and 8 October. The inclusive price is £1,999 with your 747 flight. The five night holiday costs £999 flying both ways by 747.

For your colour brochures, please telephone

081-992 6991

or write to:

SUPERLATIVE TRAVEL

43 Woodhurst Road, London W3 6SS

ABTA A8037

3 Key word: *take*

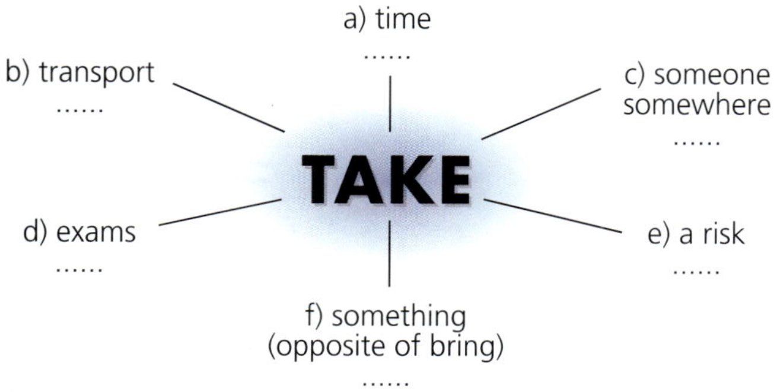

1 Match each sentence below to one of the uses of *take* above.

1	... You'll ... Go on **I'll take a chance.** Oh ..., e
2	e clever enough. **You could take an exam,** like an en
3	**We use the bus rather than take the car in daily.** '
4	or about an hour. ... **That takes about an hour** that
5	ence, okay? ... **You're not taking all that money** ar
6	wave goodbye to grandma. **I took her to the train.** Y

From the *British National Corpus* (Spoken)

2 Make questions to ask another student. Find out about:

a) the last exam she/he took and passed. What was it?
b) the last time she/he took someone somewhere. Who and where?
c) the last time she/he took a chance. What was it?
d) the last time she/he took public transport. How long did it take?

4 Reading

1 Before you read about the writer Agatha Christie, answer these questions together. Then check your answers in the article.

1 Is Agatha Christie still alive?
2 What sort of books does/did she write? How successful are they?
3 What is her connection with the Orient Express?

2 Read the article again. Is a), b) or c) correct in each of these sentences?

1 Compared to the Bible and Shakespeare, Agatha Christie has sold:
a) more books b) fewer books c) about the same number of books.
2 Hercule Poirot is in:
a) all of b) most of c) nearly half of her crime novels.
3 Agatha ran away to:
a) the Pera Palas Hotel b) a hotel in Harrogate c) Hollywood.
4 In the Pera Palas hotel, they found:
a) her diary b) a key c) a copy of *Murder on the Orient Express.*
5 It is now in the possession of:
a) the hotel staff b) Tamara Rand c) the hotel management.

Agatha's life of crime

ONE HUNDRED YEARS after her birth, Agatha Christie is still making crime pay.

Matched only by the Bible and Shakespeare, Agatha Christie has sold more than one billion copies of her books in English and the same number again in 63 foreign languages.

She is most famous for her 78 crime novels and her famous Belgian detective, Hercule Poirot, who has appeared in 33 of these, including her most successful UK paperback *Murder on the Orient Express.*

Her life, as well as her books, was riddled with mysteries, and the greatest of all was in 1926 when, her first marriage in difficulties, she vanished for 11 days. With the press in full chase, she was found in a Harrogate hotel, booked under a false name.

Some think room 411 at the Pera Palas Hotel in Istanbul – where she is said to have written *Murder on the Orient Express* – could literally hold the key. In 1978, two years after the author's death, Tamara Rand, a Hollywood psychic, declared the answer to the missing days was, in fact, a key hidden in room 411. If she held that key, she claimed she would be able to communicate with the late Agatha Christie and find her diary.

Whether Agatha Christie kept a diary is not known. But a rusty key was found. A strike among the staff at the hotel stopped it from reaching Miss Rand and it was locked in the hotel safe where it remains to this day.

From *TVTimes*

Must have/ might have/ can't have done (past deduction)

5 Grammar: *must have/might have/can't have done*

1 Match sentences with the same meaning from column A and B.

How sure?	A	B
100% Yes	She was definitely sad.	
	I'm sure she was sad.	She might have been sad.
		She was sad.
50%	Perhaps she was sad.	She can't have been sad.
		She wasn't sad.
	I'm sure she wasn't sad.	She must have been sad.
100% No	She definitely wasn't sad.	

2 Answer these questions about the sentences in column B above.

1 Do the sentences refer to present or past time?
2 Which verb form comes after *must have/might have/can't have*?
3 What do you think? How is *have* pronounced in these sentences?

3 Complete these sentences with ideas from the article on page 115.

1 Agatha Christie *can't have wanted* to be found because . . .
2 Tamara Rand *might have been* right because . . .
3 The hotel staff *must have felt* strongly because . . .

4 Tell other students what you think *might have/can't have* happened in those missing days. Did Agatha:

write a new book? need time to think? meet another man?
want the publicity? take a holiday? lose her memory?
phone her husband? other?

6 Speaking

1 Before you discuss Agatha Christie's mystery *Murder on the Orient Express*, read this summary of the beginning of the story.

1 Who has been murdered? How?
2 Who are the suspects? Why?
3 Who will try to solve the case?

AN AMERICAN, Samuel Ratchett, is found murdered on the Orient Express, stabbed many times with a knife. Hercule Poirot, the celebrated Belgian detective, is travelling on the train along with other passengers of many different nationalities. He is asked by his friend M. Bouc, of the Wagon Lit Company, to investigate the crime.

It has been impossible for anyone to leave the train since the murder because of a snowstorm which has brought the train to a standstill.

Poirot discovers that Ratchett was in fact Cassetti, the infamous American child murderer responsible for the deaths of Daisy Armstrong and her parents. Although Cassetti was obviously guilty, he had been acquitted on a technicality and had left America.

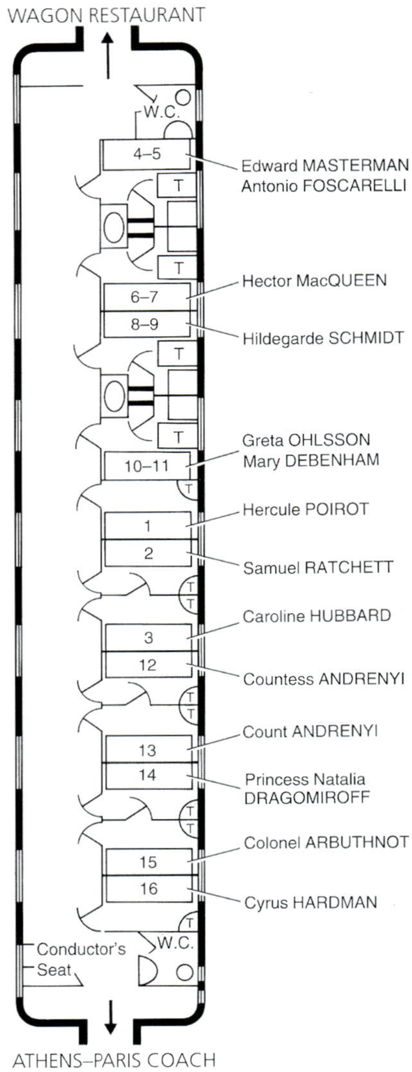

2 Look at the train plan and the passengers' names above with another student.

1 What nationality do you think each person might have been?
2 Where was the dead man's compartment?
3 Who had the compartment with a connecting door?

3 Make up a story to explain the crime. Use the train plan and the pictures opposite it of the clues Poirot found. What might have happened?

4 Tell your story to other students.

1 Which things do you all feel must have happened?
2 Which other things do you think might well have happened?

7 Listening

1 Listen to interviews between Poirot and fellow-passengers. After each extract:

a) complete the chart below.
b) discuss what must/might/can't have happened.

	clues referred to
Constantine (the Greek doctor)	1 2 3
Hector MacQueen (Ratchett's secretary)	1 2
Caroline Hubbard (an American woman)	1 2

2 In two groups, read Poirot's two solutions to the crime and answer the questions below.

Group A: Read Solution 1 on page 125.
Group B: Read Solution 2 on page 126.

1 Are any of the clues above explained?
2 Who was the murderer?
3 What do you think? Is this the true solution? Why/why not?

3 Talk to a student who read the other solution.

1 What do you think? Which is the true solution?
2 What will M. Bouc tell the frontier police?

4 Listen to the end of the story.

1 Who is the woman ?
2 Which *is* the true solution?
3 What did M. Bouc decide to do?
4 Would you do the same thing in his situation? Why/why not?

8 Grammar: question tags

1 Match each statement in column A to a question tag in column B. What rules can you see?

A	B
You would tell the police,	can they?
Ratchett was murdered,	hasn't he?
They can't leave the train,	does she?
Mrs Hubbard isn't honest,	wouldn't you?
She doesn't feel like a criminal,	is she?
They all knew the Armstrongs,	wasn't he?
Poirot has solved the case,	aren't they?
They are all guilty,	didn't they?

2 Listen, check and repeat. At the end of each question tag, does the speaker's voice go:

a) up and suggest she doesn't know the answer?
b) down and suggest she is checking her facts?

Speaking

1 Solve a murder as a class. Two of you are suspects and the rest are detectives.

SUSPECTS: Go outside and prepare your alibis.
- Where were you at the time of the crime?
- What were you doing, wearing, eating, etc?

DETECTIVES: Prepare questions for the suspects.
- What were they doing at the time of the crime?
- What can they remember about each other's actions?

2 Detectives work in two groups. Each group, question each suspect individually in turn. Check the facts and find inconsistencies.

3 Detectives compare notes and decide if the two suspects are guilty. Do both groups agree?

Win the trip of a lifetime

This week readers are given a chance to win seats on one of the most exciting railway trips ever. Ten lucky readers – five couples – will enjoy two days' first-class travel on the world's most famous train, the Venice-Simplon Orient Express.

At the same time, cars old and new will leave London's Victoria Station heading for Milan. Driving by special rules, their aim will be to reach Milan before the Orient Express.

So, if you are not lucky enough to win a seat on the train, why not enter the race from London to Milan in your own car?

The entry fee of £3,000 (Ecu 3,600) covers all expenses, including five-star accommodation, cuisine matching that on the Orient Express, a Milanese banquet and grandstand seats at the Italian Grand Prix.

Before leaving London, both winners and drivers will enjoy a champagne send-off. Train passengers will travel in traditional Orient Express luxury. Winning couples will have their own twin compartments, lunch and supper on 9 September and breakfast, lunch and supper on 10 September. They will win three nights, including continental breakfast, at a five-star Milan hotel, attend the victory banquet on 11 September and receive tickets and hospitality for the Italian Grand Prix. The winners will then fly back to London.

To win one of the five places for couples on this luxurious rail journey, collect six of the voucher-pictures appearing today and over the next five weeks in The European.

Then, in no more than an additional 15 words, complete the following sentence: 'I would like to travel on the Venice Simplon-Orient-Express because ...'

From *The European*

YOU ARE GOING TO ENTER A COMPETITION IN 'THE EUROPEAN' NEWSPAPER.

1
First, look at the headlines and photographs. What do you think the prize will be?

2
Read the article quickly and answer these questions.

1 What *is* the prize?
2 If you don't win, what does it suggest you do instead?
3 What two things do you have to do to enter the competition?

3
Read the article again and tick the chart below. What will participants get on their trip?

	The competition winners	The drivers
a goodbye drink		
twin-bedded train accommodation		
seats for the Italian Grand Prix		
a celebration dinner in Milan		
meals on the Orient Express		
a flight home		
five-star accommodation in Italy		

4
With your partner, complete the competition sentence in no more than 15 words.

5
Listen to the sentences and choose the five lucky pairs.

CONGRATULATIONS! SOME OF YOU HAVE WON THE TRIP ON THE ORIENT EXPRESS. THE REST OF YOU HAVE BEEN ACCEPTED AS DRIVERS FOR THE RACE. ENJOY YOUR TRIP!

Language review 19

1 Verbs: *must have/might have/can't have* + past participle

Use modals of deduction to express degrees of certainty about the past.

How sure?			
100%	Yes	She was	unhappy.
	▲	She *must have been*	
50%		She *might have been*	
	▼	She *can't have been*	
100%	No	She wasn't	

a Complete these sentences using *must have* or *can't have* and the verb in brackets.

Example: 1 She *must have gone* out.

1 She didn't answer the door. She . . . (go) out.
2 I can't find my umbrella. I . . . (leave) it on the train.
3 In spite of not studying, he passed the exam. It . . . (be) very difficult.
4 She's bought a new house. She . . . (win) a lot of money.
5 They knew exactly what we said. They . . . (listen) to our conversation.
6 My purse was here a minute ago. I . . . (lose) it.

b Jo is late home from work. His mother is worried. Write sentences using *might have* and the ideas below to show what she imagines.

a) have an accident b) forget the time
c) go for a drink d) miss the train
e) meet a friend f) have to work late

c Read the puzzle below and then write sentences to explain the situation using *must have/might have/can't have* + verb.

Example: Roger and Deborah might have been friends because . . .

> Roger and Deborah have just been found lying dead on the floor of the living room of a large flat. There is water and glass all around them. The window to the living room is open and the curtains are moving in the wind.

NB The solution to the puzzle is on page 126!

2 Question tags (checking facts)

Use question tags with a falling intonation to check facts. They are made with auxiliary verbs.
be can have do will should must might
Use a negative tag with a positive sentence and a positive tag with a negative sentence.

Be	Can
I *am* . . . *aren't* I? She *isn't* . . . *is* she? You *were* . . . *weren't* you? He *wasn't* . . . *was* he?	We *can* . . . *can't* we? They *can't* . . . *can* they? I *could* . . . *couldn't* I? She *couldn't* . . . *could* she?

Do	Have
I *do* . . . *don't* I? You *don't* . . . *do* you? She *swims* . . . *doesn't* she? We *ate* . . . *didn't* we? They *didn't go* . . . *did* they?	You *haven't* got . . . *have* you? She *has eaten* . . . *hasn't* she? He *doesn't* cry . . . *does* he? We *have* dinner, . . . *don't* we?

***NB* When *have* is a full verb use auxiliary *do*.**

d Complete these sentences with the correct question tag. Then answer the questions.

Example: 1 You are in your twenties, aren't you? That's right./No, I'm in my thirties.

1 You are in your twenties, . . . you?
2 You speak French, . . . you?
3 You didn't go to school in Brazil, . . . you?
4 You weren't in class yesterday, . . . you?
5 You've got three sisters, . . . you?
6 You'd like a cup of tea, . . . you?
7 You couldn't read when you were three, . . . you?
8 You'll come to class tomorrow, . . . you?

e Put the correct question tag at the end of each sentence.

1 Sophie isn't here, . . .?
2 They won't mind if we leave early, . . .?
3 He's written a beautiful poem, . . .?
4 We have to go home now, . . .?
5 I shouldn't have got angry, . . .?
6 You don't like bananas, . . .?
7 He might be at home, . . .?
8 We'd never met them before, . . .?

20 *Consolidation*

Excess baggage

FAST FOOD

Divorce bar

Top names

Back in saddle

Art sentence

1 Across cultures: the press

Revises
Vocabulary: Countries; politics
Grammar: Narrative tenses; likes/dislikes; modals (future + deduction); advice

A Michael and Emma are the most fashionable Christian names, according to a Gallup survey.

The Daily Mail

B Two Dutch nationals were imprisoned for five years for stealing three Van Gogh paintings worth more than £45 million and demanding a £1.35 million ransom for the works before they were all recovered undamaged.

The Times

C Dentist Max Forbes has refused to accept Debbie Johnson, 16, as a trainee receptionist in case her parents' divorce disturbed her work.

The Daily Mail

D The philosopher-emperor Marcus Aurelius was lowered back on to his horse after spending eight years suspended in mid-air during a cleaning of the city's famous statue.

The Independent

E Police found two scorpions, a snake and a toad in a bag left at Gatwick airport by Mr Kevin Dunster, aged 26, a student, after a holiday abroad.

The Times

F A 12ft alligator was found by social workers at a flat in Dublin. They were called in when the pet-owner's wife complained that a mouse, meant to be part of the animal's diet, was running loose.

The Independent on Sunday

NEWSPAPERS

1 Look at the newspapers above. Which countries do/might they come from?

2 Now, listen to two British people talking about the newspapers they read. Complete this chart.

	Mike	Sarah
Names of papers		
Political position		
Why liked		

3 Tell another student about the newspapers/magazines you read in your country.

1 Why do you like them? What's in them?
2 Which other things, if any, would you like to see included?

HEADLINES

4 Before you read the articles above, look at the headlines above them. What do you think each article will/might be about?

5 Now, match the headlines to the articles.

6 Read the articles again and complete a sentence below with information from each one. Use *should/shouldn't/must/might/can't + have +* verb.

1 A lot of people . . . their children these names.
2 They . . . a longer sentence if they had damaged the paintings.
3 He . . . her to work with him very much.
4 The statue . . . very dirty.
5 He . . . the animals into the country. It's against the law.
6 What a waste of the social workers' time! The owners . . . more careful.

HOME NEWS

FOREIGN NEWS

BUSINESS

FASHION

GOSSIP

ENTERTAINMENT

SPORT

Schools close in south-east

Princess to divorce

Inter Milan win again

Charity concert a sell-out

Possible tax rises alarm Stock Exchange

Earthquake hits India

Mini-skirts are back in

MAKE A CLASS NEWSPAPER

7 **First, discuss things in the news at the moment. What do you think will/might/should happen next?**

8 **Match each headline above to the appropriate section of a newspaper. In which section would you find the things you discussed?**

9 **Decide how to produce your own paper. Think about:**

- Size, length, appearance
- Who is your newspaper for?
- Will it have world news, local news or both?
- What will you call it?
- How many sections will you include? Which ones, and how long will they be?
- How will you work? Should each group/person provide one section, or one article for each section?

10 **In groups, consider all the contributions for a particular section. Cut and rephrase them as necessary to fit the space you have.**

1 What photographs/illustrations will you use?
2 What headlines will you give them?

11 **Produce and read your newspaper. Tell other students what you think of it.**

1 Which articles did you find most interesting?
2 How would you change the newspaper if you produced it again?
3 What advice would you give other students who are going to make a class newspaper?

PROGRAMMES

BBC English Radio Guide

Professor Grammar This is adapted from 'Professor Grammar' in the magazine. By answering listeners' questions, he improves your English grammar with exercises and rules. (Intermediate)

Broadcast to: *Latin America on Saturdays; South Asia and Burma on Saturdays and Sundays; Southeast Asia on Saturdays and Thursdays; Indonesia and Malaysia on Saturdays, Sundays and Thursdays; Northern and Eastern Europe on Saturdays, Sundays and Fridays, and the rest of Europe on Saturdays and Fridays.*

Professor Grammar

Useful rules to help you with English grammar

Hello again!

Do you speak **Ing**lish? No, your old friend Professor Grammar hasn't forgotten his spelling. I'm talking about the **-ing** form, e.g. ***swimming***, ***laughing***, ***dancing***.

When one verb follows another, the second often has an **-ing** form:

I enjoy eating.
Do you mind staying late?

Enjoy and ***mind*** are NEVER followed by an infinitive (**to** etc.).

- ***I enjoy* to eat.** ✗
- ***Do you mind* to stay *late?*** ✗

The above sentences are absolutely incorrect – a catastrophe!

However, there are some verbs which are followed by an infinitive, never by an **-ing** form.

***He refused* to go.**
***They decided* to move.**
She promised* to see *me.

Unfortunately you'll have to memorise this table!

VERBS FOLLOWED BY **-ING** FORM		
admit	mind	deny
postpone	enjoy	resent
finish	suggest	keep

VERBS FOLLOWED BY **INFINITIVE**		
agree	refuse	ask
seem	decide	want
expect	wish	promise

Now try the exercise.

Cheerio,
Professor Grammar

From *BBC English Magazine*

2 Language in context: the radio

Revises
Vocabulary: Radio/television programmes
Grammar: Likes/dislikes; *to/so that* (purpose); *to have something done*; verbs + *-ing/infinitive*

1 Talk together about listening to the radio.

1 Which do you do more often, listen to the radio or watch TV? Which do you prefer? Why?
2 Which of these radio programmes do/would you like to listen to most?

chat shows	plays	book/film reviews
phone-ins	pop music	other?

3 Have you ever studied English by radio or television? What do you think the advantages could be?

2 Read the programme section above from the magazine *BBC English for Language Learners*. What do you think?

1 Why do listeners write to Professor Grammar?
2 What happens on the radio programme?
3 What day can you listen to it in your country?

3 Listen to and join in a radio programme as Professor Grammar and his assistant, Wayne, discuss *to have something done*.

4 Now read Professor Grammar's article above and do the exercise on verbs + *-ing/infinitive*.

5 Look at the grammar index at the back of this book with another student. Choose a grammatical area you would like to know more about and write a question for Professor Grammar.

EXERCISE

Change the verb in brackets into the correct form.

1 Would you mind (open) the door.
2 I asked (see) him.
3 He seems (like) the idea.
4 We postponed (go) there.
5 They want (visit) the BBC.
6 I wish (make) a complaint.
7 I have finished (read) his book.
8 He suggested (go) by plane.
9 He refuses (answer) my questions.
10 They have agreed (lower) the price.
11 Would you like (come) over for lunch?
12 I enjoy (sit) by the sea.
13 He admitted (rob) the bank.
14 He denies (know) anything about it.
15 I resent (be) told what to do!

Answers

1 opening
2 to see
3 to like
4 going
5 to visit
6 to make
7 reading
8 going
9 to answer
10 to lower
11 to come
(***Would*** and ***like*** means the same as ***want*** and so is only followed by the infinitive. ***Would you like to...*** is more polite than ***Do you want to...***)
12 sitting
13 robbing
14 knowing
15 being

3 Thinking about learning: letter-writing patterns

Revises
Vocabulary: Letter-writing expressions; everyday actions
Grammar: Mixed tenses

1 Before you write to Professor Grammar, match the beginning and endings of letters below. Which patterns would you use to write to the following?

the manager of a company whose name you don't know;
the head of your company/school; a newspaper advertisement
a member of your family; Professor Grammar; a friend

1 Dear Sir/Madam,	a) Love from, *or* Best wishes from,
2 Dear Sarah,	b) Yours sincerely,
3 Dear Mr/Mrs/Miss/Ms Jones,	c) Yours faithfully,

2 Separate the formal and informal letters jumbled below.

1 Which paragraph does each sentence come from, the first or last?
2 What main differences can you see between the formal and informal language? Think about:
  a) contracted forms.
  b) length of sentences.
  c) difficulty of structures/vocabulary.

A I am looking forward to hearing from you in the near future.
B Thanks for your letter.
C Please send me ...
D I am writing to enquire about / inform you ...
E Well, I must stop. Write back soon.
F I would be grateful if you would ...
G Thank you for your letter of 20 May.
H I'm writing to ask about / let you know...

3 Rearrange and correct this date and writer's address.

1 Where do they go in formal/informal letters?
2 Which information should not appear in this part of a letter?

alan tomkins
england
dalston road 106
1994 january 31st
N16 0QL london

4 With your partner, write a letter to Professor Grammar. Ask for your question to be answered on his programme.

5 Listen and write the address to send your letter to.

6 Write to your teacher after your course has finished.

- Say how you are and what you are doing.
- Explain what you have done/been doing since the end of this course.
- Say what your immediate and long-term plans are.
- Ask her/him some questions.
- Say goodbye!

Check What You Know!
Test what you have learned in Units 16–20 by completing Check What You Know 4. (See Teacher's Book.)

Communication activities

Unit 4 Exercise 3

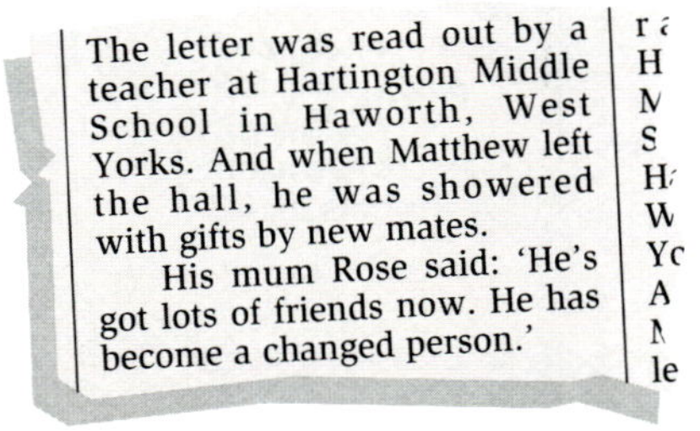

The letter was read out by a teacher at Hartington Middle School in Haworth, West Yorks. And when Matthew left the hall, he was showered with gifts by new mates.

His mum Rose said: 'He's got lots of friends now. He has become a changed person.'

From *The Daily Mirror*

Unit 9 Exercise 4

Student B

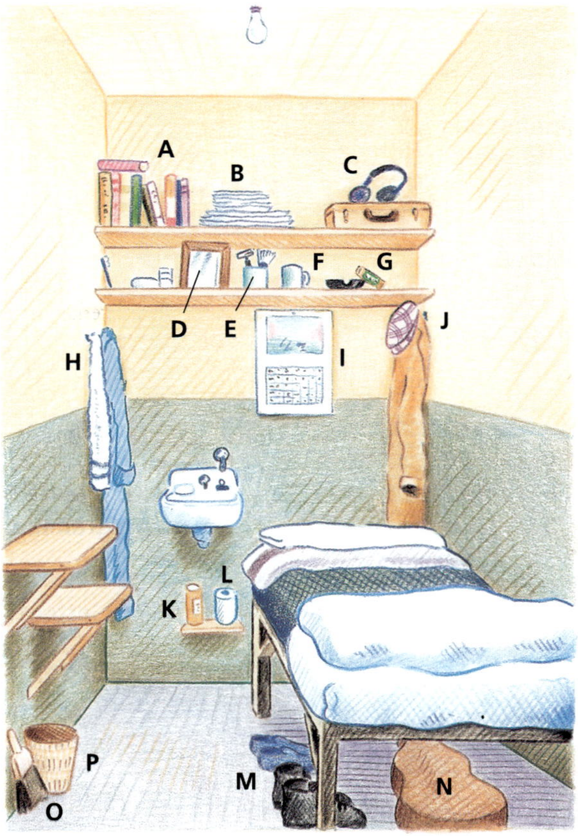

Regulations for inmates, Alcatraz
Possessions allowed in cells

A	12 books (maximum)	**I**	Calendar
B	Personal papers	**J**	Coat & cap
C	Radio headphones	**K**	Cleaning powder
D	Mirror	**L**	Toilet tissue
E	Shaving things	**M**	Extra shoes & slippers
F	Drinking cup	**N**	Musical instrument/case
G	Cigarettes & ashtray	**O**	Brush
H	Bathrobe	**P**	Wastepaper bin

Unit 14 Exercise 4

What has been done to adapt the kitchen for a disabled person?

Unit 14 Language review

Exercise c: What *has been done* to the house?

Unit 15 Across cultures

Guidelines for acceptable behaviour at meals in Britain

Don't whisper to the person next to you.
Don't start eating until the host does.
Don't put your elbows on the table.
Don't put your feet on the table.
Don't drink straight from a bottle.
Don't talk with your mouth full.
Don't eat off your knife.
Eat peas off the back of your fork.
Eat bread off a plate.
Don't lean past people to get things, e.g. salt.
Don't smoke when eating with non-smokers.
When drinking soup, move the spoon *away* from you.
Don't leave the table until everybody has finished eating.

Unit 16 Exercise 2

The results of a British Gallup Survey on therapy for New Woman Magazine

1 A third talk about problems to their partners, 24% talk to their families.
2 91% have never had any kind of therapy; 64% don't know anybody who has.
3 20% think therapy can offer little or no help.
4 Both sexes feel women are more likely to need therapy.
5 A third said 'under no circumstances at all'.
6 42% see therapy as a problem solver; the development of creativity came low on the list.
7 Mainly 30–37 year olds with good, professional careers and 2.2 children.
8 Any of these things, but b) is high on the list for the group above.
9 Most people were suspicious of therapy and felt it was self-indulgent.

Unit 16 Exercise 7

The **FOREST** represents your past, especially your childhood. If it was dark and frightening, for instance, then your childhood may not have been happy.

Your description of the **WEATHER** indicates the 'conditions' of your childhood – the sunnier the better.

The **BEAR** represents other people, society in general – and how you see them. The more friendly the bear, for instance, the more at ease you feel with people.

The way you saw the **WATER** can tell you a lot about your emotions and romantic relationships. A large body of water (i.e. the sea or a big lake) shows that you're very open-minded when it comes to love. A small body of water, such as a puddle, shows a very narrow-minded approach to relationships. The best, most healthy and well-balanced attitude would be represented by a waterfall.

Your description of the **CUP** is, in fact, a straightforward description of the way you see yourself.

The **CAVE** represents death. If it was big and frightening, then the thought of death frightens you; and what you did – entered the cave, looked at it, or walked past it – shows how much it worries you.

Unit 19 Exercise 7

Group A

Solution 1
Mr Ratchett had an enemy. When Colonel Arbuthnot and Mr MacQueen forgot to replace the bar on the train door at Vincovci Station, Ratchett's enemy got on the train. He wore a Wagon Lit tunic over his clothes and had a pass key to Ratchett's compartment. The man stabbed Ratchett many times with a knife and left via Mrs Hubbard's compartment where he hid the knife in her washbag ... Without knowing it, he lost the button off his tunic. Dressed in ordinary clothes, he got off the train just before it left Vincovci station.

Unit 17 Exercise 8

Group 2

Reggae Music In the mid 60s, a new form of popular music was being explored in Jamaica, in the West Indies. It had a distinctive bass and drum rhythm and was called reggae – a mixture of Rhythm and Blues (R&B), blue beat and ska; a mingling of Indian, European and above all African sounds.

At first, reggae was played in the small ghettos of Jamaica, but it spread throughout the island very quickly. A small handful of musicians pioneered what's now a universally respected form of music – and those people included Bob Marley and the Wailers, Gregory Isaacs and Jimmy Cliff.

In those days, the sound was very different to what we hear today. The musicians were not very technically advanced, and most records sounded as if they had been recorded in someone's living room ... Reggae was also very confined to Jamaicans and black people, because of the language and pronunciation used in the songs.

Today, reggae music is far more widely appreciated. It has even crept into TV commercials advertising the beauty of Jamaica and Bob Marley's Three little birds has been used in an advertisement for soap powder.

From *Just 17*

Unit 19 Language review

Solution to puzzle:

Roger and Deborah are goldfish. A cat came in the open window and knocked the bowl over. It smashed on the floor.

Unit 19 Exercise 1

Concorde offers:

- speed and comfort
- a three-course meal with champagne
- duty-free shopping

The Princess offers:

- cabins with colour TV, radio and satellite telephone and private bathroom
- four swimming pools
- a health club
- a business centre
- a theatre
- a shopping gallery
- seven elegant bars
- five magnificent restaurants with award-winning cuisine
- the liveliest disco afloat
- a casino

The Orient Express offers:

- five course lunch + champagne and fine wines
- a bar car
- on board boutique for souvenirs
- cabin + original wash basin cabinet

Unit 19 Exercise 7

Group B

Solution 2
The passengers represented people who had known or been employed by the Armstrong family: an Italian chauffeur, a Swedish nurse, etc. They had *all* stabbed Mr Ratchett with the knife in revenge for the murder of Daisy Armstrong and her family. Clues had been left to confuse the police: the H on the handkerchief was in fact a Russian N pointing at Princess Natalia Dragomiroff; Colonel Arbuthnot smoked a pipe and the washbag belonged to Mrs Hubbard. Each passenger was a suspect, but each passenger had an alibi.

Revision exercises

Unit 1: Past Simple vs Present Perfect

> a) I'*ve been* to America.
> b) I *went* to America last year, with my parents.

a) Use the Present Perfect to talk about general experience.
b) Use the Past Simple to talk about specific time/detail in the past.

Are the underlined parts of these sentences correct (C) or incorrect (I)? Correct the incorrect sentences.

1 He has gone to America three weeks ago.
2 Have you ever eaten snails?
3 She went to Brazil by plane.
4 When they were there, they have stayed with my parents.
5 That year he passed his exams and went to work in a museum.
6 We have received her letter last week.
7 I hear they are happily married. They have been married in Rome, you know.
8 I haven't been to Jim's before. Have you?

Unit 2: asking for descriptions

a) age	How old is she/he?
b) health	How is she/he?
c) appearance	What does she/he look like?
d) character and/or appearance	What is she/he like?
e) interests	What does she/he like doing?

Complete the gaps and use each question above once only in this conversation about Sophie's grandmother.

ROBERT: ... your grandmother these days?
SOPHIE: She's fine, considering her age.
ROBERT: ... exactly?
SOPHIE: Eighty nine but you'd never think it.
ROBERT: ..., then?
SOPHIE: Well, she's really young-looking. Her hair is going grey of course but she's still a very beautiful woman. She keeps herself active too.
ROBERT: ...?
SOPHIE: Well, everything really. Gardening, visiting friends, photography...
ROBERT: She sounds fantastic . ... as a grandmother?
SOPHIE: Wonderful. She's the kindest person I know.

Unit 3: *will* vs *going to* (decisions)

> A: I'*m going to* take some cheese to the party.
> B: OK. I'*ll* take some fruit.

A made the decision before speaking.

B made the decision at the moment of speaking.

Complete each gap with *am/are/is going to* or *will*:

1 I ... visit my mother in Scotland at the weekend. I booked the tickets this morning.
2 If you have decided to stay at home and work tonight, I think I ... go and see that new film.
3 A: Did you hear that Marisa has lost her job?
B: I know. Someone said she ... move abroad.
4 Why ... (you) leave him? It seems like a stupid idea!
5 A: What do you plan to do when your children leave home in October?
B: I don't know. Maybe I ... start painting again. I haven't done any for years.
6 A: The taxi's arrived.
B: OK. I ... go and open the front door.

Unit 4: *must/might/can't be*

How sure?		
100% Yes	She is	
	She *must be*	
50%	She *might be*	an actress.
	She *can't be*	
100% No	She isn't	

Use *must/might/can't* + *be* to show degrees of certainty and logical deduction.
Complete each gap with *must be*, *might be* or *can't be*.

A: Where's Xavier?
B: I'm not sure. He ... at the shops or he ... at his mother's.
A: He ... at the shops. They closed hours ago.
B: Then he ... at his mother's. Have you seen my glasses?
A: No, have you looked in the bathroom? They ... there, or in your bedroom?
B: I've looked in my bedroom and they're not there. They ... in the bathroom, but I don't think so. And they ... in the kitchen because I didn't go in there.
A: Then they ... in the bathroom. It's the only place left.

Unit 6: Past Continuous (interrupted)

The Past Continuous shows an action in progress when another action (Past Simple) interrupted it.

Example: He was reading when the phone rang.

Choose the correct alternative.

1 I had/was having a bath when the door bell rang.
2 I saw/was seeing the police cars when I walked/was walking down the high street.
3 We played/were playing tennis when it started/was starting to rain.
4 While I did/was doing the shopping this man stole/was stealing my handbag.
5 The train came/was coming while I talked/was talking to my friend.

Unit 7: Present Simple/Continuous

a) She's smoking a cigarette. b) She smokes 40 a day.

a) is talking about her action at this moment.
b) is talking about a present habit which she may not be doing now.

Complete the sentences below with either the Present Simple or the Present Continuous. Use each of these verbs once only.

do play paint go come take

1 I usually ... the dog for a walk twice a day.
2 I'm sorry but she ... her homework.
3 He ... the bathroom ceiling just now but he'll be free later.
4 We never ... out during the week.
5 He (not) ... home before 7 pm very often.
6 We ... tennis quite a lot in the summer.

Unit 8: positive and negative imperatives

positive imperative infinitive (– to)	negative imperative *do* + *not* + infinitive (– to)
stay	*don't stay*

1 Match each imperative below to its opposite.

come in	pick it up	take it away	go out
put it down	stand up	bring it back	sit down

2 Now use each imperative in its negative form and complete the instruction so that it makes sense.

Example: Don't come in, I'm getting dressed.

Unit 9: *don't have to/mustn't/shouldn't*

Not a good idea	You *shouldn't* smoke so much; it's not good for you.
Not permissible	You *mustn't* smoke on public transport.
Not necessary	You *don't have to* smoke just because your friends smoke.

Now use *shouldn't/don't have to/mustn't* twice each in these sentences.

1 You ... drink and drive. It's against the law.
2 She ... wear that colour. It doesn't suit her.
3 We ... phone home every week, but our parents are pleased if we do.
4 They ... go to bed so late. They find it hard to get up in the morning.
5 I'm sorry. We ... sell alcohol to people under 18.
6 We ... buy anything for her birthday but it would be nice.

Unit 11: reported statements

Direct speech	Reported statements
'I *am* hungry.' 'I *can* swim.' 'I *will* go.'	S/he said (that) s/he *was* hungry. S/he said (that) s/he *could* swim. S/he said (that) s/he *would* go.

In reported statements, verbs generally move back one tense.

Complete the reported versions of these statements.

1 'I like playing tennis.'
She said ...
2 'We are too hot.'
They said ...
3 'He thinks he will see him tomorrow.'
He said ...
4 'I don't have time.'
She said ...
5 'We are going to buy a new house.'
They said ...
6 'They can't stay very long.'
He said ...

Unit 12: Present Perfect Simple + *for/since*

Present Simple	Present Perfect Simple
I live in Rome.	I've lived here *since* 1990/*for* ages. (*not* I live here since 1990/for ages.)

The Present Perfect Simple can be used for situations which started in the past but continue in the present.

For refers to a period of time.
Since refers to a point in time.

Use *for/since* + Present Perfect Simple to make one sentence from each pair of sentences below.

1 She is in the States. She went three months ago.
2 He got the job in the bank. He started working there in January.
3 Nigel is my best friend. I met him in 1979.
4 I like living in Spain. I moved there five years ago.
5 The guitar is my favourite instrument. I began playing when I was nine years old.
6 That's my car. I got it last March.

Unit 13: *some/any; much/many/a lot of*

A: Let's make a shopping list. Have we got *any* coffee? B: No, we've got *some* tea but we haven't got *any* coffee. A: How *much* tea have we got? B: We've got *a lot of* tea but we haven't got *many* biscuits and there isn't *much* milk.

Some/a lot of is often used in positive sentences and *any/many/much* in negative sentences and questions.

NB *Much* is generally used with uncountable nouns, many is used with countable nouns.

Choose the best alternative in these sentences.

1 I've got some/any biscuits but unfortunately I haven't got some/any cake.
2 How much/many times have you been to America?
3 I haven't got much/many time. I don't want to be late.
4 He's got much/a lot of money but he doesn't like people to know.
5 There aren't much/many people here today.
6 Have you got any/many information about what happened last night.

Unit 14: *can/can't* + levels of ability

We use subject + *can/can't* + verb to express ability.

NB Don't put words expressing levels of ability, e.g. *not at all/badly/not very well/quite well/very well* between *can* and verb. 'I can very well cook.' is wrong.

Decide if these sentences are correct or incorrect. Correct the incorrect sentences.

1 She can drives a little.
2 Can they speak very well French?
3 How well can you dance the tango?
4 I can't play tennis not at all.
5 I can play the piano but not very well.
6 We cannot see the actors at all.
7 He could read quite well as a child.
8 Did he could ride a bike? Yes, very well.
9 He couldn't swim at all so he drowned.

Unit 16: ways of giving advice

You *should* (*shouldn't*)	speak to her about it. (?)
If I were you, I'*d* (*wouldn't*)	
Why don't you	

Give advice to your friend in each of these different situations. Use each of the above forms twice.

1 Your friend says she feels sick and has a high temperature.
2 A friend tells you he has met someone at work he really likes but he doesn't know how to invite her out for a date.
3 A friend's son is mixing with some fairly unpleasant boys from his school, he is out a lot and is getting behind at school.
4 A friend has recently been for a job interview but was turned down. She feels strongly that it was because she was a woman and is very angry.
5 Your friend has just got a letter from the tax office saying that she owes them a large amount of money for tax in previous years. She doesn't understand why.
6 Your friend wants to marry someone but her parents disapprove. They want her to marry someone else that she quite likes but doesn't love deeply.

Unit 17: expressing likes/dislikes

generally/always (verb + noun/*-ing* form)	**now/at a specific time** (*would* + verb + noun <u>or</u> *would* + verb + *to* + verb)
I *like* (*love/prefer*) chocolate. I *like* (*love/prefer*) eat*ing* chocolate.	I'*d like* (*love/prefer*) a cup of tea. I'*d like* (*love/prefer*) *to have* a cup of tea.

Choose the correct alternative in each sentence.

1 Would you/do you usually prefer tea or coffee for breakfast?
2 We'd love/we love to see you this Sunday.
3 Would you/do you like a coffee?
4 She'd prefer/she prefers going out alone.
5 I'd love/I love to come to the party this evening.
6 They'd like/they like listening to music at night.

Unit 18: *very/too/enough*

She's *very* intelligent and passed her exams easily.
Some of the questions were *too* difficult for Jose.
The car wasn't fast *enough* to win the race.

- ***very*** **+ adjective intensifies the adjective**
- ***too*** **+ adjective says there's a problem**
- **adjective +** ***enough*** **expresses as much as is necessary**

Use the adjectives in brackets + *too, very* and *enough* twice each to complete these sentences.

1 The coffee was (hot) to drink, so I left it.
2 He's (generous); he gives his parents half of what he earns.
3 I'm (fat) for this skirt. I'll have to get a bigger size.
4 Is he (sensitive) to understand what we meant?
5 He is (clever) to pass the exam but he's a bit lazy.
6 She's (confident), I'm sure she'll get the job.

Unit 19: *must/might/can't* + verb

She *must* know Anne. Everyone does.
You *can't* know Pete, he's our new neighbour.
They *might* know his wife. She works at the bank.

Use *must/might/can't* + verb to express degrees of certainty.

Rewrite each example using *must/might/can't* + verb.

1 Quite possibly Mary has your umbrella.
2 I'm sure she's French. She speaks French fluently.
3 I think you know Carl but I'm not sure.
4 I'm sure he hasn't got the book. He didn't have anything in his hands when he left.
5 Perhaps Joao knows the answer.
6 Of course he loves her. He went all the way to Mexico for her.
7 I'm certain she doesn't hate swimming. She goes to the pool every week.
8 Of course they don't believe him. They know he lies.

Tapescript

The complete tapescript can be found in the Teacher's Book.

UNIT 1

Exercise 3 Vocabulary: Listening: 1

1

I've actually travelled quite a lot, I suppose, one way and another. But the most fantastic bit, the most memorable bit of sightseeing I've ever done was in fact on my honeymoon. That's eleven years ago now. My husband and I decided to go to, on a tour of the Middle East and we began in Jordan. We got to Petra and booked into a hotel, I remember. And then we hired horses the next morning and went on horseback along this sort of gorge, a tunnel. And suddenly there it was in front of us, this most amazing sight. It was carved out of pink rock. It looked like a palace. I mean, it was just breathtaking and behind this incredible facade was just a cave.

2

Well, it was something I had talked about wanting to do for quite a while and then when my boyfriend gave it to me as a birthday present last April I think I was more shocked than anything. I would actually have to do it. On the day I woke up terrified. At first I refused to go but then my boyfriend said how marvellous it was so we drove out to Kawarau bridge which is just over 20 kms from my home in Queenstown, New Zealand. Everything was ready and I got careful instructions for what to do. Standing on the edge of the bridge I had a real sense that 'this was it' and I suppose my life did pass before my eyes! Then I jumped ... and it was all over so fast, and there I was bouncing about at the end of this rope just a few metres above the river. Unbelievable ... I can quite honestly say it was a once in a lifetime experience.

English in action: 3

I: Della, what is a corpus?
D: A corpus is a computerised collection of words. The British National Corpus is a very large corpus of a 100 million words, 90 million written words and 10 million spoken words, stored on a large computer.
I: How was the Spoken Corpus recorded?
D: Over half of it was recorded by volunteers actually carrying little walkman tape recorders around with them.
I: Who spoke on the recordings?
D: Every type of person that you can think of.
I: So how many words do you think there are in spoken English?
D: Well, according to the corpus there are just under 55,000 separate words, that's in spoken English. In written English there are a lot more, probably just under half a million.
I: Wow! And of all those words that you've discovered in the Spoken Corpus, I mean, what are the ten most frequent words that keep coming up?
D: Well, the ten most frequent ones are the very obvious words; they are: *the* ...
I: Yes
D: *I* ...
I: *The* and *I*, yeah ...
D: *You*.
I: Yes
D: *It, and* ...
I: *You, it, and* ...
D: *That, to, is*, that's *'s* ...
I: *That, to*, that's TO?
D: Yes and *is* is *'s* usually because obviously it's in spoken language.
I: Right.
D: *A* and *of*.
I: *A* and *of*. And how much of everyday English do these ten words make up in fact?
D: They make up about a quarter of the whole of the language that we have recorded, about 25%.
I: From a student's point of view, Della, what can the Spoken Corpus help them learn?
D: I think above all it can help them to learn the grammar of natural English. It can also help them to learn vocabulary in context and it can certainly show them how functional language actually works in speech.
I: When you say functional language ...?
D: So how you make a suggestion to a friend you know whether you say 'let's do something' and so on.
I: Yes, so compared with written work it does show how the English language is in its natural form.
D: Yes, it's much more natural, yes.

UNIT 2

Exercise 2 Pronunciation: 1

OPERATOR: Hello. International telegrams. How can I help you?
CUSTOMER: I'd like to send a telegram to the States.
OPERATOR: Fine. Can I have your telephone number, please?
CUSTOMER: Yes, it's 0171 735
OPERATOR: Yes
CUSTOMER 8294
OPERATOR: 8294. And your name?
CUSTOMER: Barbara Young.
OPERATOR: Barbara Young... and your address is?
CUSTOMER: 130 Manor Road.
OPERATOR: Manor .. is that M-A-N-O-R?
CUSTOMER: Yes, that's right. Manor Road, London N16 OQL.
OPERATOR: OQL. Fine and who are you sending it to?
CUSTOMER: Jeff Thomson, T-H-O-M-S-O-N.
OPERATOR: Right, and is that Jeff with a G or a J?
CUSTOMER: J. .... J-E-double F.
OPERATOR: Fine, and he lives at..?
CUSTOMER: 655 Post Street, San Francisco.
OPERATOR: Have you got a zip code for that?
CUSTOMER: Yes. CA 94108.
OPERATOR: OK. Right, can we have the message then?
CUSTOMER: Yes. It's 'Arriving British Airways (Flight BA 703). 6.30 am Saturday.'
OPERATOR: And who do you want that signed by?
CUSTOMER: Me. Barbara Young.
OPERATOR: Fine, that should arrive in San Francisco by 9.00 am.
CUSTOMER: Great. Could you tell me the price now?
OPERATOR: Certainly. It's £5.35 standing charge ...

Exercise 4 Vocabulary: 4

Words for *I like that stuff* on page 13.
(See Teacher's Book for completed version.)

Exercise 6 Listening: 2

Words for *The girl from Ipanema* on page 14.
(See Teacher's Book for corrected version.)

English in action: 1

1

A: It works perfectly alright, it's just that, well you see the thing is we need a much bigger one now, it really doesn't have enough space in the freezer compartment for us.
B: Oh that's OK, I'm on my own so it doesn't have to be very big. Just so long as it works alright. Anyway it's mainly for keeping fresh food and drinks in.
A: Well that should be OK. It really does ...

2

C: It sounds like a real bargain. Are you sure there's nothing wrong with it?
D: Basically no. But, remember it's not terribly big .... it's got a 20 inch screen but that means you can move it around fairly easily.
C: And you always get a good clear picture?
D: Yes, it's got an excellent indoor aerial. The only problem is that the picture does look a little green sometimes.
C: Green?
D: Yes, I'm afraid so.

3

E: Well, madam, I think you'll find it is an absolute bargain. I'm really giving it away as I need the space out front.
F: You said it was a dark blue, didn't you?

E: Yes, that's right.
F: ... and how many miles has it done?
E: Under 50,000 which I can assure you is far fewer than most models at this price. And it's good on petrol. It uses much less petrol than its size suggests.
F: And has it had regular servicing.
E: Oh yes I have the service records all here at the garage.

4

G: Is it still for sale?
H: Oh yes.
G: Can you tell me if it's in good condition?
H: Perfect. In fact it's almost new. Someone gave it to me as a birthday present but I've got a computer now, so I really don't need it.
G: I see. So it all works.
H: Yes perfectly and it's got a built-in corrector ribbon.
G: That's good.
H: And it's very light and easy to carry around. Really, it's very good value for only £100.

Bossa Nova

Tapescript for *The girl from Ipanema* as for Unit 2 Exercise 6 Listening: 2 (see Teacher's Book for corrected version).

UNIT 3

Exercise 6 Listening: 1

1

I just got some really good news. I went for a job interview last week. I really wanted it. The only thing is, it's... it's not in this country. I'd have to go abroad. But, anyway, I got the news that I got the job. It's really exciting. Certainly, I'd like to take the job. The only thing is I've got to talk to the employers. They're not exactly sure about how much I'll get paid. I mean, the salary is negotiable. Well, that's what they said at the interview, anyway. But they're going to come back to me about the money and basically I've got to decide whether to take it by next Monday. It's a big decision.

2

Well, I'm going to tell you something you never thought you'd hear me saying. I have got to decide whether or not to get married to Paolo. I've got all the family on both sides on at me because we had a phone call a couple of days ago and his father wants him back in Argentina. And it just depends on whether I can accept living abroad permanently. But if I go to live in Argentina, and we'll go by next month so I have to make up my mind really quickly, I've got my parents who want me to get married here. And so I've got to make the decision by the end of next month. I really don't know what to do.

3

Well luckily, I won't have to make that decision until I get my results, my 'A' level results. So part of the big decision about which university to go to, isn't left up to me because so much of it depends on my 'A' level results which don't come out till August. And then I'll be in a better position to choose because I have to make a decision by 10th September. Ideally, I'd like to go to Oxford ...

English in action: 3

Camp America
37A Queens Gate
London SW7 5HR
England

UNIT 4

Exercise 6 Listening: 2

I: Is it true Monica that you were a bit of a bully when you were younger?
M: Well, I don't think it is but you, I'm the eldest and if you ask my sister and my brothers, you only have to mention the word bully when we're all out for a meal at the moment and they all say 'Oh yes, we all know about that!' So I think that probably, you know, democratically, I probably am considered a bully. My sister...
I: What did you do?
M: Well, I think it was partly, I think it was partly because I was always the youngest at school so although I was the eldest at home, um you know, I had to take advantage of it really to have any power. I think I was just a good organiser but my sister says that the methods I used were a little strange.
I: What sort of methods did you use?
M: Well, I used to keep her in check by, we had an old house and every single night, I used to go upstairs and hide in the linen cupboard at the top so that when she came up the stairs I would leap out on her. And I persuaded her that there were chickens under the bed so when she had to get up to go to the toilet in the middle of the night, she had to jump off the bed. She had to stand on the bed and then jump off so..
I: But you didn't actually hit her or anything?
M: No, it was all psychological bullying – not very often anyway. It was very subtle. We used to live near the sea and when we used to go along the beach, I used to make them all walk in a line.
I: What, you, the brother and sister?
M: Yeah, and um in size order. I think it was just good management.

Exercise 8 Grammar: 1

I'd like to meet someone
that is sensitive and fair
whose passion is strawberries and
who lives in a castle
where we'd talk about tigers
which are made of silk
that might, if I close my eyes, taste like honey.

English in action: 2

a) It's just not possible to finish this work in time.
b) I hate him and I won't work with him.
c) Why don't we give all our students free lessons for a month?
d) At this point I'd like us to make a list of all the advantages and disadvantages.
e) According to my calculations, the final cost will be $150,000.
f) Of course they can do it – they're young and enthusiastic.

UNIT 5

Exercise 1 Across cultures: 3

Have you seen the old man,
In the closed-down market,
Kicking up the papers with his worn-out shoes?
In his eyes you see no pride;
Hand hung loosely at his side.
Yesterday's paper telling yesterday's news.

CHORUS
So how can you tell me you're lonely,
And say for you that the sun don't shine?
Let me take you by the hand
And lead you through the streets of London.
I'll show you something
To make you change your mind.

And have you seen the old girl,
Who walks the streets of London,
Dirt in her hair and her clothes in rags?
She's no time for talking;
She just keeps right on walking.
Carrying her home in two carrier bags.

CHORUS

And in the all-night café,
At a quarter past eleven,
Same old man sitting there on his own.
Looking at the world
Over the rim of his tea-cup.
Each tea lasts an hour and he wanders home alone.

CHORUS

And have you seen the old man,
Outside the seaman's mission,
Memory fading with the medal ribbons that he wears?
And in our winter city
The rain cries a little pity
For one more forgotten hero and a world that doesn't care.

CHORUS

UNIT 6

Exercise 8 Function: 1

1

A: Oh, hi Rachel what can I do for you?
B: Well, I hate to complain but your bonfire is filling our garden with smoke and we've got friends coming round for a barbecue lunch and ...
A: Oh, dear I am sorry. I didn't realise. I'll put it out immediately.
B: Great. Thanks. Come over for a drink and a sausage later if you feel like it.
A: OK, thanks I will.

2

C: Oh hello. I'm glad I've seen you.
D: Oh hello. How are things?
C: Fine. Well no, not really. I'm afraid it's the dog again.
D: The dog? Our dog?
C: Yes, we're not getting any sleep. It barks all night. It can't carry on like this, I'm afraid.
D: Well, I don't know what we can do really. I mean, all dogs bark.
C: Yes, well all people need sleep so you've got to do something or else I'm afraid...

3

E: OK OK I'm coming.
F: About time. Look this just isn't good enough. Do you think you could park in front of your own house? How am I supposed to get my car out with yours blocking the drive?
E: OK OK. Keep your hair on. It's not the end of the world.
F: I'm sorry but this isn't the first time and I'm in a hurry.
E: I'm moving it as fast as I can.

English in action: 2

C: Excuse me.
SA: Yes. Can I help you?
C: Yes, I hope so. It's about a wardrobe which I bought here last weekend.
SA: What seems to be the problem?
C: Well, when we got home and opened the box, we discovered that the mirror was cracked.
SA: Oh, I see, but you didn't check it when you bought it?
C: No, we assumed it would be alright.
SA: I see. Well, I'm afraid I can't do anything about it. You accepted it when you bought it.

English in action: 3

SA: I see. Well, I'm afraid I can't do anything about it. You accepted it when you bought it.
C: Well, I'm afraid that's not good enough. I'll keep the wardrobe but I'd like a new mirror.
SA: I'm sorry but we don't sell mirrors separately so that's not possible.
C: Um well, in that case ...

UNIT 7

Exercise 2 Listening: 1

Right. Well shall we get started then? I'm going to tell you your duties. You are meant to work 30 hours a week, I think it is, which works out at six hours a day.
So you get her up at half past seven, quarter to eight in the morning. She comes down for breakfast. She has her breakfast after she's dressed so she's down here by eight o'clock. She's finished her breakfast by quarter past eight. So she leaves here at half past eight and then gets back, again it varies, but she has a few after-school activities. So she will come back you'll give her just a little snack and then you'll make her her supper and then she'll have a bath. You wash her hair perhaps twice a week. She has her um, gets into her pyjamas, dressing gown and slippers, has her hair brushed and then she can come down and watch television for a little bit. She does have homework which I would like you to oversee and make sure she does it.
Now what else? Now in the mornings the sort of domestic things is to come down, to clear up in here, if there are any glasses or anything, just to do the cushions and make it look tidy and to open the curtains. The same in the kitchen, open the curtains and just put things away, and do the dishwasher. What else is there? Oh yes, just to sweep the floor, just in the mornings and then one day a week just to give this a little bit of a vacuum and just wash the kitchen floor.
You get £35 a week with me which is just cash which we give you every Friday. £35 isn't an awful lot ... but London is quite expensive. I don't know, is Sweden expensive? (Yes it is) It is expensive isn't it? (very expensive) Yes it is very expensive. So I mean are you used to having pocket money from home or? (Yes, I have pocket money). You do.

Exercise 7 Listening: 3

Birds do it
Bees do it
Even educated fleas do it
Let's do it
Let's fall in love

In Spain the best upper sets do it
Lithuanians and Letts do it
Let's do it
Let's fall in love

The Dutch in old Amsterdam do it
Not to mention the Finns
Folks in Siam do it
Think of Siamese twins

Some Argentines, without means, do it
People say in Boston even beans do it
Let's do it
Let's fall in love

Sponges they say do it
Oysters down in Oyster Bay do it
Let's do it
Let's fall in love

Cold Cape Cod clams against their wish do it
Even lazy jellyfish do it
Let's do it
Let's fall in love

Electric eels I might add do it
Though it shocks them I know
Why ask if shad do it
"Waiter, bring me shad roe."

In shallow shoals, English soles do it
Goldfish in their privacy of bowls do it
Let's do it
Let's fall in love (x 3)
Let's ...

UNIT 8

Exercise 1 Diagnosis: 2

Stand up straight
Take a deep breath
Stretch your arms up
Bring your arms down
Touch your toes. Don't bend your knees!
Stand up straight again and
Sit down, ready to work

Exercise 4 Listening 1

CHRIS: Come on it's going to rain... Hey, Anita did I tell you? I'm going to India at the end of the month.

ANITA: No! Oh, I'm jealous. It's such a long time since I've been there. What part are you going to?
CHRIS: I don't know, I can't really decide but I...
ANITA: Oh go to Calcutta. There's so much to see and the food is fantastic.
CHRIS: OK, OK, I'll go to Calcutta, then. (pause)
CHRIS: Hey wait a minute. Isn't that where you come from?
ANITA: Originally, yeah. My family not me. Hey, listen, why don't you go and stay with my grandmother, she'd love to have you? I've told her so much ab...
CHRIS: Would she really? Hey that would be wonderful. (pause)
ANITA: I'll write to her immediately. By the way, have you had all your shots, all your vaccinations?
CHRIS: Yeah, everything. I've even got malaria tablets but I don't think I'll bother with ...
ANITA: Wait a minute, malaria can be very dangerous. You need to be really careful. (pause)
CHRIS: OK but I don't usually get ill when I'm abroad.
ANITA: Well, there's always a first time and remember, it'll be terribly hot.
CHRIS: I know. (pause)
CHRIS: Anyway, I'm taking lots of suntan lotion.
ANITA: Well, if I were you, I wouldn't go out in the middle of the day at all. Lie down and have a siesta then. (pause)
CHRIS: OK I will. Thanks for the advice.
ANITA: That's okay. Will you send me a postcard? (pause)
CHRIS: Of course. Listen, will everybody speak English?
ANITA: Not in my family they won't. I know, I'll teach you a few words of Bengali before you ...
JON: But I haven't got time.
ANITA: Yes, you have and you're so good at languages. I know you'll be really good and they'll love it. Come on let's start now. To ask 'how are you?' is ...

UNIT 9

Exercise 6 Listening: 2

The magic of the city when I was young came to me as language. So I could go to South of Market, I could go to the Mission district and hear Spanish, Mexican Spanish and Spanish that's spoken by people from South America and maybe from Spain. And there is Russian Hill, and there was a German area and Chinatown and I lived in an area which had been populated by Japanese. And nobody seemed to reject me. I don't know whether I was insensitive to rejection or just so caught up by the mystery of San Francisco that I just didn't notice it. I seemed to be able to waft like the fog itself in and out of these various areas of San Francisco.

Exercise 6 Listening: 4

I live in North Carolina now but I'm in San Francisco about every two or three months. And when I go to San Francisco the people treat me as if I have come home again. And I never feel I've really left San Francisco. I mean, one is not obliged to be born in San Francisco, to be a San Franciscan. I suppose you, one is asked to be loyal to the city, to have some flair, some grace about oneself, some tolerance. One is not really considered a San Franciscan if one is intolerant of everything. There are so many races, so many styles of living. There have been blacks and asians and whites and all sorts of people involved in San Francisco; new languages, new attitudes so there is no way, I think, of people being intolerant, totally intolerant and calling themselves San Franciscans.

English in action: 3

1 Dracula by Bram Stoker

Suddenly he felt the touch of a hand and heard a voice wish him good morning. The count was standing by his side. Jonathan jumped. The count was a quiet walker, and could have entered the room unheard – but hardly unseen.
'Why didn't I see him in the looking glass?' thought Jonathan. 'He is standing in front of it even now, but although I can see myself I can't see him.'
As Jonathan continued to stare into the looking glass he noticed that he had cut himself. A little stream of blood was flowing down his neck. He looked at the count again to make sure that he really was in the room, and froze with fear! Dracula was watching the blood as it ran down his neck, watching like a hungry animal. He looked as if he was going to attack him!

2 The Great Gatsby by F. Scott Fitzgerald

As I went over to say goodbye I saw an expression of uncertainty on Gatsby's face, as if he felt some doubt about his present happiness. Almost five years! All that time he had been building up his dream of her. How could any real person equal the immense power of that dream? There must have been moments that afternoon when Daisy had disappointed him.
As I watched him his expression changed. His hand took hold of hers, and when she said something low in his ear he leaned towards her with a rush of feeling. Her voice had a magic that was beyond all dreams.
They had forgotten me, but Daisy looked up and held out her hand; Gatsby didn't know me now at all. I went out of the room and down the marble steps into the rain, leaving them there together.

3 Brave New World by Aldous Huxley

The Director walked slowly down the long line of little beds. Eighty little boys and girls lay softly breathing. There was a whisper under every pillow...
'Alpha children wear grey. They work much harder than we do, because they are so very clever. I'm really very glad I'm a Beta; because I don't work so hard. And then we are much better than the Gammas and Deltas. Gammas are stupid. They all wear green, and Delta children wear khaki. Oh no, I don't want to play with Delta children. And Epsilons are still worse. They are too stupid to be able ...'
The soft clear voice continued to whisper beneath the eighty pillows.
'Sleep teaching,' said the Director, 'is the greatest moralising and socialising force of all time ... At last,' he said 'the child's mind is completely formed of these suggestions. And the men and women too, all their lives, are conditioned. And all these suggestions are our suggestions! Suggestions from the World State.'

UNIT 10

Exercise 1 Language in context: 2

Words for *Sitting on the Dock of the Bay* on page 62.
(See Teacher's Book for completed version.)

Exercise 3 Across cultures: 7

See Additional tapescript at the end of the Teacher's Book.

UNIT 11

Exercise 5 Listening: 1

1

Well, I actually got revenge on somebody fairly recently which I have to say I was pretty pleased about. It was my ex-girlfriend, Alison, and well I suppose the reason she's my ex-girlfriend is because she left me and went off with somebody else. Anyway, she went on holiday with this guy, Kevin, and I still had a key to her flat, so when I knew she was away I went round there, and I just stood in the flat for a moment. I didn't quite know what to do, I thought of sort of rearranging all her records out of alphabetical order or something but to be honest I couldn't be bothered to do that. So I decided what I would do is I'd make a phone call and I was going to call my aunt in Australia, but in the end I decided to phone the talking clock in America. And I got through after a while and I left the phone off the hook, so I suppose the phone call lasted for about three or four hours. In the end I ended up having to pay half the bill, but believe me it was worth it.

2

Oh yes, it was a ... it was a holiday job I had as a student. And this boss was absolutely impossible to work with, you know, I mean, he was really so demanding. And we, well listen, we were at the Christmas party and he suddenly started complaining again about things that I'd gone over with him ages before and I'd had enough.

So, he'd just bought himself a large drink and I thought right, this is it and I threw it all over him. And it felt wonderful. I mean he just stood there in front of me dripping. Well, of course I lost my job. Well, naturally, he sacked me on the spot. But, even so, it made me feel absolutely wonderful.

3
Well, I went into this shop and I asked the shopkeeper a simple question, and he was so rude to me that I got extremely angry on the spot. And I used to have quite a temper. So I went out and there was a shop just quite close where I bought a can of spray paint, and I came back and I just covered his shop front windows with spray paint. And, of course, he phoned the police and I got arrested. And looking back it was really a stupid thing to do, and I do regret it.

UNIT 12

Exercise 2 Listening: 2

I: Perhaps I could start off by just trying to get some sort of life overview picture of yourself um. Now you were born in 1937, is that right?
G: 36
I: 36 right 36. And um and you went to drama school?
G: Yes.
I: When, when was that?
G: Um when I was 19. That must be 1955
I: And how many years was that? Was that three?
G: Two years.
I: Two years. And when did you then go on to act in your first film?
G: Oh that was a long time after that. I think, the first film that I did was probably the film version of a play that I'd done with the Royal Shakespeare Company called the Marat Sade.
I: And what year was that?
G: Well we did the play in 1964 so presumably the film must have been about 1966.
I: 66 hm hm. Now you've been a member of the Labour Party for quite some time haven't you? Have you always voted Labour?
G: Ever since I've had the right to vote, ever since the age of 21.
I: Right. When did you actually stop your acting career and start moving into politics as a full time thing?
G: I would think possibly... well... virt... no, I think exclusively from when uh the date of the general election in 92 was announced. I had worked up until that point. But actually stopping all acting work, it was really from the announcement of the date of the actual general election in 1992.
I: So you were actually elected and became an MP in 1992?
G: That's right.

Exercise 2 Listening: 3

I: Was there anything particular that surprised you um about the working of the House of Commons when you, when you first arrived, anything you hadn't really expected?
G: The thing that surprised me most, although I had been warned to expect it, is the marked lack of facilities provided for MPs. You become the Member of Parliament, you become the representative, in my case of more than 60,000 people, ... you have no office, you have no staff. I had to wait six months before I obtained an office which I shared with another MP. You have to provide all your own office equipment with the exception of a desk, two filing cabinets and a telephone. Um you have to hire your own staff. And I do find that, given that we are in a modern age of technological information, absolutely bewildering.
I: Yes... At the moment are there any special areas of, of interest or concern for you politically that you are working on or promoting?
G: My own particular interest over several years has been the issue of housing or rather the lamentable lack of housing in this country. The problem over and above housing is unemployment and everything attached to that which is obviously poverty.
I: A last question. What do you enjoy most really about being an MP? What are the areas that give you most satisfaction?
G: ...Certainly life, the job itself is never ever boring, and it is a great privilege to be a Member of Parliament.
I: That's been most interesting. Thank you very much.
G: Thank you.

English in action: 6

See film script on page 75.

UNIT 13

Exercise 1 Diagnosis: 4

A: Hi. I'm home. Can you help me unpack the shopping?
B: Yeah. Oh good, you got some chips for lunch. But why did you get so little bread? And you've bought so few biscuits.
A: They're fattening and there weren't any chocolate ones which are the only ones I really like. I've bought a lot of milk – you said we needed some.
B: Good. But why have you bought so many razors?
A: We didn't have any left and we haven't got much washing powder either so I decided to get some more.
B: I hate it when you go shopping. You never get any chocolate.
A: Listen, *you* go next time.

Exercise 6 Listening: 1

1
The prospect of a dinner party terrifies me. I have literally had sleepless nights. I cannot cook like a restaurant. I cannot cook like a magazine illustration and it's my impression that nowadays this is increasingly what's required if one invites people for dinner.

2
We're too busy to cook so we employ somebody to prepare the food beforehand and to bring the food round, ready for us to reheat, or simply just to serve up to people. Now the dilemma is whether we actually admit to the fact that we haven't prepared the food ourselves, because I think most people, certainly most of our friends, when they come round to dinner they expect that you've gone to the effort to prepare an exciting meal for them. I would be quite happy to admit that somebody else has done the food but Susie, my wife, is dead against admitting the fact...

3
I don't see myself as a sort of old-fashioned housewifey hostess kind of helping the husband's job by holding big dinner parties and hiding smells and hiding sounds. I actually like the idea that everybody comes into my kitchen and eats there and when they walk in the room they kind of lift the lids on saucepans to find out what's cooking.

UNIT 14

Exercise 5 Listening: 2

Part 1

I: So we started off by asking Celeste when she realised that she might actually be able to dance again..
CD: Well, it was strange. Darshan Singh Bhuller, he just called me one day and he said, 'I have an idea for a dance film and I'd like you to be in it' and I did say to him 'Well, but haven't you forgotten something, you know' and he said 'No', that he had this idea, he wanted to talk to me about it and he was very convincing and I felt that what his idea of the film would be a very positive view of disability, exploring the relationships and how they break down. It's not just the point that you can't walk or whatever, it was much more intimate than that. And he didn't know what I could do, and I didn't know what I could do but some little voice said in me 'Yes, yes do it' and it was almost, it was a real adventure into discovering different ways of moving.
I: And how does it work? How does she 'dance'?
CD: Well, I dance in the wheelchair and out of it. And, in fact, a lot of the work that I did for this film 'The Fall' was out of the chair and that was a very liberating experience ...

Part 2

It comes from inside and I don't think you can do anything with your legs and arms and your head and your back and the rest of your body and it can mean nothing unless there's something inside you and although OK parts of my body don't work any more, you can, you can move an arm or a head and it can mean all those things, it can be just minimal movement, and also you can do some quite unusual things that I couldn't do before.

UNIT 15

Exercise 2 Thinking about learning: 1

1

A: Hello?
B: Oh hello, is that Sophie?
A: Yes?
B: Hi! This is Frank.
A: Frank! How are you?
B: Great! How are you?
A: Fine. I was going to phone you.
B: Listen, have you heard about Anna?
A: Yeah, terrible isn't it? What happened exactly?
B: Well, she went to the cinema and when she got back, they'd broken into her house.
B: Did they take much?
A: No but it's a horrid feeling, you know, someone else in your house. Anyway, the worst thing is she doesn't feel comfortable there at night now.
B: No I can understand that. Of course, she could always stay here.
A: Could she? I think she'd appreciate that.
B: Well, I'll phone her. Why don't you come round later?
A: OK, listen I'll bring dinner.
B: Great. Right, well, I'll phone Anna now. See you later.
A: OK fine. Bye.

2

C: Trish, hi!
D: Hi!
C: Did you have a good weekend? What did you do?
D: Yes, great, I did nothing. What about you? What did you do?
C: I went to the country with friends. It was fantastic. Listen, I'm glad I've seen you. I wanted to ask you a favour.
D: Oh yes, what?
C: Well, I was wondering if you still had that big frying pan.
D: Yeah. Did you want to borrow it?
C: Would you mind? (no problem) You see, I'm having some friends round for dinner and ...
D: No problem at all. Anyway, I never use it.
C: Of course, I'd be really careful.
D: I'm not worried at all. But, I've got to go. I'm meeting Terry from school.
C: OK, fine. I'll phone you.
D: OK. Bye.

Exercise 3 Language in context: 4

Words for *Somebody to love* on page 93.
(See Teacher's Book for completed version.)

UNIT 16

Exercise 1 Diagnosis: 1

1

DR: Well the calls are coming in. I'll start taking them now. 0171 802 9733. Let's start with Nathalie. Are you there?
N: Yes.
DR: Good evening Nathalie. What can I do for you?
N: Good evening. Well, it's silly really but I don't know what to do. You see I keep getting these strange phone calls.
DR: What sort of strange phone calls? Nasty phone calls?
N: No, not really. Someone just says 'Hello Nathalie' and asks me how I am and then puts the phone down when I ask who it is.
DR: So it's someone who knows you?
N: I don't know. I don't recognise their voice. I feel a bit frightened really and I don't dare tell my husband because he's the jealous type and ...
DR: I see. Well, Nathalie, I think ...

2

DR: Hello, is that Dewan from London?
D: Yes.
DR: Hello. How can I help you?
D: Well, I'm sorry to trouble you but I don't really know what to do. You see I love my parents very much ...
DR: Well that's great.
D: Yes but you see, they came to England from Pakistan originally. And I've always lived here and I've met someone I really like.
DR: A girlfriend?
D Yes an English girlfriend and it's getting rather serious.
DR: And your parents don't like her?
D: Well, I haven't told them about her.
DR: Oh dear.
D: But I know they'd prefer me to marry a Pakistani girl. And it's true that the differences are very big. You know, the cultural differences and the religious differences and sometimes I wonder if maybe it would be better...

3

DR: Is that Lucia?
L: Yes, hello. In fact, I'm phoning about my brother, not me really.
DR: Your brother? What's the problem?
L: Well, I think he might be anorexic.
DR: Anorexic? You mean he's afraid of becoming fat, afraid of eating?
L: Well, yes.
DR: How old is he?
L: He's seventeen. I'm nineteen and we're very close. He's always been very careful about what he eats. He cares a lot about how he looks but lately it seems to have got out of control. He's incredibly thin and he hardly eats anything. And he refuses to talk to me about it.
DR: Have you told your parents?
L: Yes, but they think I'm exaggerating. They don't really believe boys can be anorexic and they ...
DR: I see. Well Lucia, I think ...

Exercise 5 Listening: 2

I: Can you, can you tell us how how big your immediate family was when you were a child?
V: Not at all big. It was my mother and father and me. I was an only child.
I: Of your parents, who do you feel you are most like?
V: Um I think probably my father. I can feel myself often being my father. I look exactly like my mother though.
I: Were there any particular characteristics of your father that you think you have?
V: He was an extremely rational and controlled man and I'm very like that except for the fact that I am also fantastically vulnerable and helpless.
I: Were there any special things that you remember that you liked doing together as a family?
V: No. My parents weren't I don't think happy together at all. It was a very tense household, very unhappy. And I was sitting there thinking what have I done?
I: As you were growing up what were your relationships with your mother and then your father like? How would you characterise them?
V: Well, I looked after my mother from a very early age. She was exceptionally vulnerable and had no self-confidence at all. She was a kind of brilliant, artistic woman who became head of the fashion school at a college in London. And my father was, we were like a couple of sort of sensible adults looking after my mother really, um my mother was this temperamental difficult child.

Exercise 5 Listening: 4

I: Were there any things about your childhood you felt affected you in a significant way as you were growing up?
V: I think looking after my mother and having to give in to most of her desires. And the particular time I remember is when she had fashion shows at the college which were very big events. The whole of London would be there and she would always want me to model the children's clothes in these shows. And I used to hate it um but I would always have to do it . And there would be oohs and ahs from the audience as I came down in a nightdress or a, you know, some tiny mini-skirt or something. Didn't like it.

Exercise 5 Listening: 6

I: If now as a professional you had someone come to you with the problem that you have just described in relation to their mother, what advice would you give them, someone in that situation?

V: I would, if a child wrote to me in that situation, I would say, 'Find an adult who is on your side, who will back you up when you want to say no.' I, I think I should have stood up to my mother and I shouldn't have gone along with all her manipulative requests. It's easy for me to say that now as an adult but I think it would have been interesting to know what would have happened if I'd just said, 'No, I won't.' I think I was too frightened. Would she not have loved me any more? What would have happened? Who knows!

English in action: 2

The first thing I remember really, about my young life, my childhood, was going to boarding school when I was about six. It was a very small school; it was a very caring school; the people who looked after me were were very very kind but I hated it. I hated it because it was so different. I hated not being near my parents. I suppose I felt a bit rejected.

I kept some friends though from that time, even though I left that school when I was ten/eleven. So the importance of friendship in my life, I think, comes from that time.

When I went to secondary school, I went to the local comprehensive school in London, and I remember feeling that the friends I was making were not so, so close, not so much like brothers and sisters. I was an only child so, now being on my own at home, I wanted to be with my friends a lot. And, but I became quite independent during this time too. I used to travel to France a lot because I loved French. I became very close to a French family who acted like a second family to me, a French mum, a French dad and then lots of sisters in that family so they they really gave me a feeling of family which I hadn't had up to that point. And then when I left secondary school, I went to university in the north of England, and again what I remember I suppose, are how important the friendships were that I formed there. I think I worked hard too but what I remember are the parties, and the good times, and the social occasions. And when I left university, well, I was married by that time. And I went on then to study to become a teacher and I've been working as a teacher ever since.

The unicorn in the garden

See the short story on pages 100–101.

UNIT 17

Exercise 6 Listening: 1

1

I certainly will send my daughter to an all girls' school if possible. I believe in giving girls the best education they can get and single-sex schools have been shown to do this. Girls can be as good as boys at studying sciences, for example, if they are given the chance. I agree with mixing the sexes ouside of lessons but not in class. I'm asking other parents who feel like me to sign a petition or write to their school heads. If we work together I'm sure we can get them to separate boys and girls for subject teaching, even in mixed schools.

2

I am horrified by the way the environment is being destroyed. I used to love where I live, in the South-East. It was beautiful but now I'm thinking of moving. In fact I'm thinking of going to live abroad somewhere where they value the natural countryside. In this country, they insist on making the roads bigger and bigger and building more and more factories but they are not interested in giving us a pleasant environment to live in.

3

All expectant mothers should have to listen to music for three hours a day in the week before their baby is born. Just a little pre-birth music means the baby won't be punished for having a stressed or anxious mother. The music helps the mother to stay calm and the baby is born with a friendly, happy character. Mothers-to-be are always accused of doing the wrong thing like smoking or drinking but here is a simple way to have a healthy, happy baby.

Exercise 3 Reading: Listening 1

Words for *Three little birds* on page 105.
(See Teacher's Book for reorganised version.)

Exercise 9 Writing: 5

Words for the poem *When* on page 105.
(See Teacher's Book for completed version.)

UNIT 18

Exercise 3 Listening:1

1

I've had a nose job done and a chin implant. I wasn't happy with the way I looked. The surgeon that interviewed me before I had my operation said that he felt there was absolutely nothing wrong with my nose. Having said that I felt that it was rather long and pointed and it wasn't a nose that I found attractive and I think I did the right thing because I really got a confidence boost from it.

(Do you have plans to make any other alterations to yourself?)

I'm going to have some fat transferred from my waist to my cheeks to fill them out slightly and hopefully to reduce the size of my waist. I see it more or less as, shall we say, continual maintenance really. It's not a one-off thing, it's just something that periodically something has to be done and I will have it done to keep myself looking as good as I possibly can.

2

I think the face-lift has made an enormous difference to how I feel about myself. I feel far more confident, I feel happier. I think if anybody was to be told that you could have something that would make you feel and look ten years younger than you actually feel, they'd go for it. The whole thing has cost me just under £5000 and I feel it's worth every penny.

3

I had jumbo ears, ears sticking out. My wife had cosmetic surgery done. She said 'Why don't you have it done?' So I came along and got my ears done and I wish I'd done it ten years ago...

UNIT 19

Exercise 7 Listening: 1

1

Poirot began his investigation by examining the dead man's compartment with Doctor Constantine.

'Our friend the chef de train was right. There is a woman concerned in this.'

'And most conveniently she leaves her handkerchief behind!' said Poirot. 'Exactly as it happens in the books and the films – and to make things easier for us, it is marked with an initial.'

'What a stroke of luck for us!' exclaimed the doctor.

'Is it not!' said Poirot.

Something in his tone surprised the doctor. But before he could ask for elucidation, Poirot had made another dive on to the floor.

This time he held out on the palm of his hand – a pipe cleaner.

'It is perhaps the property of Mr Ratchett?' suggested the doctor.

'There was no pipe in any of his pockets, and no tobacco or tobacco pouch.'

'Then it is a clue....Ah!' The doctor had been delicately exploring the pyjama pockets of the dead man.

'I overlooked this,' he said. 'I unbuttoned the jacket and threw it straight back.'

From the breast pocket he brought out a gold watch. The case was dented severely, and the hands pointed to a quarter-past one.

'You see?' cried Constantine eagerly. 'This gives us the hour of the crime.'

2

Later, Poirot asked Mr MacQueen what he and Colonel Arbuthnot had done on the evening of the murder.

'During the evening. Did you leave the train at all?'

'Arbuthnot and I thought we'd get out at – what was the name of the place? – Vincovci to stretch our legs a bit. But it was bitterly cold – a blizzard on. We soon hopped back in again.'

'By which door did you leave the train?'

'By the one nearest to our compartment.'

'By the one nearest to the dining car?'

'Yes.'
'Do you remember if it was bolted?'
MacQueen considered.
'Why yes, I seem to remember it was. At least there was a kind of bar that fitted across the handle. Is that what you mean?'
'Yes. On getting back into the train did you replace that bar?'
'Why, no – I don't think I did. I got in last. No, I don't seem to remember doing so.'
'One more question. Do you smoke a pipe, M. MacQueen?'
'No, sir, I do not.'

3
When Poirot interviewed Mrs Hubbard she insisted that the murderer had been in her compartment.
'You do not think, Madame, that what you heard was the noise of someone moving about next door – in the murdered man's compartment?'
'No I do not, Mr – what is it? Poirot? The man was right there in the same compartment with me. And what's more, I've got proof of it... You see this button? Well, it's not one of my buttons. It's not off anything I've got. I found it this morning when I got up.'
As she placed it on the table, M. Bouc leaned forward and gave an exclamation.
'But this is a button from the tunic of a Wagon Lit attendant!'

Exercise 7 Listening: 4
'Well,' she said 'you know everything, M. Poirot. What are you going to do about it? If it must all come out, can't you lay the blame upon me and me only? I would have stabbed that man twelve times willingly. It wasn't only that he was responsible for my daughter's death and her child's, and that of the other child who might have been alive and happy now. It was more than that. There had been other children before Daisy – there might be others in the future. Society had condemned him; we were only carrying out the sentence.'
Poirot looked at his friend.
'You are the director of the company, M. Bouc,' he said. 'What do you say?'
M. Bouc cleared his throat.
'In my opinion, M. Poirot,' he said, 'the first theory you put forward was the correct one – decidedly so. I suggest that that is the solution we offer to the Yugo-Slavian police when they arrive.'
'Then,' said Poirot, 'having placed my solution before you, I have the honour to retire from the case.'

UNIT 20

Exercise 1 Across cultures: 2
M: Sarah you don't read the Daily Mail, do you?
S: Yes, why shouldn't I?
M: But it's awful. Its politics are terrible.
S: I know it's a bit conservative but
M: A bit conservative? It's right wing.
S: Not very. A bit right of centre perhaps. Anyway I like it. It's got a good mix of news news and other things.
M: Yeah, scandal.
S: No, oh OK a bit. I admit I like reading about the rich and famous and all their problems but it's got a really good woman's page too (Yeah, true) and I really like that. Anyway, what do you read?
M: The Guardian usually.
S: Yes, that's a good paper too.
M: It doesn't compare. The Guardian is a real quality paper. It's serious. And the world news coverage is excellent.
S: Yes, but it's not unbiased politically either. It's pretty left of centre isn't it?
M: Yes, it's often seen as a pro-Labour paper but at least that's a change from most of the other papers. I read the Daily Mirror too. Now, that's not so serious but the sports coverage is good and ... it's not right wing either.
S: No, it's another pro-Labour paper. So you read a paper because of where it stands politically?
M: Yes, don't you?
S: No not really. I read it for the content. And honestly, I think the Daily Mail is good. It has good variety, a really good mix of the serious and the not so serious.

Exercise 2 Language in context: 3
G: But, Wayne, I keep telling you, there's a rule ...
W: I know there's a rule for everything but I don't know the rule for this sentence 'I have my hair cut for 50 pence'.
G: The structure 'to have something done' is often called 'causative have'.
W: Causative have?!
G: ... but I prefer to call this structure the 'service passive'. Think about all the services that we have done for us – that we pay for. Wayne for instance – why do you go to the barber?
W: To have my hair cut of course.
P: And what do you have done ... at a garage for instance?
W: I ... I have my car repaired.
P: And at a dry cleaner's?
W: I have my suit cleaned. Great well it's just about the end of the programme. I'd just like to say ...
P: Wait a minute Wayne. Wait a minute. I haven't finished. More exercises.
W: More?
P: I want you at home to change these sentences from an active construction, into a service passive – to have something done. Now, here's an example. A boy delivers my newspaper ... Wayne change that sentence using a service passive.
W: I ... I have my newspaper delivered.
P: Excellent Wayne, and in the past tense – how would you say that sentence?
W: I had my newspaper delivered.
P: Correct. I had my newspaper delivered. Now you at home try it. Here are some sentences using an active construction. I want you to change the sentences using a service passive. Some of the sentences are in the present, some in the past.
No. 1 A man delivers my milk.
No. 2 A man cleans my car.
No. 3 A man repaired my watch.
No. 4 A man decorated my living room.
Now Wayne, the answers. A man delivers my milk. Change that sentence using a service passive.
W: I have my milk delivered.
P: No. 2 A man cleans my car.
W: I have my car cleaned. I think you should rename this structure the rich man's passive.
P: Wayne, no.3 A man repaired my watch.
W: I have my watch repaired.
P: Wayne I said a man repaired my watch.
W: Ah past tense... I had my watch repaired.
P: Good. And no. 4. A man decorated my living room.
W: I had my living room decorated.
P: Now, before we go, I'd like to tell you about my next programme ...

Exercise 3 Thinking about learning: 5
Professor Grammar
c/o BBC English Magazine
PO Box 76
Bush House,
London WC2B 4PH
England

Mini-dictionary

This Mini-dictionary contains the most important words in *The Intermediate Choice*. For the groups of words below, please see the following pages.

- animals 102
- clothes 20
- dance music 14
- fish 45
- hotel facilities 114
- nationalities 45, 56
- noises 36
- political systems 72
- types of books 58
- verbs of size and position 86

The Mini-dictionary contains definitions from the *Longman Active Study Dictionary of English.*

Abbreviations: *n.* noun; *adj.* adjective; *v.* verb; *adv.* adverb; *pron.* pronoun; *prep.* preposition; *pl.* plural.
/ ˈ/ shows main stress.
/ʳ/ or /ʷ/ at the end of a word means that this sound is usually pronounced when the next word begins with a vowel sound.

Phonemic chart

Consonants				Vowels			
/p/	pen	/s/	son	/iː/	eat	/eɪ/	say
/b/	bed	/z/	cheese	/i/	happy	/əʊ/	no
/t/	tall	/ʃ/	shop	/ɪ/	sit	/aɪ/	my
/d/	day	/ʒ/	television	/e/	egg	/aʊ/	how
/k/	car	/h/	hot	/æ/	taxi	/ɔɪ/	boy
/g/	go	/m/	man	/ɑː/	far	/ɪə/	here
		/n/	finish	/ɒ/	chocolate	/eə/	where
/tʃ/	chair	/ŋ/	sing	/ɔː/	door	/ʊə/	tourist
/dʒ/	jam	/l/	look	/ʊ/	book		
		/r/	read	/uː/	shoe		
/f/	four	/j/	young	/ʌ/	bus		
/v/	very	/w/	walk	/ɜː/	shirt		
/θ/	think			/ə/	butter		
/ð/	this						

Numbers are page numbers. LR means Language Review.

abroad /əˈbrɔːd/ *adv.* to or in another country: *He lived* **abroad** *for many years.* p8

accuse /əˈkjuːz/ *v.* to say that someone has done something wrong or has broken the law: *He was* **accused** *of murder.* p66

actor /ˈæktəʳ/ *n.* (*fem.* **actress**) a person who acts in a play or film or on television. **act** *v.* p74

adaptable /əˈdæptəbəl/ *adj.* able to change your behaviour or ideas so as to manage well in a new situation (opposite **unadaptable**) p29

admit /ədˈmɪt/ *v.* agree, often unwillingly, that something bad or unpleasant is true: *She'll never* **admit** *she is wrong.* p102

advice /ədˈvaɪs/ *n.* (no *pl.*) an opinion given by one person to another on how that other should behave or act: *I asked the doctor for her* **advice**. **advise** *v.* p94

afford /əˈfɔːd/ *v.* to have enough money to do or buy something without difficulty: *Can you* **afford** *£35,000 for a house?* p27

alibi /ˈæləbaɪ/ *n.* proof that a person was in another place at the time of a crime and so could not have done it: *He didn't have an* **alibi** *for the night of the murder.* p117

all-inclusive /ˌɔːl ɪnˈkluːsɪv/ *adj.* containing or including everything: *The cost of this holiday is* **all-inclusive**. p45

ambitious /æmˈbɪʃəs/ *adj.* having a strong desire to be successful, powerful, or rich: *an* **ambitious/ unambitious** *young man.* p29

amusing /əˈmjuːzɪŋ/ *adj.* making you laugh or smile: *an amusing story.* p15

ankle /ˈæŋkəl/ *n.* the part of your body where your foot joins your leg. p95

appeal /əˈpiːl/ *n.* a request to a higher court to change the decision of a lower court: *His* **appeal** *was turned down.* **appeal** *v.* p66

artist /ˈɑːtɪst/ *n.* a person who paints, draws, or produces pieces of art. **artistic/unartistic** *adj.* p74

ashamed /əˈʃeɪmd/ *adj.* feeling shame, guilt, or sorrow about something: *I was* **ashamed** *to admit what I had done.* p68

ashtray /ˈæʃtreɪ/ *n.* a small dish for cigarette ash. p55

asthma /ˈæsmə/ *n.* a disease which makes breathing very difficult at times. p50

attractive /əˈtræktɪv/ *adj.* pretty or handsome (used of a person): *an* **attractive/unattractive** *man.* p33

audition /ɔːˈdɪʃən/ *n.* a performance given by a singer, actor or dancer as a test of their ability for a particular job. p74

au pair /ˌəʊ ˈpeəʳ/ *n.* a young foreign person who lives with a family in order to learn their language, in return for doing light work in the house. p43

babysit /ˈbeɪbi sɪt/ *v.* to look after children while their parents are out: *I'm* **babysitting** *for Mrs Davis tonight.* **babysitting** *n.* p43

back up /bæk ˈʌp/ *v.* to show agreement and support of somebody. p96

baggy /ˈbægi/ *adj.* hanging loosely (used of clothes): *His trousers were* **baggy** *at the knees.* p20

bake /beɪk/ *v.* to cook in an oven: *The bread is* **baking**. **baked** *adj.* p79

be /bi/ *v.* See Key word p13

be on someone's side: agree with someone and be ready to support them in an argument. p96

beach /biːtʃ/ *n.* a shore of a sea or lake covered by sand or small stones. p45

beat /biːt/ *v.* to hit someone repeatedly, usually with a hard object: *The students were* **beaten** *by the police.* p67

behave /bɪˈheɪv/ *v.* to act in a particular way: *She* **behaved** *with great courage.* **behaviour** *n.* p90

biased /ˈbaɪəst/ *adj.* to have either a favourable or unfavourable opinion about something although all the facts are not necessarily known: *I admit I'm rather* **biased** *in favour of our candidate.* p29

birdwatching /ˈbɜːd ˌwɒtʃɪŋ/ *n.* a hobby of observing birds in their natural surroundings. p7

blanket /ˈblæŋkɪt/ *n.* a thick woollen covering used especially on beds to protect you from the cold: *We might need an extra* **blanket** *tonight.* p45

blind /blaɪnd/ *n.* a piece of cloth or other material which can be pulled down to cover a window. p86

blood pressure /ˈblʌd ˌpreʃəʳ/ *n.* the force with which blood travels through the body. p109

boil /bɔɪl/ *v.* to cause a liquid to reach the temperature at which liquid changes into a gas: *Make sure you* **boil** *the water for at least five minutes.* **boiled** *adj.* p79

bone /bəʊn/ *n.* the hard parts of your body, which are covered by flesh and skin: *He* **broke** *a bone in his leg.* p62

borrow /ˈbɒrəʊ/ *v.* to take something for a certain time, intending to return it: *Can I* **borrow** *your dictionary for a moment?* p27

brave /breɪv/ *adj.* courageous and ready to suffer danger or pain: **brave** *soldiers.* p26

broken /ˈbrəʊkən/ *adj.* damaged, spoilt, or made useless by breaking: *Be careful of the* **broken** *glass.* p40

bully /ˈbʊli/ *n.* a person who uses their strength to hurt or frighten people who are not as strong as they are: *He was bullied by* **bullies** *at school.* **bully** *v.* p26

bungee jumping /ˈbʌndʒiː ˌdʒʌmpɪŋ/ *n.* jumping for fun from great heights with feet attached to rope. p7

calendar /ˈkælɪndəʳ/ *n.* a list showing

the days and months of the year. p55
can /kæn/
1 *v.* See Key word p86
2 *n.* a small closed metal container in which food or drink is preserved: *He opened a* **can** *of beans.* p45
cancer /ˈkænsəʳ/ *n.* a serious disease in which the body's cells increase too fast, producing a growth which may cause death: *lung/skin* **cancer**. p50
caring /ˈkeərɪŋ/ *adj.* providing attention and support (opposite **uncaring**). p33
carrier bag /ˈkæriəʳ bæg/ *n.* a cheap strong paper or plastic bag with handles, for carrying away from a shop. p32
carrot /ˈkærət/ *n.* a long, thin, orange vegetable. p80
casual /ˈkæʒuəl/ *adj.* informal (used of clothes) p15
catch /kætʃ/ *v.*
1 to hold and stop something that is moving in the air: *The dog* **caught** *the ball in its mouth.*
2 to take transport: *He* **caught** *the bus to work.* p114
charge /tʃɑːdʒ/ *v.* to say officially to someone they have done something against the law: *He was* **charged** *with stealing the jewels.* p66
checked /tʃekt/ *adj.* having a pattern of coloured squares: *a* **checked** *tablecloth.* p20
cheek /tʃiːk/ *n.* the fleshy part of your face below your eyes: *plump red* **cheeks**. See picture p108
child /tʃaɪld/ (*pl.* **children**) *n.*
1 a young person, not yet fully grown: *We've known each other since we were* **children**. p24
2 a son or daughter: *We have five* **children** *but they're all grown-up now.* p8
chin /tʃɪn/ *n.* the front part of your face below your mouth. See picture p108
china /ˈtʃaɪnə/ *n.* a hard white substance made by baking fine clay. p13
clever /ˈklevəʳ/ *adj.* having a quick and able mind: *a* **clever** *student.* p29
coach /kəʊtʃ/ *n.* a bus used for long-distance travel or touring: *We're going by* **coach**. p114
cold /kəʊld/
1 *adj.* not hot: *a* **cold** *wind.*
2 *n.* an illness of the nose or throat, which is common in winter and may cause headaches, coughing, and slight fever: *He's got a bad* **cold**. p50
comedian /kəˈmiːdiən/ *n.* a person whose job is telling jokes or making people laugh. p74
compass /ˈkʌmpəs/ *n.* an instrument for showing direction, usually consisting of a magnetic needle which always points to the north. p45
complain /kəmˈpleɪn/ *v.* to express feelings of annoyance or unhappiness about something: *Mary is always* **complaining** *about something.* **complaint** *n.* p39
confess /kənˈfes/ *v.* to admit to a fault or crime: *He has* **confessed** *to the murder.* p67
conservative /kənˈsɜːvətɪv/ *adj.* unwilling to change your ideas: *He is very* **conservative** *in his views of women.* p29
controlled /kənˈtrəʊld/ *adj.* capable of not showing one's feelings. p96
cook /kʊk/ *v.* to prepare food for eating by using heat: *My mother's a wonderful* **cook**. *She enjoys* **cooking**. **cook** *n.* a person who cooks. p79
cooker /ˈkʊkəʳ/ *n.* an apparatus on which food is cooked.
cord /kɔːd/ *n.* a piece of thick string or thin rope: *a light* **cord**. p86
cotton /ˈkɒtn/ *n.* thread or cloth made from the cotton plant: *a* **cotton** *dress.* p13
could /kəd/ *v.* See Key word p27
cousin /ˈkʌzən/ *n.* the child of your uncle or aunt. p95
cracked /krækt/ *adj.* damaged so that lines appear on the surface: *Don't pour hot water into the glass or it will* **crack**. **crack** *v.* p40
crawl /krɔːl/ *v.* to move slowly on your hands and knees or with your body close to the ground: *The baby* **crawled** *across the room.* p84
creative /kriˈeɪtɪv/ *adj.* producing new and original ideas and things: *They're a* **creative** *couple: she paints and he writes novels.* p29
cricket /ˈkrɪkɪt/ *n.* a small brown insect which jumps; the male makes loud noises by rubbing its wings together. p37
crime /kraɪm/ *n.* an action which is punishable by law: *She had committed a terrible* **crime**. p67
critic /ˈkrɪtɪk/ *n.* a person who makes judgements about works of art, music, or literature, and writes about them, especially as a job. p74
cruise /kruːz/ *n.* a sea voyage for pleasure. p45
cupboard /ˈkʌbəd/ *n.* a piece of furniture with shelves and a door where clothes, plates, or food may be stored. p28
curly /ˈkɜːli/ *adj.* having curls, not straight: **curly** *hair.* p15
curtain /ˈkɜːtn/ *n.* a piece of hanging cloth that can be pulled across to cover a window or door, or the stage in a theatre. p74
customs /ˈkʌstəmz/ *n.* (pl) a place where your luggage is searched and you may pay taxes when you leave or enter a country: *I got through* **customs** *and jumped in a taxi.* p45
dark /dɑːk/ *adj.* black or nearly black in colour (opposite **light**): **dark** *hair.* p15
decisive /dɪˈsaɪsɪv/ *adj.* having or showing the ability to make decisions quickly: *We need a strong,* **decisive** *leader.* (opposite **indecisive**) p33
defence /dɪˈfens/ *n.* someone who has been charged with a crime, together with their lawyers in court: *The* **defence** *claimed unfair provocation.* p66
demonstration /ˌdemənˈstreɪʃən/ *n.* a public show of opposition or support for something, often with marching: *Some students are holding a* **demonstration** *against nuclear weapons.* See picture p106
deny /dɪˈnaɪ/ *v.* to say that something is not true: *They* **denied** *telling his mother.* p102
depression /dɪˈpreʃən/ *n.* a feeling of sadness and hopelessness: *He's suffering from* **depression**. p50
diet /ˈdaɪət/ *n.* be on a diet, go on a diet, to be trying to lose weight by eating a limited amount of food. **diet** *v.* p80
director /dɪˈrektəʳ/ *n.*
1 a person who controls or manages an organisation or company. p33
2 someone who directs a play or film, deciding how it is performed and filmed. p74
dirt /dɜːt/ *n.* an unclean substance, such as mud or dust: *The floor is covered with* **dirt**. **dirty** *adj.* p32
disabled /dɪsˈeɪbəld/ *adj.* unable to use your body properly: *He's been* **disabled** *since the war, when he lost his arm.* **disability** *n.* p84
dish /dɪʃ/ *n.* (*pl.* **dishes**)
1 all the plates, cups, knives, and forks that have been used for a meal: *Put the* **dishes** *in the dishwasher.*
2 cooked food of a particular kind: *a wonderful* **dish** *of salmon baked in the oven.* p82
do /duː/ *v.* See Key word p44
dock /dɒk/ *n.* a place where ships are loaded and unloaded, or repaired: *The ship left the* **dock**. p62
draw /drɔː/ *v.* to make pictures using a pencil or pen. p55
drunken /ˈdrʌŋkən/ *adj.* resulting from or connected with too much drinking of alcohol: **drunken** *driving* p67
dry cleaner's /ˌdraɪ ˈkliːnəz/ *n.* place where clothes can be taken to be cleaned with chemicals instead of water. **dry clean** *v.* p109
duty-free /ˌdjuːti ˈfriː/ *adv.* allowed to come into the country without tax: *We bought some* **duty-free** *whisky at the airport.* p45
ear /ɪəʳ/ *n.* part of your body used for hearing: *Rabbits have long* **ears**. p108
earth /ɜːθ/ *n.*
1 the world in which we live: *They returned from the moon to the* **earth**. p13
2 soil in which plants grow: *He planted the seeds in the* **earth**. p13
easy-going /iːziˈ gəʊɪŋ/ *adj.* not easily worried or annoyed: *He's an* **easy-going** *sort of person.* p15
electric socket /ɪˌlektrɪk ˈsɒkɪt/ *n.* the place to connect an electric plug to electricity. p86
encourage /ɪnˈkʌrɪdʒ/ *v.* to try to persuade someone to do something: *We* **encouraged** *him to go to university.* p48
energetic /ˌenəˈdʒetɪk/ *adj.* very active: *an* **energetic** *tennis player.* p50
entrance /ˈentrəns/ *n.* a gate, door or other opening by which you go into a place. p86
even-tempered /ˌiːvən ˈtempəd/ *adj.* having a balanced nature; not moody:

She never gets angry; she's really **even-tempered**. p29
execution /ˌeksɪˈkjuːʃən/ *n.* a lawful killing as a punishment: Executions *used to be held in public.* p66
experience /ɪkˈspɪəriəns/ *n.* something that happens to you and has an effect on your mind and feelings: *Our journey by camel was quite an* **experience**. **experience** *v.* p7
experienced /ɪkˈspɪəriənst/ *adj.* good at something because you have spent a lot of time doing it: *an* **experienced/ inexperienced** *doctor*. p33
eyebrow /ˈaɪbraʊ/ *n.* the line of hairs above each of your eyes. p108
eyelash /ˈaɪlæʃ/ *n.* one of the small hairs which grow from the edge of each eyelid. p108
face /feɪs/ *n.* the front part of your head, which has your eyes, nose, and mouth on it. p108
fair /feəʳ/ *adj.*
1 just or reasonable; not biased: *a* **fair** *decision.* (opposite **unfair**) p29
2 light in colour (used of someone's hair or skin). p15
faithful /ˈfeɪθfəl/ *adj.* loyal to someone, especially your partner: *He was* **unfaithful/faithful** *to his wife.* p33
fatalistic /ˌfeɪtlˈɪstɪk/ *adj.* believing events are decided by powers outside human control. p87
favour /ˈfeɪvəʳ/ *n.* something you do from kindness to help and not because you have to: *do someone a* **favour**. p44
filing cabinet /ˈfaɪlɪŋ ˈkæbɪnɪt/ *n.* a set of drawers in an office, used for storing important papers. p72
fine /faɪn/
1 *n.* an amount of money paid as a punishment: *a parking* **fine**.
2 *v. to be* **fined** *$100*. p38
fire /faɪəʳ/ *n.*
1 a pile of burning coal or wood used to heat a room or to cook food over: *We sat in front of the* **fire**. p65
2 flames, light, and great heat: *People discovered* **fire** *many years ago.* p13
fish hook /ˈfɪʃ ˌhʊk/ *n.* a curved piece of metal for catching fish. p45
flat /flæt/
1 *adj.* smooth and level not pointed, or sticking out: *He's got quite a* **flat** *nose.* p108
2 *n.* a set of rooms on one floor which are a home in a building or block: *The house is divided into* **flats**. See picture p36
flea /fliː/ *n.* a small jumping insect without wings, that feeds on human or animal blood. p45
flight /flaɪt/ *n.* a trip by plane: *'Did you have a good* **flight**?' p45
fluent /ˈfluːənt/ *adj.* able to speak or write a language easily and well: *She speaks* **fluent** *English*. **fluently** *adv.* p85
fog /fɒg/ *n.* weather of very thick mist which makes it difficult to see. p56
for /fɔːʳ/ *prep.* See key word p73
forecast /ˈfɔːkɑːst/ *n.* a statement of what is expected to happen in the future: *The weather* **forecast** *said it would rain.* **forecast** *v.* p51
forehead /ˈfɒrɪd/ *n.* the part of your face above your eyes and below your hair. See picture p108
forest /ˈfɒrɪst/ *n.* a large area of land with many trees growing close together; a large wood. p97
forgetful /fəˈgetfəl/ *adj.* having the habit of forgetting things: *My elderly aunt has become rather* **forgetful**. p75
fork /fɔːk/ *n.* an instrument for eating which has a handle at one end with two or more points at the other. p55
friendly /ˈfrendli/ *adj.* acting in a kind and pleasant way, like a friend: *He's not very* **friendly** *to newcomers.* (opposite **unfriendly**) p33
fry /fraɪ/ *v.* to cook in hot fat or oil: *Shall I* **fry** *the fish for dinner?* **fried** *adj.* **fried** *rice.* p79
full board /ˌfʊl ˈbɔːd/ *adj.* with all meals provided: *Is your holiday half or* **full board**? p45
furniture /ˈfɜːnɪtʃəʳ/ *n.* large objects that are used in houses, like beds, tables, or chairs. p55
game /geɪm/ *n.* a form of play or sport: *He's very good at ball* **games**. p74
generous /ˈdʒenərəs/ *adj.* willing to give money, help, and kindness: *It was very* **generous** *of you to lend them your new car to go on holiday.* p56
gene /dʒiːn/ *n.* the part of the cell which controls the development of all the qualities in a living thing passed on from its parents. p109
genetic engineering /dʒɪˌnetɪk endʒɪˈnɪərɪŋ/ *n. tech.* the changing of the nature of a living thing by changing its genes. p109
get /get/ *v.*
1 See Key word p8
2 to enter/leave transport. *She* **got** *on/off the bus. He* **got** *into/out of the car.* p114
give in /gɪv ˈɪn/ *v.* to accept unjust treatment or defeat in an argument or fight. p96
glass /glɑːs/ *n.* a hard easily-broken substance that lets light through and is used for windows and bottles: *I've cut my hand on broken* **glass**. p13
go along with /gəʊ əˈlɒŋ wɪð/ *v.* to agree with someone. *They* **went along with** *my ideas.* p96
gold /gəʊld/ *n.* a valuable yellow metal: *A* **gold** *medal is made of gold.* p13
graceful /ˈgreɪsfəl/ *adj.* attractively and effortlessly smooth in movement: *a* **graceful** *dancer.* p56
grass /grɑːs/ *n.* a common low-growing green plant that covers wide areas of ground on hills and in fields, gardens, parks, etc.: *The sign said 'Keep off the* **grass**'. p13
grill /grɪl/ *v.* to cook food under direct heat: *We* **grilled** *the sausages and tomatoes.* **grilled** *adj.* p79
guest /gest/ *n.* a person who is in someone's home by invitation to stay for a short time or for a meal. p81
guilty /ˈgɪlti/ *adj.* having broken a law or disobeyed a moral or social rule: *He was* **guilty** *of murder.* (opposite **innocent**) p66
hairdresser's /ˈheəˌdresəʳs/ *n.* a shop where you go to get your hair cut and washed. p109
hang /hæŋ/ *v.* to kill someone, usually as a punishment, by putting a rope around their neck and dropping them so all their weight is taken by it: *He was* **hanged** *for murder.* p66
happiness /ˈhæpinɪs/ *n.* the state of being pleased or satisfied. (opposite **sadness**) p62
have /hæv/ *v.* See Key word p51
heart attack /ˈhɑːt əˌtæk/ *n.* a very dangerous medical condition in which a person's heart suddenly stops working properly: *He died of a* **heart attack**. p50
helicopter /ˈhelɪkɒptəʳ/ *n.* an aircraft which is made to fly by a set of large fast-turning metal blades fixed on top of it. p114
helpless /ˈhelpləs/ *adj.* unable to look after yourself: *a* **helpless** *child.* p96
hero /ˈhɪərəʊ/ *n.* a person remembered or admired for bravery or goodness. p32
hit /hɪt/ *v.* to bring your hand, or something held in your hand, forcefully against someone or something: *She* **hit** *the burglar on the head.* p69
hobby /ˈhɒbi/ *n.* an activity which you enjoy doing in your free time. p7
homeless /ˈhəʊmˌləs/ *adj.* having nowhere to live. **homelessness** *n.* p32
hooligan /huːlɪgən/ *n.* a noisy, violent, young person who causes trouble by fighting and breaking things. p67
horseracing /ˈhɔːsˌreɪsɪŋ/ *n.* the sport of racing horses. See picture p6
housework /ˈhaʊswɜːk/ *n.* work done in a house, such as cooking, washing, and cleaning. p43
hum /hʌm/ *v.* to sing a piece of music by making a continuous sound with your lips closed. p105
hurt /hɜːt/*v.*
1 to cause you pain: *My back* **hurts**. p95
2 to upset someone and make them unhappy: *She knew that she had* **hurt** *him very badly.* p95
if /ɪf/ *conj.* supposing that something happens or is true: See Key word p22
independent /ˌɪndɪˈpendənt/ *adj.* not dependent on other people or things for help, money, or support: *She's a very* **independent/dependent** *person.* p56
ingredient /ɪnˈgriːdiənt/ *n.* one of the things that goes into a mixture when something is made, especially in cooking: *Let me check the* **ingredients** *for this recipe.* p82
intelligent /ɪnˈtelɪdʒənt/ *adj.* having or showing powers of reasoning and understanding: (opposite **unintelligent**) p33
invitation /ˌɪnvɪˈteɪʃən/ *n.* a spoken or written offer of a chance to go to something such as a meal or party or to do something: **invite** *v.* p82

iron /ˈaɪən/ *v.* to make clothes smooth with an iron. **ironing** *n. I've been doing the* **ironing** *all day.* p45

irritable /ˈɪrɪtəbəl/*adj.* easily made angry: *Don't take any notice, he's always* **irritable** *in the mornings.* p50

jaw /dʒɔː/ *n.* one of the two bony parts of your face in which your teeth are set. p108

jealous /ˈdʒeləs/ *adj.* feeling fearful and protective because you think someone may try to take something that belongs to you: *He's insanely* **jealous** *of his wife's love.* **jealousy** *n.* p67

jelly /ˈdʒeli/ *n.* a soft sweet food made with fruit and eaten as part of a meal: **jelly** *and ice cream.* p80

journey /ˈdʒɜːni/ *n.* a trip from one place to another, usually by land: *He made the long* **journey** *by train.* p45

judge /dʒʌdʒ/ *n.* a public official who has the power to decide questions brought before a court of law. p66

jury /ˈdʒʊəri/ *n.* a group of people chosen to hear all the details of a case in a court of law and give their decision on it: *The* **jury** *found him guilty of murder.* p66

keep /kiːp/ *v.* to have something in a particular place: *Where do you* **keep** *the coffee?* p55

knife /naɪf/ *n.* a sharp blade fixed in a handle and used for cutting or as a weapon. p55

law /lɔː/ *n.* the system of rules developed by a government/society to control social and business relationships: *If you break the* **law** *you will be punished.* p66

leader /ˈliːdəʳ/ *n.* a person who guides or directs a group, team, or organisation: *the* **leader** *of a political party.* **lead** *v.* p29

leather /ˈleðəʳ/ *n* treated animal skin used for making things like shoes and bags: *a* **leather** *coat.* p13

lend /lend/ *v.* to give someone the use of something for a limited time: *Can you* **lend** *me some money?* (opposite **borrow**) p39

lifebelt /ˈlaɪfbelt/ *n.* a belt/ring that will float, to wear if you fall into water to stop you sinking. p45

like /laɪk/ *v/prep.* See Key word p95

linen /ˈlɪnɪn/ *n.* a kind of heavy cloth, often used for sheets, etc. p13

lip /lɪp/ *n.* one of the two edges of your mouth: *He kissed her on the* **lips**. p108

lonely /ˈləʊnli/ *adj.* alone and unhappy: **loneliness** *n.* p32

look after /lʊk ˈɑːftəʳ/ *v.* to take care of someone or something: *Who will* **look after** *the baby?* p43

loose /luːs/ *adj.* not tight (used of clothes): *He lost so much weight his trousers were quite* **loose**. **loosely** *adv.* p32

looting /ˈluːtɪŋ/ *n.* stealing things after a riot. p67

loyal /ˈlɔɪəl/ *adj.* faithful to people, places, or things. (opposite **disloyal**) p33

lucky /ˈlʌki/ *adj.* having good fortune: *He's a* **lucky/unlucky** *man.* p33

make /meɪk/ *v./n.* See Key word p37

management /ˈmænɪdʒmənt/ *n.* the control of something such as a business or money. **manager** *n.* person p29

market /ˈmɑːkɪt/ *n.* a building or open place where people meet to buy and sell goods. p32

match /mætʃ/ *n.*

1 a short thin stick of wood that produces a flame when it is struck against a rough surface: *a box of* **matches.** p45

2 a game or sports event: *a football* **match**. p74

material /məˈtɪəriəl/ *n.* a substance from which something is or can be made. p13

medal /ˈmedl/ *n.* a flat piece of metal, usually round or cross-shaped, given as an honour for an act of bravery or skill: *The old soldier wore his war* **medals** *on his jacket.* p32

migraine /ˈmiːgreɪn/ *n.* a severe headache. p50

mint sauce /mɪnt ˈsɔːs/ *n.* sauce, eaten particularly with lamb in Britain, made from the leaves of a small fresh-smelling plant, often used in tea. p80

miss /mɪs/ *v.* to fail to do something that was intended or possible: *He arrived too late and* **missed** *the train.* p114

missing /ˈmɪsɪŋ/ *adj.* not in the expected place: *I noticed he had a finger* **missing** *from his left hand.* p40

moody /ˈmuːdi/ *adj.* having feelings that change often and quickly, unpleasant for other people. p29

moon /muːn/ *n.* the object which moves round the earth once every 28 days, and can be seen shining in the sky at night. p62

mother-in-law /ˈmʌðəʳ ɪn lɔː/ *n.* the mother of your husband or wife. p95

mugging /ˈmʌgɪŋ/ *n.* a robbery with violence, especially in a dark street. p69

murder /ˈmɜːdəʳ/ *n.* the crime of killing a human being illegally. **murderer** *n.* person who murders. p66

neck /nek/

1 *n.* the part of your body which joins your head to your shoulders. p108

2 *adj.* having a certain shape or style of neck: *a v-***necked** *dress; a round-***necked** *sweater.* p20

neighbour /ˈneɪbəʳ/ *n.* someone who lives next to or near someone else. p36

nephew /ˈnefjuː/ *n.* the son of your brother or sister or your brother-in-law or sister-in-law (fem. **niece**). p95

nervous /ˈnɜːvəs/ *adj.* frightened or worried: *I always get* **nervous** *before exams.* p14

newspaper /ˈnjuːsˌpeɪpəʳ/ *n.* a set of large folded sheets of paper containing news, articles and advertisements, printed and sold daily or weekly. p32

nibble /ˈnɪbəl/ *v.* to eat slowly as a snack. p80

noise /nɔɪz/ *n.* a sound, often unwanted, unpleasant, or confused: *Try not to make a* **noise** *when you go upstairs – the baby's asleep.* **noisy** *adj.* p37

nose /nəʊz/ *n.* the part of your face above your mouth through which you smell and breathe. p108

nylon /ˈnaɪlɒn/ *n.* a strong man-made material made into clothes, cords, and plastics. p13

oar /ɔːʳ/ *n.* a long pole with a wide flat blade at one end, used to move a boat through the water. p45

obedient /əˈbiːdiənt/ *adj.* willing to do what you are told to do by someone, for example a parent or teacher: *an* **obedient/disobedient** *child.* p33

oil /ɔɪl/ *n.* a fatty liquid used for burning, for making machines run easily, for cooking or light: *an* **oil** *lamp.* p45

omelette /ˈɒmlɪt/ *n.* eggs beaten together and cooked in hot fat in a pan. p80

only child /əʊnli ˈtʃaɪld/ *n.* a child with no brothers or sisters. p95

operate /ˈɒpəreɪt/ *v.* to cut someone's body in order to remove/repair a diseased or damaged part. **operation** *n.* p109

optimistic /ˌɒptɪˈmɪstɪk/ *adj.* feeling hopeful about the future. p29

organised /ˈɔːgənaɪzd/ *adj.* able to arrange things well (opposite **disorganised**). **organise** *v.* **organiser** *n.* person who organises. p29

orphan /ˈɔːfən/ *n.* a child whose parents are dead. p95

own /əʊn/ *v.* to possess something: *We only rent the house, we don't* **own** *it.* **owner** *n.* person who owns. p73

package tour /ˈpækɪdʒ tʊəʳ/ *n.* a completely planned holiday arranged by a company at a fixed price. p45

parent /ˈpeərənt/ *n.* the father or mother of a person. p95

parsnip /ˈpɑːsnɪp/ *n.* a cream-coloured vegetable which grows under the ground. p80

patient /ˈpeɪʃənt/ *adj.* having the ability to wait or deal with difficulties for a long time without getting angry. (opposite **impatient**) p33

performance /pəˈfɔːməns/ *n.* an act of performing: *There are two* **performances** *a day.* p74

persuade /pəˈsweɪd/ *v.* to cause someone to do something they had been unwilling to do by giving good reasons: *She didn't want to come, but I* **persuaded** *her.* p48

pessimistic /ˌpesɪˈmɪstɪk/ *adj.* thinking whatever happens will be bad. p29

pet /pet/ *n.* an animal you keep in your home as a companion: *a* **pet** *dog.* p102

plain /pleɪn/ *adj.* simple, without decoration or pattern. p20

plastic /ˈplæstɪk/ *n.* a light man-made material which can be made into different shapes when soft and keeps its shape when hard: *The chairs are made of* **plastic**. p13

play /pleɪ/
1 *v.* to take part in a game. p14
2 *n.* a piece of writing that is acted in a theatre or on television: *You must go and see the new* **play** *in town.* p74

pointed /ˈpɔɪntɪ̈d/ *adj.* shaped to a point at one end: *long,* **pointed** *fingernails.* p108

polite /pəˈlaɪt/ *adj.* having good manners, and showing respect and consideration for others. (opposite **impolite**) p33

pottery /ˈpɒtəri/ *n.* substance made out of baked clay. p13

poverty /ˈpɒvəti/ *n.* the state of being poor. p32

practical /ˈpræktɪkəl/ *adj.* concerned with real situations and actions, rather than with ideas. p21

pride /praɪd/ *n.* a feeling of satisfaction and pleasure in something you or someone else has done, or in something you own: *He looked at the new baby with* **pride**. **proud** *adj.* p32

producer /prəˈdjuːsəʳ/ *n.* a person who has general control of the money for and preparation of a play, film, or broadcast. p74

promise /ˈprɒmɪs/ *v.* to state that you will certainly do something: *She* **promised** *to phone me later.* **promise** *n.* p111

properly /ˈprɒpəli/ *adv.* in a correct or acceptable way: *I believe in doing a job* **properly**. p40

psychotherapist /ˌsaɪkəʊˈθerəpɪst/ *n.* person who treats disorders of the mind using psychology rather than drugs. **psychotherapy** *n.* p94

pudding /ˈpʊdɪŋ/ *n.* the sweet dish at the end of a meal. p80

punishment /ˈpʌnɪʃmənt/ *n.* the act of making someone suffer for a fault or crime. **punish** *v.* p67

quick-tempered /ˌkwɪk ˈtempəd/ *adj.* having a tendency to get angry very easily. p75

radish /ˈrædɪʃ/ *n.* a small strong-tasting red and white vegetable which is eaten raw. p80

rags /rægz/ *n.* [pl] torn old clothes: *The beggar was dressed in* **rags.** p32

rational /ˈræʃənəl/ *adj.* having the ability to think and understand things clearly and make decisions based on reason. (opposite **irrational**) p96

raw /rɔː/ *adj.* not cooked: **raw** *vegetables.* p80

recipe /ˈresɪpi/ *n.* a set of instructions for cooking a particular type of food. p82

rehearsal /rɪˈhɜːsəl/ *n.* practice as preparation for a public performance: **Rehearsals** *will take place every Saturday.* p74

relative /ˈrelətɪv/ *n.* a member of your family: *My uncle is my nearest* **relative**. p95

reliable /rɪˈlaɪəbəl/ *adj.* that you can trust to perform well at all times. (opposite **unreliable**) p33

remain /rɪˈmeɪn/ *v.* to stay or be left behind after others have gone: *She* **remained** *at home with the children.* p62

remind /rɪˈmaɪnd/ *v.* to make someone remember something. p48

retired /rɪˈtaɪəd/ *adj.* no longer working. **retire** *v.* p46

revenge /rɪˈvendʒ/ *n.* action taken against someone who has done something to harm you: *a* **revenge** *attack.* p68

review /rɪˈvjuː/ *n.* a magazine, newspaper, or article giving judgements on things like new books or plays. p74

rheumatism /ˈruːmətɪzəm/ *n.* a disease causing pain and stiffness in the joints or muscles. p50

ribbon /ˈrɪbən/ *n.* a long, narrow piece of silk or other cloth used for tying your hair or for decoration. p32

roam /rəʊm/ *v.* to walk around with no clear purpose. p62

roast /rəʊst/ *v.* to cook with fat in an oven. **roast** *adj. a* **roast** *chicken.* p79

robbery /ˈrɒbəri/ *n.* the crime of taking someone else's property. p67

rock climbing /ˈrɒk klaɪmɪŋ/ *n.* a hobby climbing cliff and mountain sides. p7

roll /rəʊl / *v.* to move by turning over and over or from side to side. *The ship* **rolled** *with the waves.* p62

romantic /rəʊˈmæntɪk/ *adj.* showing strong feelings of love. (opposite **unromantic**) p21

sadness /ˈsædnɪs/ *n.* a feeling of unhappiness. p62

salad /ˈsæləd/ *n.* a mixture of vegetables served cold and usually raw, sometimes with other foods added: *We'll have a green* **salad** *with the steak, so I need to get a lettuce.* p80

satisfied /ˈsætɪsfaɪd/ *adj.* pleased or contented: *There goes another* **satisfied** *customer!* p68

scene /siːn/ *n.* a part of a play, film, or book which describes the events happening in one place over a short period of time: *Is that the* **scene** *in which he kills his sister?* p74

scenery /ˈsiːnəri/ *n.* the set of painted backgrounds and furniture used on a theatre stage to give an idea of the place where the action happens. p74

scramble /ˈskræmbəl/ *v.* to mix the white and yellow parts of eggs together while cooking them. **scrambled** *adj.* **scrambled** *eggs.* p79

script /skrɪpt/ *n.* a written form of a speech, play, film, or broadcast. p74

sea /siː/ *n.* the salty water that covers much of the Earth's surface. p6

seaside /ˈsiːsaɪd/ *n.* a place by the sea where people stay on holiday. p6

self-catering /ˌself ˈkeɪtərɪŋ/ *adj.* in which you cook your own meals (used of a place where you stay). p45

self-confident /ˌself ˈkɒnfɪdənt/ *adj.* believing in your own power to do things successfully. **self-confidence** *n.* p29

selfish /ˈselfɪʃ/ *adj.* caring only about yourself and not caring about other people. (opposite **unselfish**) p33

semolina /ˌseməˈliːnə/ *n.* a powder made from wheat, used in producing pasta, couscous and a sweet dessert in Britain. p80

sensible /ˈsensɪ̈bəl/ *adj.* reasonable and practical. *She was* **sensible** *and went to bed early.* p96

sensitive /ˈsensɪtɪv/ *adj.* showing delicate feelings or judgment. (opposite **insensitive**) p96

sentence /ˈsentəns/ *v.* (of a judge or court) to give a punishment to someone: *He was* **sentenced** *to three years in prison.* p66

serious /ˈsɪəriəs/ *adj.* solemn and not joking or cheerful: *a* **serious** *expression on his face.* p15

shave /ʃeɪv/ *v.* to cut hair from your face or body. p55

shelf /ʃelf/ *n.* (*pl* **shelves**) a long board fixed against a wall or in a cupboard so that things can be kept on it. p55

ship /ʃɪp/ *n.* a large boat for carrying goods or people on the sea. p62

shocked /ʃɒkt/ *adj.* feeling very upset, angry, or unpleasantly surprised: *His sudden death* **shocked** *me.*

shoplifting /ˈʃɒpˌlɪftɪŋ/ *v.* taking things from a shop without paying for them. p67

short-sighted /ˌʃɔːt ˈsaɪtɪ̈d/ *adj.* unable to see things clearly if they are not close to your eyes (opposite **long-sighted**) p26

show /ʃəʊ/ *v.* to allow or cause something to be seen: He *was* **showing** *them his holiday photographs.* p32

shy /ʃaɪ/ *adj.* nervous and uncomfortable in the company of other people. p29

sightseeing /ˈsaɪtˌsiːɪŋ/ *n.* going about as a tourist on holiday, visiting places of interest: *Allow three days for* **sightseeing** *in Paris.* p7

signal flare /ˈsɪgnəl fleəʳ/ *n.* an object which sends out a bright light to show someone needs help. p45

silk /sɪlk/ *n.* fine smooth thread which is made into cloth: *a* **silk** *dress.* p13

silver /ˈsɪlvəʳ/ *n.* a soft precious metal, greyish-white in colour, that can be brightly polished, and is used in jewellery and for making coins. p13

skin /skɪn/ *n.* the natural outer covering of your body. p13

sleeve /sliːv/ *n.* a part of a piece of clothing that covers your arm. **short/long-sleeved** *adj. a* **short-sleeved** *shirt.* p20

smart /smɑːt/ *adj.* neat and stylish in appearance: *You look very* **smart** *in that new shirt.* p15

smoked /sməʊkt/ *adj.* preserved by hanging in smoke: **smoked** *salmon.* p80

so /səʊ/ *adv.* See Key word p57

solitary confinement /ˈsɒlɪtəri kənˈfaɪnmənt/ *n.* alone in a prison cell without seeing the other prisoners. p60

son /sʌn/ *n.* a male child (fem. **daughter**) p95

sore /sɔːʳ/ *adj.* painful because of infection, hard use, or a wound: *I've got a* **sore** *throat.* p50

spoon /spuːn/ *n.* an object used for mixing, serving, and eating food: *two* **spoons** *of sugar, please.* p55

stamp collecting /stæmp kəlektɪŋ/ *n.* a hobby finding and keeping postage stamps from different countries. p7

stand up to /stænd 'ʌp tu:/ *v.* to refuse to accept unjust treatment from someone. p96

stay /steɪ/ *v.* to remain somewhere: *I* **stayed** *late at the party last night.* p62

stepmother /'step,mʌðə'/ *n.* a woman who is not your natural mother, but whom your father has married. p95

sticking out /stɪkɪŋ 'aʊt/ *adj./adv.* protruding; not flat: *He had* **sticking out** *ears.* p108

straight /streɪt/ *adj./adv.* not bent or curved: *Draw a* **straight** *line.* p108

string /strɪŋ/ *n.* narrow cord made of threads wound together. p45

stripe /straɪp/ *n.* a long narrow band which is different in colour from what surrounds it. **striped** *adj. She wore a* **striped** *sweater.* p20

stroke /strəʊk/ *n.* a sudden illness in part of someone's brain which can cause death or loss of movement in certain parts of their body. p50

stuff /stʌf/ *n.* (uncountable) a substance of any sort: *What's this sticky* **stuff** *on the floor?* p13

stupid /'stju:pɪd/ *adj.* silly or foolish: *I think you were* **stupid** *to agree.* p29

sun /sʌn/ *n.* the burning star in the sky. p62

sunbathe /'sʌnbeɪð/ *v.* to sit or lie in strong sunlight in order to make your body brown. **sunbathing** *n.* p45

sunburn /'sʌnbɜ:n/ *n.* sore, red skin from spending too much time in strong sunlight. **sunburnt** *adj.* p45

supplement /'sʌplɪment/ *n.* an additional cost. p45

surgery /'sɜ:dʒəri/ *n.* the performing of medical operations: *He had cosmetic* **surgery** *to change his appearance.* p109

suspect /'sʌspekt/ *n.* a person who is thought to be guilty, especially of a crime. p66

sympathetic /,sɪmpə'θetɪk/ *adj.* feeling or showing pity for another person's problems or suffering: *She was* **sympathetic** *when I was ill.* p40

take /teɪk/ *v.* See Key word. p115

take care of /teɪk 'keə' əv/ *v.* to be responsible for someone. p96

tanned / tænd/ *adj.* brown as a result of being in strong sunlight. p14

tea-cup /'ti:kʌp/ *n.* a cup from which you drink tea. p32

telescope /'telɪskəʊp/ *n.* a long scientific instrument which makes distant objects appear nearer and larger. p45

temperamental /,tempərə'mentl/ *adj.* having frequent and sudden changes of feeling. *The actor was so* **temperamental** *that people refused to work with him.* p96

the /ðə/ *definite article.* See Key word p80

threat /θret/ *n.* a warning that someone will hurt or punish you if you do not do what they say. p111

tide /taɪd/ *n.* the regular movement of the sea level up and down the shore: *The sea comes right up to the cliffs when the* **tide** *is in.* p62

tidy up /taɪdi 'ʌp/ *v.* to make a place neat: *When are you going to* **tidy** *your room* **up**? p43

tight-fitting /taɪt 'fɪtɪŋ/ *adj.* fitting part of your body closely: **tight-fitting** *shoes.* p20

to /tu:/ *prep.* See Key word p103

toenail /'təʊneɪl/ *n.* nail on a toe. p13

toffee /'tɒfi/ *n.* a hard brown sweet made by boiling sugar and butter: *a sticky* **toffee**; **toffee** *apples.* p80

tolerant /'tɒlərənt/*adj.* allowing people to behave or think in a way that may not please you, without becoming annoyed. (opposite **intolerant**) **tolerance** *n.* p33

tram /træm/ *n.* a vehicle for the public, driven by electricity. p56

travel /'trævəl/ *v.* to make a journey from one place to another: *He* **travelled** *across the States on a Greyhound bus.* p45

trial /'traɪəl/ *n.* the legal process of hearing and judging a person or case in a court: *The murder* **trial** *lasted six weeks.* p66

trimmings /'trɪmɪŋz/ *n.* something added to the main thing, often for decoration: *duck served with all the* **trimmings**. p80

trip /trɪp/ *n.* a journey from one place to another and back again: *They went on a day* **trip** *to the country.* p45

uncle /'ʌŋkəl/ *n.* the brother of your father or mother, or the husband of your aunt. (fem. **aunt**) p95

unemployment /,ʌnɪm'plɔɪmənt/ *n.* the number of people in a society without a job: *The level of* **unemployment** *has increased by 5000 this month.* p72

vacuum /'vækjuəm/ *v.* to clean with a vacuum cleaner. **vacuuming** *n.*: *I've done the* **vacuuming** *this morning.* p43

vandalism /'vændəlɪzəm/ *n.* intentional and pointless damage and destruction of public property. p67

vegetable /'vedʒtəbəl/ *n.* a plant that is grown for food to be eaten in the main part of a meal. p79

vegetarian /,vedʒɪ'teəriən/ *n.* a person who does not eat meat or fish. p80

verdict /'vɜ:dɪkt/ *n.* the official decision made in a court of law, at the end of a trial: *Members of the jury, what is your* **verdict**? *Guilty, or not guilty?* p66

vulnerable /'vʌlnərəbəl/ *adj.* easily hurt in body or mind. p96

waist /weɪst/ *n.* the narrow part of your body just above your hips. p108

warn /wɔ:n/ *v.* to tell someone of a possible future problem or danger so they can try to prevent it or avoid it: *He* **warned** *his students that they would have to work very hard to pass.* p48

washing up /,wɒʃɪŋ 'ʌp/ *n.* to wash the dishes, knives, forks, etc., after a meal: *I'll* **wash up.** *or I'll do the* **washing up**. p43

wastepaper bin /,weɪst'peɪpə ,bɪn/ *n.* a small container on the floor of a house or office in which you put unwanted paper. p55

watch /wɒtʃ/ *v.* to look at and pay attention to a person or object. p62

water skiing /'wɔ:tə' ,ski:ɪŋ/ *n.* the sport in which you move over water on skis, pulled by a boat. p7

wavy /'weɪvi/ *adj.* having regular curves; not straight: **wavy** *hair.* p15

wheelchair /'wi:ltʃeə'/ *n.* a chair with large wheels used by a person who cannot walk. p87

will /wɪl/ *v.* See Key word p111

window-shopping /'wɪndəʊ ʃɒpɪŋ/ *n.* looking at the goods in shop windows without intending to buy anything. p7

windsurfing /'wɪnd,sɜ:fɪŋ/ *n.* to move along on the water on a flat board with a sail. p7

wish /wɪʃ/ *n.* a feeling of wanting something: *I am sure everyone shares my* **wish** *for these peace talks to succeed.* **wish** *v.* p92

witness /'wɪtnɪ̥s/ *n.* a person who sees something happen and can describe it to other people: *There were no* **witnesses** *to the accident.* p66

wood /wʊd/ *n.* the substance of which trees are formed. Also a small forest. p13

wool /wʊl/ *n.* thick thread or cloth made from thick woollen hair from animals, especially sheep: *another ball of* **wool** *for my knitting.* p13

word processor /'wɜ:d ,prəʊsesə'/ *n.* a small computer used for typing and storing information. p72

work /wɜ:k/ *v.*

1 to be employed: *She* **works** *in an office.* p42

2 to operate properly: *This light doesn't* **work**. p40

worn-out /,wɔ:n 'aʊt/ *adj.* no longer usable because of so much use in the past: **worn-out** *shoes.* p32

would /wʊd/ *v.* See Key word p69

yacht /jɒt/ *n.* a boat with sails or a motor, used for pleasure. p114

Grammar index

Numbers are page numbers. RE means Revision Exercise. LR means Language Review.